Financial management in education

OPEN UNIVERSITY PRESS

Management in Education Series

Editor
Tony Bush
Senior Lecturer in Educational Policy and Management
at The Open University

The series comprises five volumes which cover important topics within the
field of educational management. The articles present examples of theory
and practice in school and college management. The authors discuss many
of the major issues of relevance to educational managers in the post-
Education Reform Act era.

The five readers are components of The Open University M.A. in
Education module *E818 Management in Education*. Further information about
this course and the M.A. programme may be obtained by writing to the
Higher Degrees Office, Open University, PO Box 49, Walton Hall, Milton
Keynes, MK7 6AD.

Financial management in education

EDITED BY
Rosalind Levačić
at The Open University

OPEN UNIVERSITY PRESS
MILTON KEYNES · PHILADELPHIA
in association with The Open University

Open University Press
Celtic Court
22 Ballmoor
Buckingham MK18 1XW

and

1900 Frost Road, Suite 101
Bristol, PA19007, USA

First Published 1989. Reprinted 1991, 1993

British Library Cataloguing in Publication Data

Financial management in education.—(Management in
  education)
   1. Great Britain. Educational institutions. Financial
  management
  I. Levačić, Rosalind   II. Series
  371.2'06'0941

  ISBN 0-335-09247-0
      0-335-09246-2 (paper)

Library of Congress Cataloging-in-Publication Data

Financial management in education / edited by Rosalind Levačić.
      p.   cm.—(Management in education series)
    ISBN 0-335-09247-0.—ISBN 0-335-09246-2 (pbk.)
     1. Education—Finance.   2. School management and organization—
  Great Britain.   3. School budgets—Great Britain.   I. Levačić,
  Rosalind.   II. Series
  LB2826.6.G7F56   1989
  379.1'1—dc20   89–8863 CIP

Typeset by Rowland Phototypesetting Ltd
Bury St Edmunds, Suffolk
Printed and bound in Great Britain by
Biddles Ltd, Guildford and King's Lynn

Contents

Acknowledgements

All possible care has been taken to trace ownership of the material included in this volume, and Open University Press would like to make grateful acknowledgement for permission to reproduce it here.

1   R. Levačić (1989). Commissioned for this collection.
2   A. R. Anthony and R. E. Herzlinger (Revised Edition 1980). *Management Control in Nonprofit Organizations*, pp. 1–10, pp. 14–21, Illinois, Richard D. Irwin, Inc.
3   P. Crisp (1987). 'Case study A: a metropolitan LEA', *Coombe Lodge Report*, Vol. 19, No. 12, Bristol, The Further Education Staff College.
4   J. Stewart and C. Holtham (1986). *Decentralized Resource Management*, pp. 1–4, Luton, Local Government Training Board.
5   H. Howard (1988). 'Financial management in schools', *Local Financial Management in Schools* edited by P. Downes, pp. 112–27, Oxford, Basil Blackwell.
6   J. Arnold and T. Hope (1983). *Accounting for Management Decisions*, pp. 264–81, Hemel Hempstead, Prentice-Hall.
7   R. Levačić (1989). Commissioned for this collection.
8   Coopers & Lybrand (1988). *Local Management of Schools*, extracts from Chapters 5 and 6, produced under contract with the Department of Education and Science and reproduced with the permission of the Controller of Her Majesty's Stationery Office.
9   F. J. Brockmann (1972). 'Program budgeting: implications for secondary principals', *NASSP Bulletin*, Vol. 56, Pt. 366, October, pp. 34–42, Virginia, National Association of Secondary School Principals.
10 H. J. Hartley (1979). 'Zero based budgeting for secondary schools', *NASSP Bulletin*, Vol. 63, Pt. 431, December, pp. 22–8, Virginia, National Association of Secondary School Principals.

11   J. Fielden and P. Pearson (1968). *Costing Educational Practice*, from Foreword and pp. 19–52, London, National Council for Educational Technology.

12   D. Jones (1986). Accountability and budgets in colleges: a practical unit cost approach, *Coombe Lodge Report*, Vol. 19, No. 1, pp. 15–66, Bristol, The Further Education Staff College.

13   D. Birch (1988). *Managing Resources in Further Education*, pp. 67–75, Bristol, The Further Education Staff College. Reproduced with the permission of the Controller of Her Majesty's Stationery Office.

14   R. Levačić (1989). Commissioned for this collection.

15   T. Simkins (1989). Commissioned for this collection.

16   D. Esp (1989). Commissioned for this collection.

17   P. Young (1989). Commissioned for this collection.

18   G. Hulme (1989). Commissioned for this collection.

19   C. T. Fitz-Gibbon (1989). Commissioned for this collection.

20   E. R. House (1973). Reprinted with permission from McCutchan Publishing Corporation. From Ernest R. House, 'The Dominion of Economic Accountability', in *School Evaluation: The Politics and Process*, ed. Ernest R. House, pp. 234–8. Copyright 1973 by McCutchan Publishing Corporation. All rights reserved.

The development of this Reader has benefited greatly from the comments and suggestions of the E818 course team and external assessors. I would also like to express my appreciation to the headteachers, governors and staff of Fenstanton and Oakwood Schools and Linton Community College for giving their time and co-operation in order to inform me about local financial management. I would also like to thank my secretary, Betty Atkinson, for word processing articles and assembling the Reader, with such efficiency and unfailing good humour. Additional thanks are due to Nicky Lowe for her painstaking work in assembling articles for the Reader.

Thanks are also due to the following contributors, whose work was specially commissioned for this volume:

Derek Esp   Education consultant and former Director of Education for Lincolnshire

Dr Carol T. Fitz-Gibbon   Senior Lecturer, School of Education, University of Newcastle upon Tyne

Geoffrey Hulme   Director, Public Expenditure Policy Unit, Public Finance Foundation

Tim Simkins   Senior Lecturer in the Centre for Education Management and Administration at Sheffield Polytechnic

Dr Pamela Young   Senior Lecturer, University of London Institute of Education

Section I

Functions and practice of budgeting: the educational context

1

Financial management in education: an emerging function

Rosalind Levačić

The 1988 Education Reform Act has catapulted financial management to the top of the education management agenda. Under the previous system of centralized resource allocation by local education authorities, school managers had little financial responsibility apart from managing the school fund and a limited capitation allowance, though this had been considerably extended in scope by some authorities. School governors had virtually no financial responsibilities and, until the implementation of the 1986 Education Act, were not even informed of the costs of running their school. Further education colleges had greater responsibility for managing their budgets, but were constrained by being unable to carry over under- or overspending to the next financial year or to vire money between budget heads. Real resources, such as staff posts, larger items of equipment and maintenance, had to be negotiated on an item-by-item basis with the LEA.

Under the provisions of the 1988 Act all secondary schools and all primary schools and colleges with rolls of 200 or more must receive delegated budgets by the start of the 1993/4 financial year. Their governing bodies will be responsible for managing a budget which will cover around 80 per cent of the total resources available to the institution. Many schools and colleges will be brought into financial delegation schemes at an earlier date and smaller primary schools and special schools may also have delegated budgets, if the LEA so decides. The Act makes specific provision for the governors to delegate budget management to the head or principal and to set up a finance subcommittee to undertake the bulk of the governors' work with respect to budgeting. Similar provisions for financial delegation are proposed for Northern Ireland. For Scotland the government has proposed that the newly created school boards can apply to have additional resource management responsibilities delegated to them.

The prime responsibility for financial management will, in most cases, rest with the head or principal and be shared, to differing degrees, by a senior management team, with local circumstances determining the degree of involvement of particular governors. These are the key people in schools and colleges on whom the emerging task of financial management will rest. Other key personnel are those in local authorities responsible for setting up and operating schemes of financial delegation and for providing operational support to colleges and, especially, to schools which being smaller may not have the resources for specialized financial staff of their own. The reader is thus aimed particularly at actual or aspiring senior managers in schools and FE colleges and those in local authorities with responsibility for financial systems and support services for schools and colleges.

What is financial management in education?

The activities which in educational institutions have come to be referred to as financial management are encompassed in business organizations by the functional areas known as management accounting and management control. These are concerned with providing the information and systems which enable managers to plan and control the organization's activities. Because of the pre-eminence of money as a unit of account in the market sector, the provision of information and systems for planning and control purposes has been dominated by accountancy.

Accounting serves two distinct functions. The first, just mentioned, that of providing information and systems for internal management planning and control, is the province of management accounting. The second branch of accounting is for stewardship purposes – to serve the needs of users outside the organization. In the business sector the main interests served by stewardship accounts are the firm's creditors and shareholders. Stewardship accounting is concerned with fulfilling the legal requirements that annual company accounts are published and that the organization's transactions are audited to ensure the probity of its managers and other employees.

Public sector organizations, including local authorities, have similar legal requirements to publish accounts of their use of public funds and to conduct audits. In this case the external interests being served are those of taxpayers and electors. Under the provisions of the 1988 Education Act, local education authorities will be required to draw up their budgets for educational expenditure according to quite strict rules, in particular those relating to formula funding of schools and colleges. These institutional budgets will be derived from the LEA's planning of its educational provision (within the limits allowed by the Act) and are also to be used as instruments for decentralized control of schools and colleges. However, for the managers of school and colleges, the main focus of 'financial management' of the delegated budget will be internal management (the tasks of planning and control) rather than the stewardship functions of accountancy. Hence school and college managers will be more concerned with drawing upon relevant techniques from management accounting rather than with those of stewardship accounting. Nevertheless, school and college managers under the 1988 Act will be held accountable by the LEA for the use of the resources delegated to them. This involves having their institution's financial transactions audited and drawing up budgets which show how financial resources were allocated. In addition, the Act places more emphasis than before on educational audit as a way of motivating and controlling school and college managers; they are to be held accountable for their management of budgets by means of external evaluation of their institution's educational outcomes.

Though school and college managers need to be highly aware of the implications of educational audit and their role in it, their main concerns are those of setting the institution's broad policy framework (or aims), linking these to detailed operational goals and controlling the activities of the organization. Financial management in education is a key part of these management tasks; it therefore embraces far more than managing money. One of the main messages emerging from existing LEA financial delegation schemes (such as those in Solihull and Cambridgeshire) is that delegated budgeting does not just bolt on a separate set of accounting tasks; it becomes integrated with all the other aspects of managing a school. It was to emphasize this close interrelation between financial and other management tasks that the policy was renamed 'local management of schools' (Coopers & Lybrand, 1988).

Schools and colleges will not be in the business of managing finance in the sense of managing monetary assets. Rather, delegated budgets give educational institutions the means to have a greater say over their *real* resources, such as teaching and support staff, books, equipment, materials and maintenance work. School and college managers have always been engaged in real resource management, but its chief focus has been organizing student time around the curriculum and deploying staff and materials in order to deliver the curriculum. The familiar activities of hiring staff, timetabling and allocating capitation moneys are all part of real resource management. Financial management enlarges the scope for schools and colleges to determine what real resources they acquire and how they deploy and develop them.

In a sense, financial management is something of a misnomer, since in the business world the 'finance' function refers to raising money to finance the business and investing this in short-term financial assets or in stocks and capital assets. Apart from a concern with the formula which determines the school or college budget and with any additional income generation, schools and colleges are unlikely to be much concerned with the other aspects of business finance.

They will have very few financial assets and liabilities to manage as the

LEA is likely to act as banker. In fact at least one LEA is withdrawing cheque book facilities from its schools on the introduction of financial delegation. Obtaining the best return from short term investment of cash is an activity enjoying economies of scale, so local authorities are unlikely to wish to forgo these advantages by paying school and college budgets into individual bank accounts. Neither will LEA schools and colleges be making investment decisions (except for equipment and minor works financed out of their own budgets), since capital expenditure and debt charges are mandatory exceptions which, under the 1988 Act, must not be delegated. Given these considerations, the term 'financial management' in education relates to a broad set of management tasks concerned with planning and controlling what the institution (or, from the LEA perspective, what the education service) does. In particular, it is concerned with the acquisition and allocation of financial and real resources and with using budgets to plan and control the deployment of real resources. To undertake these tasks education managers do not need qualifications in accountancy; rather they need to make common sense applications of a few key techniques and approaches, suitably adapted from the practice of management accountancy in other kinds of organization.

The financial management cycle

Financial and real resource management within an institution involves a number of distinct stages which form a coherent and interrelated cycle of activities.

First is the acquisition of resources. Under the 1988 Act the bulk of resources will be received as money – from the institution's budget share distributed by the LEA (and determined by a formula) plus some additions from other sources, such as letting premises. Some real resources will still be provided by the LEA; others may be obtained from the community, such as parents' time or donations of equipment.

The next stage in the cycle is making decisions about how to allocate resources. With delegated budgeting, schools and colleges will need to decide how to convert the financial resources acquired into real resources; this in turn will be determined by what educational activities school and college managers intend to provide. In the short run such decisions are highly constrained by the real resources the institution has already acquired in the past, in particular its staff and buildings, but over time more options for changing real resources become available. These real resource constraints and decisions are reflected in the budget plans drawn up for the coming financial year. A basic budget plan shows the amount that it is expected to spend on each of the individual budget heads, such as teaching, supply cover, ancillary staff, fuel etc. In a formal budget planning and resource allocation system these planned expenditures are derived from educational decisions about the curriculum and its delivery. In a less formal (and more common) planning system the links between the educational activities being resourced and the planned budget expenditures on different kinds of resources are not made explicit, though they may well have been considered informally, at least by some of those involved in budget preparation.

The third stage in the real resource and financial management cycle is putting the budget plan into operation. Broadly interpreted this task encompasses all the management activities of staffing, timetabling, running the premises, ordering supplies, and so on, which incur expenditures. Other activities, such as hiring school premises or selling courses for a fee, bring in additional income. The specifically financial task is monitoring the budget regularly through the year in order to compare actual income and expenditures under the various budget heads with those intended. If divergences occur, as is likely, management decisions are made to correct such divergences, if they seem likely to persist and unbalance the budget. This may involve adjusting certain expenditure plans or implementing better financial control on internal budget holders (such as heads of departments) in order to curtail or stimulate spending as required. Budget monitoring is the most conspicuous of the additional tasks financial delegation brings in its wake: inadequate or inaccurate financial information systems considerably increase the burden.

The fourth stage of the resource management cycle is evaluation, currently its most underdeveloped aspect. While considerable educational evaluation is undertaken, very little of it relates the value of the resources used to the resulting educational outcomes. Currently educational evaluation is undertaken by LEA advisers and inspectors and HMI while, quite separately, local authority auditing is restricted to conventional financial auditing to check the probity of transactions undertaken by LEA employees. The Audit Commission has been crusading for value for money auditing: this assesses the efficiency and effectiveness of resource utilization by relating service outcomes to policy objectives (effectiveness) and resource utilization (efficiency). The DES, in circulars 7/88 and 9/88, requires LEAs to monitor and evaluate their financial delegation schemes, as an essential ingredient in holding governing bodies accountable for their budget management. Colleges have also been urged by outside bodies to provide information for external value-for-money auditing (the performance indicators recommended by the Joint Efficiency Study, adopted by the government) and to develop complementary systems for internal evaluation (such as the Responsive College Programme funded by the Training Agency and run by the Further Education Unit (FEU)). However, there is a long way to go before such systems become installed, let alone feed back systematically into resource allocation decisions.

Perspectives on financial management

Texts on management accounting are almost invariably explicitly normative, in that they purport to show how it ought to be done. Most texts implicitly assume that the principles, rules and techniques they explain are those that are actually practised; but what is practised is, in turn, based on distinct ideas of how the management accountancy function ought to be undertaken. These ideas and practices ·are embedded in the professional attitudes, values and expectations of accountants, auditors and management consultants. The prevailing presumption of accountancy texts is that organizations are purposeful goal-seeking entities which use these techniques to enhance their ability to survive and prosper. The presumed underlying model is the rational bureaucratic one (Bush, 1989).

The discussion above, which outlined four distinct stages in the cycle of real resource management, was implicitly predicated on a rational view of the organization, in which real resource allocation decisions and the resultant budget planning are determined in relation to the organization's aims. Both aims and the means available to attain them are made explicit; those activities which are judged to best promote the organization's aims are resourced. Implementation is carefully monitored and modified by management in the light of unfolding circumstances to ensure that the organization achieves its intended objectives as closely as possible. Evaluation is undertaken to ascertain how closely objectives are achieved, why discrepancies arise, and what action can be taken to improve performance. Thus the results of evaluation feed directly back into resource allocation. Close attention is given to goal congruence; that is, to ensuring that individuals in the organization are motivated by sanctions and incentives to act in accordance with the goals of the organization.

Within this rational perspective there has over the years developed a growing adherence in managerial circles to the view that detailed hierarchical control of subordinates by their superiors is not an effective way to run an organization. It requires superiors to have a vast amount of information about their subordinates' working environment and fails to motivate individuals lower down the hierarchy. Decentralized management is regarded as more effective; it involves giving individual junior and middle managers considerable discretion within a clear framework of targets to be achieved within a set of constraints, particularly those imposed by a budget. Superiors control subordinate managers not through detailed instructions and daily negotiations, but through holding them accountable for the results achieved with the means supplied. Superiors do not spend time and effort on seeing how subordinate managers do their jobs, but on evaluating their actions.

Directly translated into the educational setting this means giving school and college managers the discretion to determine within a budget what real resources they need and how they should be deployed. Centralized hierarchical control is replaced by an arm's-length relationship. Local managers are given a one-line budget and are, in principle, to be held accountable for its management. In the absence of the bottom profit-and-loss line of the commercial organization, the government envisages putting in place a series of performance indicators for schools and colleges which would serve an analogous function, giving information to 'customers' (pupils, students, parents and employers) and to the 'shareholders' (the electors and their representatives, the LEA). The organization of the education service put in place by the 1988 Act is based on a rational model adapted from commercial organizations. Governing bodies take on more of the features of a board of management, with budgetary and staffing responsibilities; they set strategic goals, approve the executive management's policies for attaining those goals and consider evaluative reports on the organization's performance.

However, the model is more complex than the commercial analogy because the lines of accountability are more diffuse. LEAs retain statutory responsibilities for the provision of education in their area. Local government shares with central government the articulation of public demand for education, doing so by raising finance for education locally and by distributing central government grants and locally raised revenues between education sectors, programmes and institutions. At the same time, governing bodies have been strengthened both in their powers and in their local community representation, in order to provide an alternative channel to the election of local councillors, whereby the local community can influence schools and colleges. Thus there is not the clear line of hierarchy and accountability, discernible in other settings, which runs from subunits through to subsidiary firms and then to the parent company's board of management. Given, moreover, that the outputs of schools and colleges are multidimensional and difficult to quantify, the scope for ambiguity remains much greater in the educational setting.

Much of the advocacy of how financial management in education should be conducted is informed by the rational perspective and reflects the prevailing professional values of management specialists. It is currently reinforced by the government's attempt to put in place a more market oriented, and, as it sees it, more efficient and effective education system, in which its practitioners are not only more responsive to the requirements of their clients but take decisions in the light of their resource implications. A book on financial management in education must give the rational perspective a good run for its money since many of the skills widely accepted to be useful in managing resources and budgeting are drawn from the rational perspective.

However, educationists are probably more aware than commercial managers of the rich menu of alternative perspectives on understanding organizations. The political and subjective perspectives share the view that the concept of an organization's goals is meaningless. In the political model resource allocation and budget decisions are the outcome of interactions between interest groups within the organization. If objectives are pursued at all they are those of particular interest groups not of the organization as a whole. The subjective approach focuses on the meanings individuals attach to organizational activities. Thus resource allocation results from individual interactions; the process and its outcomes are interpreted and understood differently by the various members of the organization.

However, accountancy texts, at least modern ones, make clear that budgets are negotiated between budget givers and budget holders and that budgeting is affected by contingent factors which characterize the organization and its environment. When participating in or attempting to direct such negotiations, practitioners will find it useful to draw on the collegial, political, subjective and ambiguity approaches (developed in Bush, 1989), as well as the rational perspective, so as to amalgamate those elements of the various approaches which are relevant to their own personal and institutional circumstances.

Outline of this reader

This volume contains some theoretical articles, which set out concepts and techniques for financial management. These are interleaved with articles of a more applied nature, including case studies, which exemplify principles and techniques. The reader is divided into four sections:

- Functions and practice of budgeting;
- Principles of financial management: the rational perspective;
- The political and organizational context;
- Performance evaluation.

Functions and practice of budgeting

In Chapter 2, which sets out a conceptual framework for studying financial management, Anthony and Herzlinger develop the concept of management control in the context of non-profit organizations. They see management control as the process of making and implementing decisions so that the purposes of the organization are attained. They consider that management control exists in all organizations except perhaps the tiniest. It comes in different forms. It may be undertaken by means of a strong hierarchical structure dominated by formal decision making or it may be very informal, emerging from regularly confirmed consensus in a collegial setting. Budgeting is an important part of a management control system.

The 1988 Education Act can be seen as changing the management control system for education which embraces three levels – central government, the local authority and the institution. Under the 1944 Act there was considerable ambiguity regarding the relative powers of central and local government, while the local authority exercised detailed control of the resources allocated to its institutions. This centralized system of resource allocation is described in the case study by Paul Crisp (Chapter 3). The provisions of the 1988 Act reflect the prevalent view within management consultancy and the government that decentralized decision making within organizations promotes the efficient use of resources and improves the quality of output. A case for decentralized resource management in local government service provision is put by Stewart and Holtham in Chapter 4. How it operates in education is described and assessed by Haydn Howard (Chapter 5) in relation to Cambridgeshire's local financial management scheme which began in 1982.

Having indicated the general framework within which educational institutions will practise delegated financial management, we need to examine how this is undertaken within the school or college. One of the key tasks is budgeting – planning and preparing the budget, monitoring and fine-tuning it and, finally, evaluating budget decisions and using the information in further rounds of budget preparation. The budgeting process is explained by Arnold and Hope in Chapter 6. How three schools which participated in the Cambridgeshire local financial management scheme practised financial management is examined in Chapter 7.

The rational perspective

The 1988 Education Act can be seen as an attempt to restructure the education service along the lines of a rational model of a decentralized management control system. In this framework the national curriculum and its attainment targets serve as a control device whereby the DES sets out what schools and LEAs should achieve with their resources and leaves the detailed decisions as to how to deliver the prescribed educational outcomes to local managers. LEAs are cast in the role of intermediate-level management controllers; they are specifically charged with the responsibility for providing resources, evaluating and monitoring institutional performance and seeking improvements where necessary. (The changed role of LEAs is discussed in Chapter 16 by Derek Esp, which appears in Section III.) A further control device for improving local managers' performance (as conceived by the government) is competition for customers, to be achieved by the provisions for open enrolment and the insistence that schools and colleges are funded by a formula which is largely driven by the number of pupils or students attending the institution. The design of the budget formula as a management control device is examined by Levačić in Chapter 14.

The clear thrust of official pronouncements is that schools and LEAs should be developing 'rational' management control techniques.

It will be for the governing body, together with the head teacher, to develop and carry out a *management plan* for their school within the

general conditions and requirements of the LEA's scheme. In developing such a plan, governing bodies will need to take account of the full
range of their responsibilities for the management of schools, including
those on the curriculum and admissions set out in the Act. . . . The
head teacher will have the key role in helping the governing body to
formulate a management plan for the school, and in securing its
implementation with the collective support of the school's staff.

(DES, 1988a, p. 6)

In preparing and implementing schemes, LEAs, governing bodies and
head teachers will need to have regard to the relationship between
schemes of local management and their respective curricular duties
under the Education Acts. . . . Within this statutory framework,
governing bodies will be free to allocate resources to their own
curricular priorities from delegated budgets. . . . LEAs should,
however, provide in their schemes that governing bodies should spend
their delegated budgets in a manner which is consistent with the
implementation of the National Curriculum [and] with the statutory
requirements relating to the curriculum as a whole . . . and, for county
and controlled schools (and special schools covered by schemes), with
the LEA's curriculum policy as modified by the governing body.

(DES, 1988a, p. 35)

The rational approach to management is a strong thread running
through Coopers & Lybrand's (1988) report (from which Chapter 8 is
drawn).

Decision making will need to cover all aspects of school activities
starting with the setting of objectives, through the preparation of
detailed budgets and operating plans, the monitoring of progress and
achievement, agreement of changes and finally an annual review of the
year. . . .
   The operating plans and budgets developed at this stage should
contain proposals with estimated costs for the curriculum and extra
curricular development and training, and building and grounds maintenance. Of importance at this stage would be a review of the ways in
which continuing activities are carried out, with a view to ensuring the
best use of resources and value for money. . . . It will also be necessary
to set targets against which performance can be measured.

(Coopers & Lybrand, 1988, pp. 4–5)

If school management is to be conducted along these lines, then the
budget must be used as an instrument of management planning. As explained
in Chapters 2 and 6, the budget performs three distinct roles, accountability,
financial control and management planning. For the purposes of accountability (narrowly defined as is traditional in education and other sectors)
stewardship accounting is designed to show that money was spent for

intended and legitimate purposes. For this purpose and for financial control the traditional budget, which shows what is spent on the various inputs, is appropriate. An alternative name for the traditional budget is the subjective budget since it is constructed around the 'subjects' of expenditure such as staff, materials, fuel, building maintenance, and so on.

However, for management planning and rendering accountability in terms of ensuring value for money the traditional budget is inadequate, because it does not inform managers about the costs of the activities undertaken by the organization, or give them a longer term and comprehensive view of these activities. The rational approach to budgetary planning as an instrument of management control is to derive the planned activities or programmes of the organization from its aims. These aims, often referred to as missions, are very broad and usually qualitative. They are then translated into specific operational objectives which, if possible, should be quantified. For a school or college these operational targets are the programmes of learning provided for students which form the curriculum and supporting activities. Thus the rational approach to education budgeting requires that the budget be derived from the curriculum and supporting activities, such as pastoral care, administration and running the premises.

A budget which costs the activities or programmes of an organization is called an *objective* or *programme* budget. This type of budget enables one to evaluate the outcomes of particular programmes against the costs of providing them. Only when this is done can one obtain measures of the efficiency and effectiveness with which resources are used.

Chapters 9 to 13 present a variety of techniques used in rational approaches to budgeting. Chapters 9 and 10 outline two rational approaches to budgeting which have been adopted for school systems in the USA: these are planning, programming budgetary systems, and zero-based budgeting. In Chapter 11, Fielden and Pearson explain, within an educational context, some key cost concepts which are useful for resource planning. In Chapter 13, Derck Birch shows how programme budgeting would be applied to FE and HE colleges. Some aspects of these budgeting approaches can prove useful, as Jones demonstrates in Chapter 12 with respect to his own college.

The political and organizational context

Rational techniques are predicated on the presumption that the decision-making process proceeds in orderly stages. The organization's goals are established, then information on the relative costs and benefits of different ways of achieving those goals is assessed so as finally to select those that yield the highest expected net benefits. However, techniques such as programme budgeting and zero-based budgeting may be too demanding in terms of the resources needed to collect and analyse the necessary data and to use it for decision making. Indeed the data may be inadequate for measuring the costs that should be correctly attributed to particular activities. A lot of complex calculations do not necessarily provide relevant information. Furthermore, the rational approach to decision making and its attendant information requirements may be rejected by an institution because it clashes with its culture, with the interests of particular groups or individuals, or with its decision processes. Tim Simkins, in Chapter 15, discusses budgeting as a political and organizational process. Though written with reference to post-compulsory institutions, it is also highly relevant to schools. Thus, in practice, rational budgeting techniques have to be tempered by the organizational constraints and political realities that present unique features in each institution. Pamela Young (Chapter 17) takes this theme further in the school context, by considering the implications of the evidence drawn from research into effective schools for undertaking financial management within schools.

Performance evaluation

The final section on performance evaluation is, given the nature of the topic, a return to the rational perspective. Geoffrey Hulme (Chapter 18) considers general issues concerned with performance evaluation and the design and use of performance indicators for schools, while Carol Fitz-Gibbon (Chapter 19) outlines an example of measuring and using performance indicators in secondary schools. The final word is left to Ernest House, whose raised voice against the rationalist managerial approach reminds us that attempts to implement it have been made in the USA since the 1960s.

Conclusion

Financial management in education is a developing field. Some of the articles in this reader draw on existing literature on management accounting and control in other sectors, where the topic has been intensively studied in the last thirty years. Here there has been an increasing awareness of the limitations of the rational perspective and a growing interest in relating the practice of management accounting and control to the context of the organization. Those who are or will be engaged in financial management in education are fortunate in being able to draw upon this literature and experience, to select what seems relevant to education and to develop, through practice and research, an emerging field. The newly published articles in this reader are a contribution to this, as is the work of all those involved in the financial management of educational institutions.

References

Bush, T. (1989). *Managing Education: Theory and Practice*. Milton Keynes, Open University Press.

Coopers & Lybrand (1988). *Local Management in Schools.* London, HMSO.
Department of Education and Science and Welsh Office (1987). *Managing Colleges Efficiently.* London, HMSO.
Department of Education and Science (1988a). *Education Reform Act: Local Management of Schools.* Circular 7/88.
Department of Education and Science (1988b). *Education Reform Act: Local Management of Further and Higher Education Colleges: Planning and Delegation Schemes and Articles of Government.* Circular 9/88.

2

Management control in nonprofit organizations

A. R. Anthony and R. E. Herzlinger

In all organizations, except possibly the tiniest, there is a process called management control. The process has existed as long as organizations have been in existence, but it has not been the subject of much systematic study and analysis until fairly recently. A landmark book, Barnard's *Functions of the Executive*, which dealt with this as well as other management processes, was originally published in 1938.[1]

From this book and from a number of other studies published in recent years, there have evolved principles that are helpful in designing management control systems and in carrying on management control activities. As is the case with all principles of management, these principles are tentative, incomplete, inconclusive, vague, sometimes contradictory, and inadequately supported by experimental or other evidence. Some of them will probably turn out to be wrong. Nevertheless, they seem to have sufficient validity so that it is better for managers to take them into account than to ignore them. They seem to work in an considerable number of actual organizations.

Most studies of the management control process have been done in business organizations, and most of the new control techniques were developed in these organizations. Most descriptions of the management control process therefore tend to assume, usually implicitly but sometimes explicitly, that the process being described is taking place in a business enterprise.

This book, by contrast, is a study of management control in nonprofit organizations. Its thesis is that the basic control concepts are the same in both profit-oriented and nonprofit organizations, but that because of the special characteristics of nonprofit organizations, the application of these concepts differs in some important respects. Some, but not all, of the control techniques developed in profit-oriented organizations are applicable to nonprofit organizations. Certain other techniques are appropriate for nonprofit organizations but not for profit–oriented organizations.

Management control systems

Before discussing the similarities and differences of management control techniques in nonprofit organizations as compared to those in business, we shall provide an overview of the general characteristics of management control systems.

Planning and control processes

Two of the important activities in which all managers engage are (1) planning and (2) control. *Planning* is deciding what should be done and how it should be done, and *control* is assuring that the desired results are obtained. In most organizations, three different types of planning and control processes can be identified: (1) strategic planning, (2) operational control, and (3) management control. Since our focus is on the management control process, we shall describe the other two types of processes only briefly.

Strategic planning

Any organization has one or more goals. Its top management decides what these goals should be. Top management also decides on the general nature of the activities that the organization should undertake in order to achieve these goals; these are its strategies. *Strategic planning* is the process of deciding on the goals of the organization and on the broad strategies that are to be used in attaining these goals. These decisions are made only occasionally and at the highest levels in the organization.

Operational control

At the other extreme are processes that are used in facilitating the day–to–day activities of the organization. These consist of rules, procedures, forms, and other devices that govern the performance of specific tasks. *Operational control* is the process of assuring that specific tasks are carried out effectively and efficiently.

Management Control

Between these two types of planning and control processes is the process called management control. In this process the goals and strategies arrived at in the strategic planning process are accepted as given; management control has to do with the implementation of these strategies. On the other hand, management control does not involve the detailed operating decisions that are the focus of operational control; rather, it seeks to ensure that these operations are carried out properly. *Management control* is defined as the process by which management assures that the organization carries out its strategies effectively and efficiently.

Nature of a management control system

Any organization, except the smallest, is divided into units which are called *responsibility centers*. A responsibility center is a group of people headed by a manager who is responsible for what it does. In large organizations there is a complicated hierarchy of responsibility centers – units, sections, departments, branches, and divisions. Except for those at the bottom of the organization, these responsibility centers consist of aggregations of smaller responsibility centers. The entire organization is itself a responsibility center. One function of top management is to plan, coordinate, and control the work of all these responsibility centers; this is the management control function.

> **Example**: A university consists of a number of responsibility centers, called schools and colleges, for example, the Schools of Law and Medicine and the College of Arts and Sciences. Each of these schools and colleges is in turn composed of separate responsibility centers, for example, the language department, the physics department, and so on. These departments may in turn be divided into separate responsibility

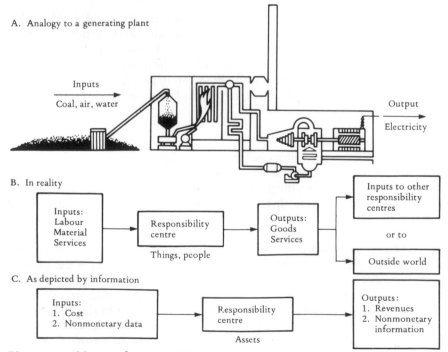

Figure 2.1   Nature of a responsibility center

centers; for example, the language department may be composed of different areas for each separate language. The management control function is to plan, coordinate, and control the work of all these responsibility centers.

Figure 2.1 shows the essence of what any responsibility center does, using a steam-generating plant as an analogy. The plant exists for a purpose, namely, to generate electrical energy. In order to accomplish this purpose, it has furnaces, turbines, smokestacks, and other physical resources. In operating, the generating plant uses fuel; this is its input. The energy that it produces is its output.

Any responsibility center exists to accomplish one or more purposes; these purposes are its *objectives*. Presumably, the objectives of an individual responsibility center are intended to help achieve the overall goals of the whole organization. These overall goals are decided upon in the strategic planning process, which means that they have been established prior to the beginning of the management control process.

A responsibility center has inputs of labor, material, and services; for example, the language department has inputs of faculty, staff, educational materials, and services. It does work with these inputs, and as a consequence it produces outputs of goods or services. The language department educates its students in language. Presumably, these outputs are related to the responsibility center's objectives, but this is not necessarily so. In any event, whatever the responsibility center does constitutes its outputs.

Measurement of inputs and outputs

The amount of labor, material, and services used in a responsibility center are physical quantities: hours of labor, quarts of oil, reams of paper, kilowatt-hours of electricity, and so on. In a control system it is convenient to translate these amounts into monetary terms. Money provides a common denominator which permits the amounts of individual resources to be combined. The monetary amount is ordinarily obtained by multiplying the physical quantity by a price per unit of quantity (e.g., hours of labor times a rate per hour). This amount is called cost. Thus the inputs of a responsibility center are ordinarily expressed as costs. Cost is a measure of resources used by a responsibility center.

Note that inputs are resources *used* by the responsibility center. The patients in a hospital or the students in a school are *not* inputs. Rather, it is the resources that are used in accomplishing the objectives of *treating* the patients or *educating* the students that are the inputs.

Although inputs almost always can be measured in terms of cost, outputs are much more difficult to measure. In many responsibility centers, outputs cannot be measured at all. In a profit-oriented organization, revenue is often an important measure of output, but such a measure is rarely a complete expression of outputs; it does not encompass everything that the organization does. In many nonprofit organizations, no good quantitative measure of output exists. A school can easily measure the number of students graduated, but it cannot measure how much education each of them acquired. Although outputs may not be measured, or may not even be measurable, it is a fact that every organization unit *has* outputs; that is, it does something.

Efficiency and effectiveness

The concepts stated above can be used to explain the meaning of efficiency and effectiveness, which are the two criteria for judging the performance of a responsibility center. The terms efficiency and effectiveness are almost always used in a comparative, rather than in an absolute, sense; that is, we do not ordinarily say that Organization Unit A is 80 per cent efficient, but rather that it is more (or less) efficient than Organization Unit B, or that it is more (or less) efficient currently than it was in the past.

Efficiency is the ratio of outputs to inputs, or the amount of output per unit of input. Unit A is more efficient than Unit B either (1) if it uses less resources than Unit B but has the same output, or (2) if it uses the same resources as Unit B and has more output than Unit B. Note that the first type of measure does not require that output be quantified; it is only necessary to judge that the outputs of the two units are approximately the same. If management is satisfied that Units A and B are both doing a satisfactory job and if it is a job of comparable magnitude, then the unit with the lower inputs, that is, the lower costs, is the more efficient. For example, if two elementary schools are judged to be furnishing adequate education, the one with the lower costs is the more efficient. The second type of measure does require some quantitative measure of output; it is therefore a more difficult type of measurement in many situations. If two elementary schools have the same costs, one can be said to be more efficient than the other only if it provides more education, and this is difficult to measure.

In many responsibility centers, a measure of efficiency can be developed that relates actual costs to some standard – that is, to a number that expresses what costs should be incurred for the amount of measured output. Such a measure can be a useful indication of efficiency, but it is never a perfect measure for at least two reasons: (1) recorded costs are not a precisely accurate measure of resources consumed; and (2) standards are, at best, only approximate measures of what resource consumption ideally should have been in the circumstances prevailing.

Effectiveness is the relationship between a responsibility center's outputs and its objectives. The more these outputs contribute to the objectives, the more effective the unit is. Since both objectives and outputs are often difficult to quantify, measures of effectiveness are difficult to come by. Effectiveness, therefore, is often expressed in nonquantitative, judgmental terms, such as

'College A is doing a first-rate job'; 'College B has slipped somewhat in recent years'.

An organization unit should be *both* efficient and also effective; it is not a matter of one or the other. Efficient managers are those who do whatever they do with the lowest consumption of resources; but if what they do (i.e., their output) is an inadequate contribution to the accomplishment of the organization's goals, they are ineffective. If in a welfare office the employees are invariably busy and if they process claims and applications with little wasted motion, the office is efficient; but if the personnel have the attitude that their function is to ensure that every form is made out perfectly rather than that their function is to help clients get the services to which they are entitled, the office is ineffective. [. . .]

The role of profits

One important goal in a profit-oriented organization is to earn profits, and the amount of profits is therefore an important measure of effectiveness. Since profit is the difference between revenue, which is a measure of output, and expense, which is a measure of input, profit is also a measure of efficiency. Thus, profit measures both effectiveness and efficiency. When such an overall measure exists, it is unnecessary to determine the relative importance of effectiveness versus efficiency. When such an overall measure does not exist, it is feasible and useful to classify performance measures as relating either to effectiveness or to efficiency. In these situations, there is the problem of balancing the two types of measurements. For example, how do we compare the profligate perfectionist with the frugal manager who obtains less than the optimum output?

Although profit is an important overall measure of effectiveness and efficiency, it is a less than perfect measure for several reasons: (1) monetary measures do not exactly measure either all aspects of output or all inputs; (2) standards against which profits are judged are not accurate; and (3) at best, profit is a measure of what has happened in the short run, whereas we are presumably also interested in the long-run consequences of management actions.
[. . .]

Structure and process

As is the case with any system, a management control system can be described in terms of (a) its structure and (b) its process; that is, what it is and what it does. [. . .]

The account structure

An account is a device for collecting homogeneous data about some phenomenon, as indicated by its title and as specified in the definition of what is to be collected therein. Accounts collect data on either inputs or outputs. They can collect data on either what has happened (i.e., historical data) or what is planned to happen (i.e., future data). A management control system contains two principal account structures, namely, a program structure and a responsibility structure. Although they are described separately, they are in practice interrelated.

The program structure

The program structure contains information on the programs that the organization undertakes or plans to undertake. In a profit-oriented company, the principal programs are the company's products or product lines because program decisions are made in terms of products or product lines. The program structure is arranged so that data collected in the program accounts are useful for three principal purposes:

1 To make decisions about the programs that are to be undertaken and the amount and kind of resources that should be devoted to each program.
2 To permit comparisons to be made among programs carried on by several organizations. For example, hospitals typically have a food service program; thus, food service costs in one hospital can be compared with those in another hospital.
3 To provide a basis for setting fees charged to clients or for reimbursement of costs incurred.

The responsibility structure

The second principal way of classifying information is by responsibility centers. Information classified in this way is used for (1) planning the activities of responsibility centers, (2) coordinating the work of the several responsibility centers in an organization, and (3) controlling the responsibility center manager. There are three principal types of responsibility centers: (1) expense centers, (2) profit centers, and (3) investment centers.

Expense centers

If the management control system measures the expenses incurred by a responsibility center but does not measure the monetary value of the unit's output, the unit is an expense center. Although every responsibility center *has* outputs (i.e., it does something), in many cases it is neither feasible nor necessary to measure these outputs in monetary terms. It would be extremely difficult to measure the monetary value that the accounting department contributes to the whole organization, for example. Although it would be relatively easy to measure the monetary value of the outputs of an individual production department, there may be no good reason for doing so if the responsibility of the factory supervisor is simply to produce a stated *quantity* of output at the lowest feasible cost.

In a business enterprise most individual production departments and most staff units are expense centers. In many nonprofit organizations, *all* the responsibility centers are expense centers. For these, the accounting system records expenses incurred, but not revenue earned.

Profit centers

Revenue is a monetary measure of output, and expense is a monetary measure of input, or resources consumed Profit is the difference between revenue and expense. Thus, in a profit-oriented business, if performance in a responsibility center is measured in terms of both the revenue it earns and the expense it incurs, the unit is called a *profit center*. Many nonprofit organizations have responsibility centers in which fees charged for services furnished approximately equal the value of these services. This is the case with most of the operating departments of a hospital; with the housing, food service, and other auxiliary services of a university; and with utilities, refuse collection, and similar enterprises of a municipality. Although the use of the term 'profit center' in a nonprofit organization may seem to be a contradiction of terms, for our purposes it is convenient to label such responsibility centers as profit centers.

Investment centers

In an investment center, the account structure measures not only profit but also the capital employed in generating that profit. Thus, the account structure in an investment center encompasses more aspects of the manager's job than is the case with the profit center, just as the profit center encompasses more aspects than does the expense center. The investment center concept is rarely used in nonprofit organizations, however.

Mission centers and service centers

It is also useful to classify responsibility centers as either mission centers or service centers. The output of a *mission center* contributes directly to the objectives of the organization. The output of a *service center* contributes to the work of other responsibility centers, which may be either mission centers or other service centers; its output is thus one of the inputs of these responsibility centers.

A service center can be either an expense center or a profit center. If the latter, it 'sells' its services to the units that it services, and its output is measured by the revenue generated by such sales. Its objective usually is not to make a profit – that is, an excess of revenue over expenses – but rather to break even. The extension of the profit center idea to service centers is relatively new, especially in nonprofit organizations. When properly set up, it can provide a powerful instrument for management control.

Relation of the program and responsibility structures

A responsibility center may work solely on one program, and it may be the only responsibility center working on that program. If so, the program structure corresponds to the responsibility structure. This is so, for example, when a group of people work on a single program, as is often the case in municipal governments when one organization unit is responsible for providing police protection, another for education, and another for solid waste disposal. In some cases this correspondence between programs and responsibility centers does not exist.

[. . .]

Other accounting information

The two main account structures described above are part of an organization's accounting system. In addition to the accounts needed for management control purposes, the accounting system must be able to collect the data needed for general-purpose financial reports prepared for outside parties. [. . .]

In addition to general-purpose financial reports, outside agencies may require reports prepared according to requirements that they specify. [. . .] These reports may or may not be useful to the management of the organization that prepares them. Ideally, the information these special-purpose reports give should be summaries of the information contained in the management control system because outside agencies presumably do not need more, or different, information from that which is useful to management. This ideal is not always achieved [. . .]

The accounting system provides historical information; that is, information on what has happened, what the costs were. In addition, the management control system provides two other types of information: (1) estimates of what *will* happen in the future and (2) estimates of what *should* happen. The latter are called standards or budgets, and the former are called forecasts.

Summary of the account structure

The essence of the preceding description can be restated by listing four questions for which a management control system is designed to communicate relevant information. Two of these arise before operations take place, and the other two arise after operations have taken place. They are as follows:

Before the event:
1 What activities should the organization undertake (i.e., its planned outputs)?
2 What resources should it use (i.e., its planned inputs)?
After the event:
3 How effectively did the organization do its job (i.e., its actual outputs related to its objective)?

4 How efficiently did the organization use resources (i.e., its actual inputs
   related to outputs)?

All four questions should be answered both in terms of programs and in
terms of responsibility centers.
[. . .]

The management control process

As already noted, the management control process takes place in an organization that already exists, that has goals, and that has decided on broad
strategies for achieving these goals. Decisions on these goals and strategies are
made in the *strategic planning process*. The strategic planning process is largely
unsystematic and informal. The management control system collects information that is useful in strategic planning. Since strategic decisions are
made only occasionally, and since each strategic issue requires information
that is tailor-made to the requirements of that issue, this information cannot
ordinarily be collected in any routine, recurring fashion but must rather be
put together when the need arises and in the form required for the specific
issue.
[. . .]
Much of the management control process is informal. It occurs by
means of memoranda, meetings, conversations, and even by such signals as
facial expressions. Such control devices are not amenable to a systematic
description. Many organizations also have a formal system. The information
in this system consists of (1) planned (or estimated) and (2) actual data on (a)
outputs and (b) inputs. Prior to actual operations, decisions and estimates are
made as to what outputs and inputs are to be; during actual operations,
records are maintained as to what outputs and inputs actually are; and
subsequent to operations, reports are prepared that compare actual outputs
and inputs to planned outputs and inputs, and action is taken on the basis of
these reports. The principal steps in the formal management control process
are the following:

1 Programming.
2 Budgeting.
3 Operating (and measurement).
4 Reporting and analysis.

Each of these steps leads to the next. They recur in a regular cycle, and
together they constitute a 'closed loop', as indicated in Figure 2.2.

Programming

In the programming phase, decisions are made with respect to the major
programs the organization plans to undertake during the coming period.

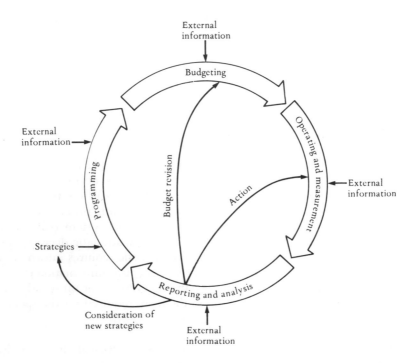

Figure 2.2 Phases of management control

These decisions either are made within the context of the goals and strategies that have previously been decided upon, or they represent changes in strategy. If the latter, they are part of the strategic planning process, rather than the management control process; the two processes merge into one another in the programming phase.

Some organizations state their programs in the form of a 'long-range plan' which shows planned outputs and inputs for a number of years ahead – usually 5 years, but possibly as few as 3 or (in the case of public utilities) as many as 20. Many organizations do not have such a formal mechanism for displaying their overall future programs; they rely instead on reports or understandings as to specific, important facets of the program, particularly the amounts to be invested in capital assets and the means of financing these assets.

In an industrial company the 'programs' are usually products or product lines, plus activities (such as research) that are not relatable to specific products. The plans state the amount and character of resources (i.e., inputs) that are to be devoted to each program, and the ways in which these resources are to be used. [. . .]

To the extent feasible, program decisions are based on an economic analysis. In such an analysis, the revenues or other benefits estimated from the proposed program are compared with the estimated costs. For many programs in profit-oriented companies, and for most programs in nonprofit organizations, however, reliable estimates of benefits cannot be made. For these programs, decisions are based on judgment and are influenced by the persuasive abilities of program advocates, and by political and other considerations.

Budgeting

A budget is a plan expressed in quantitative, usually monetary, terms covering a specified period of time. The time period is usually one year, but in a few organizations it may be six months or three months. In the budgeting process the program is translated into terms that correspond to the sphere of responsibility of those who are charged with executing it. Thus, although plans are originally made in program terms, in the budgeting process they are converted into responsibility terms. The process of arriving at the budget is essentially one of negotiation between the managers of responsibility centers and their superiors. The end product of these negotiations is a statement of the outputs that are expected during the budget year and the resources that are to be used in achieving these outputs.

The agreed-upon budget is a *bilateral commitment*. Responsibility center managers commit themselves to produce the planned output with the agreed amount of resources, and their superiors commit themselves to agreeing that such performance is satisfactory. Both commitments are subject to the qualification 'unless circumstances change significantly'.

Operating and measurement

During the period of actual operations, records are kept of resources actually consumed and outputs actually achieved. The records of resources consumed (i.e., costs) are structured so that costs are collected both by programs and by responsibility centers. Costs in the former classification are used as a basis for future programming, and those in the latter are used to measure the performance of the heads of responsibility centers.

Related to the collection of information is the process of *internal auditing*. It consists of the procedures that are intended to ensure that the information is accurate and that the opportunities for an undetected departure from plans and policies, and for theft or defalcation, are kept to a minimum. In organizations of any substantial size, a separate internal auditing organization exists to ensure adherence to these procedures. In many nonprofit organizations the internal auditing function is not well developed. In such organizations the data tend to be unreliable, and this greatly impedes the smooth functioning of the management control process.

Reporting and analysis

Accounting information, along with a variety of other information, is summarized, analysed, and reported to those who are responsible for knowing what is happening in the company and for improving performance. As indicated above, these reports essentially compare planned outputs and inputs with actual outputs and inputs. The information in these reports is used for three purposes.

First, the reports are a basis for coordinating and controlling the current activities of the organization. Using this information, together with information that is obtained from conversations or other informal sources, managers identify situations that may be 'out of control', they investigate these situations, and they initiate corrective action if investigation shows such action to be necessary.

Second, the reports are used as a basis of evaluating operating performance. Such an evaluation leads to actions with respect to managers: praise for a job well done; constructive criticism if this seems to be warranted; and to promotion, reassignment, or, in extreme cases, termination of the managers of the responsibility centers whose performance is reported. It may also lead to improved methods of operating.

Third, the reports are used as a basis for program evaluation. For any of a number of reasons, the plan under which the organization is working may turn out not to be optimum. If so, the budget and the program are revised accordingly. This is why the management control system is a closed loop. Evaluation of actual performance can lead back to the first step, a revision of the program.

General system characteristics

A total system

Ordinarily, a formal management control system is a *total* system in the sense that it embraces all aspects of the organization's operation. It needs to be a total system because an important management function is to assure that all parts of the operation are in balance with one another; and in order to examine balance, management needs information about each of the parts. By contrast, the information used in the strategic planning process is usually collected specifically for the plans under consideration, and these rarely embrace the whole organization. Also, information used in the control of operating activities (e.g., production control, inventory control) is usually tailor-made to the requirements of each such activity.

Goal congruence

It is reasonable to expect that persons will act according to what they perceive their own best interests to be. A management control system should be designed so that the actions it leads managers to take in accordance with their perceived self-interest are also actions that are in the best interest of the organization. In the language of social psychology, the system should encourage *goal congruence*. It should be structured so that the personal goals of people in the organization are, so far as feasible, consistent with the goals of the organization as a whole. Perfect congruence between individual goals and organizational goals does not exist, but as a minimum the system should not encourage the individual to act *against* the best interests of the organization. For example, if the system signals that the emphasis should be only on reducing costs, and if an individual responds by reducing costs and at the same time sacrificing quality or providing inadequate service, or by reducing costs in one department by measures that cause a more than offsetting increase in some other department, the person has been motivated, but in the wrong direction.

Financial framework

With rare exceptions a management control system is *built around a financial structure*; that is, resources are expressed in monetary units. Money is the only common denominator by means of which the heterogeneous elements of resources (e.g., hours of labor, type of labor, quantity and quality of material) can be combined and compared. This does not mean that accounting information is the sole, or even the most important, part of the system; it means only that the accounting system provides a unifying core to which other types of information can be related. Although the financial structure is usually the central focus, nonmonetary measures such as minutes per operation, number of persons, and reject and spoilage rates are also important parts of the system.

The system contains information about both inputs and outputs. In nonprofit organizations, however, output information is often difficult to express in monetary terms, in contrast with input information which can usually be expressed in terms of costs.

Rhythm

The management control process tends to be rhythmic; it follows a definite pattern and timetable, month after month, and year after year. In budgeting, certain steps are taken in a prescribed sequence and at certain dates each year: dissemination of guidelines, preparation of original estimates, transmission of these estimates up through the several echelons in the organization, review of these estimates, final approval by top management, dissemination back through the organization, operating and accounting, reporting, and the analysis of performance. The procedure to be followed at each step in this process, the dates when the steps are to be completed, and even the forms to be used can be, and often are, set forth in a manual.

Integration

A management control system is, or should be, a *coordinated, integrated system*; that is, although data collected for one purpose may differ from those collected for another purpose, these data should be reconcilable with one another. In a sense, the management control system is a single system, but it is perhaps more useful to think of it as two interlocking subsystems, one focusing on programs and the other on responsibility centers.

Line and staff relationships

The person responsible for the design and operation of the management control system is here called the controller. In practice, the person may have other titles, such as administrative officer or chief accountant.

The idea that the controller has a broader responsibility than merely 'keeping the books' is a fairly recent one in profit-oriented organizations, and it is not yet well accepted in many nonprofit organizations. Not too long ago, controllers, who were then invariably called 'chief accountants', were expected to confine their activities to collecting and reporting historical data. With the development of formal management control systems and the emphasis on information needed for planning and decision making, the controller's function has broadened.

Notwithstanding the broadened responsibilities, the controller remains, or should remain, a staff person. Decisions about management control should be made by the line managers, not by the staff. The job of the staff is to provide information that will facilitate making good decisions. In an organization whose chief executive officer is unwilling to assume overall responsibility, an operating manager with a problem of inadequate resources may be told, 'Go see the controller'. In making such a statement, the top manager abrogates line responsibility, and the controller is put in the position of acting in a line capacity. The controller then, de facto, becomes a manager, with a corresponding diminution in the responsibility of the person who nominally is charged with management. This usually leads to less than optimum management of the whole organization.

In some government agencies, this tendency for the controller to assume line responsibility became quite strong in the 1940s and 1950s. This was usually a consequence of top management's reluctance to accept overall responsibility. [. . .] With the 'power of the purse', the budget officer became one of the most powerful persons in the organization. It has been said that in some large military installations, the commanding officer was principally in charge of ceremonies, and the real boss was the budget officer. With the current tendency to select a good manager as the chief executive officer, the role of the budget officer has, fortunately, become more like the staff role that it should be.

[. . .]

Line managers

It is important to emphasize that line managers are the focal points in management control. They are persons whose judgments are incorporated in the approved plans, and they are the persons who must influence others and whose performance is measured. Staff people collect, summarize, and present information that is useful in the process, and they make calculations that translate management judgments into the format of the system. Such a staff may be large in numbers; indeed, the control department is often the largest staff department in an organization. However, the significant decisions are made by the line managers, not by the staff.

Informal systems

The system described in the preceding paragraphs is the *formal* management control system. Alongside this formal system there also exists in every organization an informal system of relationships among the members of the organization. In understanding the total management control process in a given organization, discerning the nature of this informal system is at least as important as learning about the formal system. Ideally, these informal relationships reinforce the formal system, but in many organizations the two systems work at cross purposes. Although the formal system is designed to achieve certain objectives, the behavior of individual managers and their personal relationships with one another may operate to defeat the attainment of these objectives. In this situation, although the formal system clearly describes the job that is supposed to be done, that job may not actually get done. In describing a system, however, it is impossible to include the nature of the informal system other than to point out its existence and its importance.

Boundaries of management control

Management control is an important function of management, but it is by no means the whole of management. An even more important function is to make judgments about people, their integrity, their ability, their potential, their fitness for a given job, their compatibility with colleagues. Management is responsible for building an effective human organization and for motivating the people in that organization to work toward its goals.

Note

1 Chester I. Barnard, *Functions of the Executive*, 30th anniv. ed. (Cambridge, Mass.: Harvard University Press, 1968).

3

Centralized resource allocation in education

Paul Crisp

The LEA under consideration is a district of one of the former metropolitan counties. [. . .] The FE service is delivered through seven general FE colleges, two monotechnics and a polytechnic. [. . .] Expenditure on FE colleges (excluding the polytechnic) in 1985/6 was £28.5m of which £20.5m (72 per cent) was staffing costs. Non-academic staff costs account for approximately 12 per cent of the gross expenditure. [. . .]

The policy arena of this study is marked by an absence of overt policy making. On the budgeting front the LEA has followed a cash-limited system which does not distinguish between different forms of expenditure. Personnel polices are set by the council's Personnel Department and these have impacted more significantly on support staff than teaching staff. The recent re-organization of the Education Department has included a shift of responsibility for personnel generally to within that department. It is nevertheless still the case that the department has less freedom to determine staffing levels, grades and deployment of support staff than for teaching staff, the latter being virtually wholly within Education Department control. One consequence of this is that variations in support staff establishment [. . .] are very difficult to achieve and have to undergo a lengthy and elaborate approval procedure as far as the Policy and Finance Committee. [. . .] Premises related staffing (i.e. cleaners, in the main) is determined by work study under a productivity scheme . . .

[. . .]

The Treasurer's Department supervises adherence to financial regulations in regard to matters such as virement, processing of payments, etc. In fact, there is no delegation of virement powers to institutions and all proposals to switch expenditure between heads require the agreement of Continuing Education Division, the treasurer or, in some cases, the appropriate committee. Nor is there any carry over of under- or over-spends between years. Similarly, aside from minor items paid from petty cash account, all payments to suppliers are processed through the treasurers' cashier. Approval to commit expenditure on equipment above a certain value has to be obtained centrally.

Planning and budgeting

The planning and budgeting approach of this LEA is the traditional historical/incremental one. The revenue base budget is established by bringing forward the previous year's budgeted expenditure updated for current (November) prices. Discussions at political level establish the likely level of funds to be available in the budget year in question and the marginal amount to be made available for new developments and/or savings to be achieved. The budget figure established in this process is at the service (i.e., education as a whole) and sector level and is usually fixed in February. Treasurer's Department, in consultation with the Continuing Education Division, then derives individual college budgets to conform with the budget allocation determined for FE. Individual allocations to colleges are usually announced in June/July.

Plans to revise the budgeting process to take greater account of student numbers using an SSR relationship were set out in the Work-Related NAFE Development Plan. Progress in this area has, however, been delayed. [. . .] In the current year most college budget heads were established purely historically. [. . .]

Income

The council sets targets for external income for each college. 'Income' includes 'full cost' courses funded directly by employers, students etc., and courses bought directly by MSC (e.g., YTS). It excludes the work-related NAFE funds now distributed by MSC through the planning process agreed in 1985 by the MSC and LEAs. Colleges may retain the greater part of any income earned over target, subject to a number of constraints on how the resources may be committed (e.g., no long-term commitments, no variations in permanent staffing). For those colleges which do not meet their targets there are, apparently, no penalties or sanctions applied – the LEA has not adopted a net budgeting regime. An analysis of 1985/86 out-turn figures revealed significant variations in income levels achieved by individual colleges. [. . .] Objective criteria by which to establish target levels for income earning [do not exist].

The LEA does not, in general, use formulae for distributing resources to colleges. The exception is for cleaning budgets where a formula based on floor area, type of usage and type and frequency of cleaning is used. This is related to the productivity scheme described above. [. . .]

The capital budget is set using a process similar to that for revenue expenditure, i.e. the global capital budget is determined at council level and then apportioned to service departments. It differs from the revenue budget in that a three-year rolling programme has been established which is reviewed and brought forward each year. [. . .]

Control of expenditure

Expenditure control is seen, in practice, primarily as the responsibility of the treasurer and the college. The treasurer produces a monthly analysis of expenditure against a profiled budget and this is sent to Continuing Education Division and the college principal. The treasurer would expect to follow up any gross departures from planned budget but this is rarely necessary as the principals seem to manage their institutions, by and large, within the budget set. There is, as yet, no system within Continuing Education Division for monitoring expenditure on a routine basis. In addition, college make an end-of-year expenditure return and a quarterly return on income.

Control of teaching staff is principally through a centralized advertisement process which prevents posts in excess of complement being advertised. For support staff, variations are controlled through the approval mechanism described above. Proposals to appoint support staff to part time and temporary positions can be approved if funded from the college visiting teachers allowance. In these cases colleges have to make a detailed individual submission to Continuing Education Division and demonstrate that they have the funds available. Personnel Department vet the grading proposed and the treasurer has to confirm that the college can fund the post within its budget.

Expenditure from the equipment, tools, and materials budget requires Continuing Education Division approval for items over £500. Competitive tenders have to be obtained for items over £1,500. [. . .] The appropriateness of the purchase of any individual item is judged, it appears, on individual merits – not against established criteria.

Premises related staff work to a productivity scheme which is monitored by work study officers based in the council's Management Service Unit. Building maintenance is undertaken by the Engineers Department and funded from within the global maintenance budget. The funds available appear to be inadequate to the task and at least one college has funded some maintenance work from within its own resources. Other premises costs (including energy, telephones, postage and travelling expenses) are met from central budgets and recharged to colleges. The budget for each of these expenditure heads is established on a historic basis and has not been systematically reviewed. [. . .] It is probable that there is difficulty in identifying the relevant costs for each college. [. . .]

In general, then, the LEA is primarily concerned to ensure that each college lives within its total budget. As the institutions have generally managed to do this, even where this has been educationally dysfunctional (as some colleges would claim), there has been little incentive in the past to revise the budget allocation and expenditure monitoring procedures.

[. . .]

The scope for targets [. . .]

A fundamental issue within the LEA is the availability of management information. The 1984 'value for money' review conducted by the auditors drew attention to the importance of reliable information and the absence of systems to deliver it. At the time of this study those systems were in the early stage of development. Continuing Education Division had just appointed a management information officer but he had not yet taken up the post. The current reliance on manual returns from colleges, the FESR return and the routine outputs of the council's central accounting system is intended to be supplemented or replaced by other systems, some of which are being developed within Continuing Education Division using micro-computer facilities. FEMIS (Further Education Management Information System) has been purchased for use on a trial basis in a small number of colleges and the LEA is currently considering whether to provide the system for all colleges.

The LEA is also beginning to develop its use of performance indicators across the whole service. [. . .] It is hoped eventually to use indicators to inform the budget allocation process, major structural decisions such as closures and re-organizations, periodic reports to council on the work of the Education Committee and day-to-day management decisions.

4

Decentralized resource management in local government

J. Stewart and C. Holtham

Decentralized resource management (DRM) is the delegation of greater authority to managers at identifiable cost centres to enable them to deploy resources to achieve the authority's policies. Rather than over-define the management task in detailed duties and over-limit the way resources are to be used, the management task is defined by what has to be achieved within the policies of the authority and the resources made available.

Decentralized resource management has derived from two separate sources. The first is accountable management where each manager is given responsibility for achieving agreed results for specified levels of resources. The second is the idea of cost centre management, where a cost centre manager is responsible for a financial budget, cost control of that budget and for the effective application of the resources controlled in that budget.

There is nothing particularly new in the idea of public sector managers being accountable for meeting targets or for controlling budgets. That has been seen as a necessary part of stewardship. Decentralized resource management is however seen as a means of improving management. It derives from a recognition that stewardship does not necessarily require control in the detail in which it has normally been exercised. Thus an emphasis on detailed financial control is replaced by an emphasis on overall control. It is the bottom line that is controlled. The responsibility of the cost centre manager is to keep within the overall financial limit set upon the cost centre.

Effective management of resources is more likely to be achieved if the cost centre managers can themselves manage the deployment of resources. Interest in decentralized resource management has been stimulated by the growth of modern computer systems which makes it possible, even in the very largest and most geographically dispersed organizations, for managers to have rapid access to budget and cost information.

Decentralized resource management does not mean simply allocating budgets to cost centre managers to do what they wish with the resources. Budgets and finance are a means of achieving management purposes. The management purposes are achieving the policy objective of the authority. [. . .] Giving greater managerial authority does not remove the need for accountability, rather it reinforces the need. In traditional management the manager is subject to detailed control. Formal accountability is secured by detailed control. Under DRM, the manager is free from detailed control, but remains accountable for the achievement of the Council's policy within the resources available. This is achieved through periodic review of accountability. Rather than day by day accountability, the cost centre manager is given organizational time and space to discharge managerial responsibilities. [. . .] The manager must account for the way those responsibilities have been exercised. Information systems need to be created to facilitate this accounting for performance. [. . .]

The arguments for decentralized resource management are that it increases managerial authority while ensuring effective management control with the result that the authority is likely to achieve both more efficient and more effective use of resources. Efficient and effective use of resources is more likely, it is argued, to be achieved by those who actually use those resources than can be achieved centrally.

DRM gives cost centre managers a positive organizational interest in achieving the best use of resources. If savings can be made under one budget head they can be deployed for other purposes. The manager ceases to be a mere bidder for resources and instead becomes a manager of resources.

At the same time DRM promotes effective control. By clarifying accountability not merely for containing overall costs but for policy achievement, it provides a clear basis for control. Control is concentrated on what requires to be controlled. To attempt to control all is not effective control, but frustrated control. Control is concentrated where control is required. Control being based on a system of accountability permits and ensures review. Periodic discussion of achievement ensures not the mere enforcement of control, but the review of the responsibilities given, problems encountered and opportunities available.

The original drive to decentralized resource management is essentially a managerial initiative. It derives from the belief that there are limits to the decision making capacity of the senior managers in an organization. It recognizes the importance of involving managers at all levels in the organization in decisions. Decentralized resource management is a managerial response to the problems of bureaucracy. It retains the basic structure of the organizational hierarchy, but moves certain decisions to the lowest possible level.

[. . .]

Decentralization, whether undertaken to ensure better delivery of services or to increase community involvement, or both, is likely to require decentralized resource management. Whereas such decentralization has separate origins, it is unlikely to be effective unless it is given expression through such management changes.

5

Financial management in schools

Haydn Howard

Budget generation

[. . .] There are two quite separate processes involved in the activity which is commonly referred to as budgeting. The first is the process of *generating* a budget, in the LFM context that means determining the total sum available to the scheme of local management. The second involves the *distribution* of that total sum to schools within the scheme in the authority.

The generation of the total sum available for spending in the forth-coming financial period will depend on an authority's perception of the appropriate balance between service needs and affordability. This process of generation is informed and influenced by a wide range of local and national pressures: the local demand for resources, the economic situation, government policy, political attitudes and so on. The reconciliation of all of these, mostly competing, factors leads eventually to the determination of a sum available for spending within the education service, and each of the phases within the service. [. . .]

The important point to recognize is that the product of the budget generation process is the definition of the total budgetary cake available for the service. The slicing of that cake is the process of distributing those available resources.

In most authorities the distinction between the two processes of generation and distribution is blurred by their approach to budgeting. Most authorities still adopt the time-honoured method whereby the previous year's base is incremented to take account of key variables – in particular, inflation and any growth planned by the authority.

With this traditional approach the pattern of resource distribution mirrors the means of budget generation. Indeed the anticipated pattern of distribution governs the generation of the budget. In other words the cake is sized to provide for the previous year's allocation of resources as updated for adjustment at the margin.

Authorities may adopt this approach at different levels. Some simply define a budget at phase level (say for all secondary schools), analysing planned expenditure over staffing, premises, equipment, supplies and services. Others extend this analysis down to the level of each individual school. But with the traditional approach the making of the cake and its slicing are largely determined by previous spending patterns and the system tends to preserve those patterns.

There are ways of generating a budget which are more sensitive to current needs. Some authorities already generate their budgets by reference to a particular rationale which gears resources to client needs in some structured way. The two most popular approaches are either to relate the planned inputs directly to pupil numbers or to generate a budget by reference to an agreed curriculum model. Again, the budget can be generated at a global level, i.e. for all secondary schools, or at the individual school level and then aggregated. Thereafter, the manner of distribution is likely to reflect the process of generation.

It certainly seems appropriate for the future that these more considered and structured approaches be used to generate a budget. Nonetheless the traditional approach can still be applied to generate a total fund available for the local management scheme. [. . .]

Resource allocation

[. . .]

One of the greatest challenges for authorities embarking on the process of devolving financial management is to identify a firm base, most likely a new base, for allocating resources to local management. [. . .]

The key to success is a simple and robust means of distributing the total available resources by way of formula, a structured approach to distribution which can be readily expressed. It could be that the general formula embraces a number of 'sub-formulas'. In other words:

A could equal B + C + D . . .

where B, C, D, . . . are derived by separate self-contained formulas. It is essential however that the formula can be easily understood.

[. . .]

The principle behind formula allocation is quite simply to allocate the lion's share of the budget available to the scheme of local management on a pro-rata basis to each school. [. . .]

Cambridgeshire has given detailed consideration to two different approaches to distributing the balance of funds by way of formula factors, the

Age Weighted Pupil Unit (AWPU) [and] Organization Based Staffing (OBS).

Age Weighted Pupil Unit (AWPU)

The essence of this approach is to allocate resources in relation to the pupil population in each school, but using an age weighting to vary the resource entitlement of particular age groups. It is a practice which is well established in the education service. The particular weightings presently contemplated by the Cambridgeshire system are:

Age group	Unit
Years 1 to 3	1
Years 4 to 5	20/16
Years 6+	20/11

There has been much discussion on the appropriateness of the units for the various age groups. One of the attractions of the approach is its simplicity. It would be an easy matter to vary the units from time to time.

Organization Based Staffing (OBS)

The AWPU approach takes broad account of the composition of the school population. But it is not sensitive to the implications, especially for the teaching resource, of the distribution of population within a school by each individual year group. The organization based staffing (OBS) approach attempts to be sympathetic to this issue. It would allocate funds by a financial model of organization based staff, using assumptions of how the grouping of pupils in a notional school of any particular size could be organized.
   Suggested assumptions are:

1 Basic calculations derived from:

Age group	Periods	Max. class size
Yrs 1, 2, 3	36	27
	4	20
Yrs 4, 5	32	24
	8	20
Yrs 6, 7	32	Teacher staffing 1 to 12

2 Additional calculations based on:

- a teaching contact ratio of 0.8 for Yrs 1 to 5
- 5% for special needs
- small year groups:

Age group	No. of pupils	Additional periods per year
Yrs 1, 2, 3	up to 99	4
Yrs 4, 5	up to 95	12
Yrs 4, 5	96–119	4

The two formula variants, AWPU and OBS, need not be mutually exclusive. Cambridgeshire has recently introduced a refinement to its AWPU approach which is based on OBS concepts. This is an organization factor which is related to the size of the age group entering and moving through the school. It recognizes the organizational issues of the 'smaller' school. Before applying AWPU for slicing, 1.8 per cent of the budget would be shared between schools of five forms of entry and below, on a graduated scale. A further 0.2 per cent of the total budget would be allocated to the two sixth form colleges.

Despite the elements of protection outlined above, a number of schools are still likely to lose significant amounts of resource through use of the formula allocation. To mitigate resource reductions in schools, a further level of protection is favoured in Cambridgeshire, that is, to phase the impact of any revised method of allocation over time. This simply means that losses and gains will be reduced in the early years to ease the transition. [. . .] Incidentally, there is further scope for protection by using an earlier time basis (e.g. the previous January) for pupil numbers. This would favour schools with falling rolls.

The resultant formula may be simply expressed as:

$$\text{School allocation} = \text{Direct allocations} + \frac{\text{Remainder}}{\text{AWPU or OBS}} \pm \text{Phasing factor}$$

Cambridgeshire's Education Committee has chosen the AWPU approach for allocating resources to all secondary schools in the financial year 1988–89. The Committee liked the concept of the OBS approach but felt it was more appropriate for generating a budget and preferred the simplicity of the AWPU method for allocating resources.

Budget preparation

Under LFM budget preparation becomes a task to be undertaken by the local manager within the total sum allocated to the school by the allocation process. This is not to be confused with the process of budget generation which is undertaken at the centre. What we are concerned with here is the preparation of the spending plan for the school for the next financial period.

It is normally a fresh experience for the school manager to need to prepare the budget for most of the resources within and around the school. He or she will, however, have had extensive experience of managing the likes of capitation allowances and will already well understand the tenets of financial management. It is vital, nevertheless, that strong support is given from the centre towards the process of budget preparation.

It may be that in the early stages the local manager wishes to abide by an existing base budget for the school (assuming that such exists). As long as this spending plan fits within the school's allocation it is reasonable to do so. Indeed it should not be assumed that all local managers approach the budget preparation with a clean sheet. In Cambridgeshire, most financial plans tend to be derived by adjusting a previous base at the margins. This can prove to be a safe and secure approach as long as the product provides a credible plan for the period. But obviously the culture of local financial management is for the school manager to prepare financial plans within available resources which more ably match local needs and circumstances. This will only be achieved by a structured and informed reconciliation of requirements with resources.

There are two important refinements to budget management which Cambridgeshire has practised. First, the sum allocated to a school is regarded as a cash limit and the local manager is free to prepare the school budget within that overall figure. [. . .]

The second important initiative is the carry-forward facility. Under the Cambridgeshire system, local managers are allowed to carry forward, albeit within certain limits, overspendings and underspendings into the next financial period. This eases the burden of getting everything absolutely right at the outset but again the facility must be used with extreme caution.

Control monitoring

It seems almost too obvious to say that there is a critical need for competent budgetary control, that is to say the process of managing actual expenditure to keep it in line with the budget plan. Naturally this process will be eased if the original budget is soundly based and accurately reflects the resource requirements of the school within the limits set. However, throughout the budget period changes will occur. The need to spend is likely to differ from pre-set levels. New pressures will appear and changes will need to be made to the planned pattern of spending.

There are, of course, two levels of control which need to be considered – the central level and the local school level. The crucial aspect of financial devolution is that, by definition, control over spending has been passed down to the local level. [. . .]

The tools for controlling expenditure at the centre remain much the same. The centre will have the same level of information about spending as it did before devolution. The task simply becomes harder because control has been moved down to the local level. The main task at the centre is to spot significant deviation in particular schools at an early stage, since this may indicate a lack of local control. Care must be taken, however, in following up any indicators since the local manager may be quite properly exercising local discretion. Some tolerance factor needs to be set, beyond which preliminary investigation is triggered. This could be set at a level of, say, 3–5 per cent deviation from planned spending.

It is at the local level that the process of control is now most keenly felt. It calls for substantial commitment to constant monitoring of expenditure against pre-set limits. The management functions for achieving this are simply defined. However, their execution depends very much on the quality of the financial systems which are employed to provide the information and the skills which managers demonstrate in acting upon that information.

There can be no substitute for extensive use of technology at both the centre and local level in order to capture and to manage the requisite information. There is also a need for a reliable interface between information kept at central and local levels. It will be a long time (if ever) before the likes of the payroll function can be performed at the local level. Until such time the school is dependent on the central systems for the supply of information concerning payments to staff. It is vital that this information is communicated promptly and accurately to schools. There is, however, ample scope for much of the other information about expenditure on supplies, equipment and services to be sourced and managed at the local level and maintained on a commitment basis (rather than the cash spent basis of the centre). Such a local facility for recording commitments for comparison with budgeted levels is essential for the proper management of funds.

It is extremely unlikely, in view of the numbers of transactions inherent in such a system, that a support function could be operated effectively on a manual basis. [. . .] Experience shows that the level of detail required by the local manager will put a strain on all but the most powerful and versatile of central systems. By comparison a local microcomputer system – with a friendly face – seems to have much to commend it.

Having said that, we must not lose sight of the need for a proper reconciliation of the books in the school with those of the centre. Whatever the local records say at school level, it is the central mainframe records which constitute the books of the authority. There must be a sound and demonstrable reconciliation between the two sets of records. [. . .]

The treasurer's control

There will, inevitably, be some concern among treasurers about financial control being passed down into the hands of local school managers. The degree of concern will differ between authorities, depending on their management style. Some may see it as a loss of power. Such concern is not as sharply felt within Cambridgeshire since the concept of LFM fits neatly within the Council's corporate culture of enabling the fullest delegation consistent with effectiveness. Moreover, heads are recognized as highly competent managers. [. . .] Heads are regarded as an integral part of the senior management structure of the authority. It does not feel odd, therefore, to entrust to them the financial function which, after all, is a key and integral management responsibility.

Naturally, the treasurer has to ensure that safe and efficient arrangements are implemented and maintained for the stewardship of schools' funds which are under local control. There is ample scope for realizing that objective, especially given the opportunity afforded by technology for facilitating the necessary safeguards. Inevitably, however, there will be a significant increase in the need for auditing efforts and skills.

In less enlightened environments there will, no doubt, be concern about the potential loss of power or control at the centre. The Cambridgeshire experience has been that the process of financial management is strengthened by the participation of the local manager. Heads take their financial responsibilities seriously and make a substantial contribution to better informing the processes of budget generation, resource allocation and financial control. [. . .]

6

The budgeting process

John Arnold and Tony Hope

[. . .] A vitally important task for management is to coordinate [the] various interrelated aspects of decision making. This helps first to ensure that the final results are consistent with the organization's goals and, secondly, to prevent suboptimization within the organization by ensuring, as far as possible, that individual managers are working towards the same end. This is a difficult and time consuming task. [. . .]

[. . .] One way for management to coordinate these activities is to prepare detailed and explicit financial plans of action for specific future periods, both for individual units within the [. . .] organization and for the organization [. . .] as a single entity. These detailed plans are usually referred to as *budgets*, and the coordinating activity is usually termed the *budgetary process*. The overall plan for the organization [. . .] is termed the *master budget* or *comprehensive budget*. Another way of viewing budgeting is as an exercise in communication, by which the expectations of management about the levels of performance of subordinates are communicated to the subordinates. Whether or not employees should help directly in determining these expectations (i.e. whether they should participate in the budgetary process), we discuss later. [. . .]

In order to understand the budgetary process more clearly, we should explain how it fits into the overall framework for managerial planning, decision making and control, set out in [. . .] Figure 6.1. The budgetary process begins with Step 5 of the managerial framework, i.e. once decisions have been taken to commit resources to specific plans of action, forecasts are made of the expected outcomes of these plans, in the form of budgets. Budgets thus embody the expected outcomes of particular decisions; and because decisions take account of the interdependences within the organization, budgets include the impact of these interdependences.

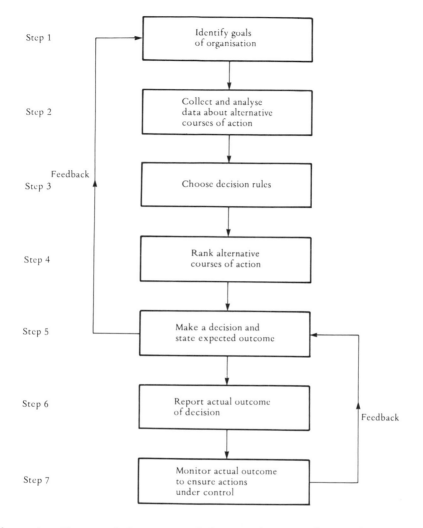

Step 1 — Identify goals of organisation

Step 2 — Collect and analyse data about alternative courses of action

Feedback
Step 3 — Choose decision rules

Step 4 — Rank alternative courses of action

Step 5 — Make a decision and state expected outcome

Step 6 — Report actual outcome of decision

Feedback

Step 7 — Monitor actual outcome to ensure actions under control

Figure 6.1   Framework for managerial planning, decision making, and control

The use of budgets is integral to the *planning process*. But the importance of budgeting does not stop with planning. In order to ensure that plans are correctly implemented, that stated targets are reached and that information is available to aid future planning, actual performance must be regularly reported and monitored, by comparison with expected performance (Steps 6 and 7 of the framework). These two steps are commonly known as the *control process*. Thus the use of budgets is important also as an aid to performance evaluation and control. We might add a third main use of budgets as a device for *motivation*, although it is not always obvious that the same budget can satisfactorily serve all three purposes. [. . .]

[. . .] Budgeting and planning

In order to better aid the pursuit of organizational goals, explicit, formal plans should be drawn up. If this is not done, then managers can use only crude, intuitive measures to judge whether their operations are successful, and their targets achieved. Budgets represent the financial expression of formal plans, and, as with successful planning, successful budgeting should also be formalized. This means that both the objectives of the budget, and the means of attaining them, should be stated explicitly. The level of sophistication and detail of any budget should be a function of the size of the organization and also the position of the particular budget within the organization. [. . .] This implies a structure of responsibility centres within the organization, each accountable for a specific level of detail within the total budgetary process. We look at this notion of responsibility accounting and its corollary activity, management by exception, in the section dealing with budgeting and control. It is very important to point out here that, as with other aspects of the planning and control process, the benefits of any system of budgeting should be judged in relation to the costs of setting up and operating the system. No managerial activity should be viewed in isolation from its attendant costs and benefits. There are, however, two interdependent aspects of the relationship between budgeting and planning which we should consider in more detail: the method by which budgets are prepared, and the time periods covered by budgets.

The preparation of budgets

Budgets do not appear out of thin air; they represent the product of much organizational thinking, and, often, internal dissension. Most large organizations commit considerable human resources to the preparation of budgets. A budget director or controller, who usually takes no part in the detailed preparation of individual budgets, is responsible for overall budget preparation and coordination, often being assisted by a budgeting committee consisting of members of top management from each of the organization's functional divisions. The task of the committee is to set general guidelines to be followed by individual managers in building up their own budgets, to resolve differences among them and to submit a final comprehensive budget for approval by the board of directors.

  The structure of budget organization and responsibility is important. Budgeting is a complicated process. Only infrequently will figures be immediately accepted without controversy. Rather, an iterative process is involved by which the plans, intentions, ambitions and constraints of individual managers throughout the organization are submitted, reviewed, changed and ultimately, by reason of the authority of the budget controller and his committee, agreed. Budgeting, in short, is a bargaining process in which individual goals are traded off for (hopefully) the overall benefit of the organization and, as in most bargaining situations, the end product is often radically different from the original submission. The end product of the whole budgeting process takes the form of the organization's expected position at some future point in time (a *budgeted balance sheet*) and the means of reaching that position (a *budgeted income statement*). A statement of the sources and applications of the organization's funds may accompany the two main statements. [. . .] These statements are usually vague, single-valued estimates of the future, derived from individual budgets for sales, purchases, cash flow etc., and as such are *static*. [. . .]

In preparing detailed budgets it must be recognised that the activities of the organization are likely to be limited by certain constraints. In consequence, the recognition of both the level of constraints, and the time at which they are likely to arise, is of critical importance. [. . .]

The time periods covered by budgets

Budgets are financial plans for future periods. But which future periods? It is normal to distinguish between two types of budgets, short-term and long-term, because they may seek to serve different purposes and because the level of detail they incorporate may differ widely.

Short-term budgets

These are related to current conditions and usually cover a period of one year. Such annual budgets are, in turn, broken down into quarterly, monthly, four-weekly or even weekly periods. The actual level of disaggregation of the annual budget is a function of the particular business, but at least some disaggregation is usually necessary. For instance, management will wish to monitor progress throughout the year, and to take any corrective action as soon as possible rather than wait until the end of the year when the final results are known. Equally, management will need information during the year to adjust current budgets for the remainder of the period if the situation warrants such changes. [. . .]

Long-term budgets

These relate to the development of the business over many years. They are usually drawn up in very general terms which cover the nature of the business, its position in the industry, the expected level of inflation and its impact on the business. A period of between three and ten years may be appropriate for a long-term budget. [. . .]

[. . .] Budgeting and control

A second purpose of budgeting is its usefulness for control purposes. The control process follows the planning process, i.e. once plans have been agreed, decisions are implemented and reports are prepared to determine whether events are going according to plan. We might say that the control process involves three sequential, but interrelated stages: the recording of actual performance, the comparison of actual performance with expected performance and, as a linking stage, the provision of regular feedback to allow continual monitoring of events. These three steps are brought together in Figure 6.2, which shows an abbreviated view of the control process.

Differences between budgeted and actual performance are termed *variances*. The generation of variances provides the feedback which entitles us to term the whole process a *control system*. Notice that the diagram of the control process takes the appearance, via the feedback mechanism, of a loop, or continuous process. This is because any time scale has been omitted from the diagram. The budget for the current period is compared with the actual performance of the current period and the variances are calculated accordingly. These variances will be useful both as a spur to immediate, remedial

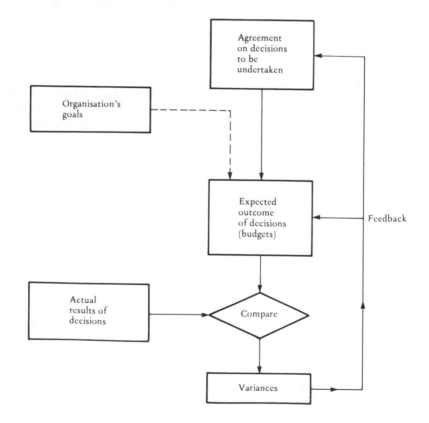

Figure 6.2   The control process

action if actual performance is less good than expected and also as input into the budgetary process for future periods. We now examine two of the aspects of the control process in more detail.

Recording actual performance

We have seen that the decisions giving rise to the formulation of plans and budgets are carried out for different areas of activity within the organization. If such budgets are to be used to assess and evaluate individual performance, managers need some criteria to determine exactly what constitutes a particular area of activity. To achieve this end, budgets should reflect *areas of responsibility* within the firm, so that individuals are charged *only* with those costs and revenues for which they can be held responsible, i.e. for those costs and revenues which they control. Thus we might define a responsibility area, or centre, as an area of activity within an organization which has control over particular resources for a specified period.

It is vital that such areas are explicitly defined, so that managers and employees know precisely what is expected of them. Conceptually, this is easy to acknowledge; in practice it is very difficult to apply. The difficulty lies in determining which costs should be assigned to specific responsibility centres. We can do no better than to cite guidelines for deciding which costs should be assigned to responsibility centres (first drawn up in the USA in 1956).[1]

1 If the person has authority over both the acquisition and the use of the services, he should be charged with the cost of such services.
2 If the person can significantly influence the amount of cost through his own action, he may be charged with such costs.
3 Even if the person cannot significantly influence the amount of cost through his own action, he may be charged with those elements with which the management desires him to be concerned, so that he will help to influence those who are responsible.

Responsibility centres are usually either cost centres or profit centres. A cost centre is the smallest area of responsibility for which costs are accumulated, for example, a single department of a firm employing few people. A manager in charge of a cost centre is held accountable only for the controllable costs of his centre. He has no control over, and is therefore not accountable for, revenues earned. A profit centre, such as an autonomous division within a firm, is a section of business for which both costs and revenues are accumulated. Thus, a manager in charge of a profit centre is responsible for the profit, or contribution margin, earned by his section of the business. [. . .] The system of responsibility accounting is intended to generate control reports which reflect the decentralization of authority within the organization. [. . .] The system has the advantage of allowing responsible officials to react speedily to any changes in their own area of responsibility, with the

result that the flow of reports through the firm will allow corrective action to
be taken at the appropriate level.

Provision of feedback information

Timely and regular feedback is vital to a successful control system, as an aid to
both managers and employees. For example, managers need speedy information on significant deviations from budget in order to take effective action
to correct such deviations and to amend future plans, in so far as deviations
signify a change in longer-term circumstances; employees need equally
speedy information to know whether or not they have achieved their targets,
and whether their performance is satisfactory. Delay in giving information
on employee performance may lead to a loss of motivation, to the detriment
of future performance.

The regularity with which control information is generated determines
in large measure the success of the entire control process. Regularity will be
largely dependent upon the activity under consideration and on the position
of the activity within the entire organization.

[. . .] Budgeting and motivation

All budgeting processes involve relationships between people, for example
manager–employee, director–manager and manager–manager relationships, and all interpersonal relationships generate, to some extent, behavioural problems. Thus budgeting entails behavioural problems. We must state
quite categorically that the present state of knowledge concerning the
behavioural implications of accounting is such that even very broad generalizations can be dangerous. Individuals, whatever their formal position
within the organization, differ in their behaviour in any given situation, and
organizational settings vary widely from firm to firm.

However, in determining the basis to be used in evaluating performance for any budget period, two related behavioural questions have given rise
to considerable debate and elicited much research output. First, how tightly
should budgets be set in order to induce maximum performance from
employees, and second, what degree of employee participation in the
budgeting process should be encouraged?

To clarify some of the issues under these two headings we shall say
something about the forms of organizational structure which can exist within
individual firms. In order to illustrate the main points, it is useful to identify
two forms of organizational structure which lie towards opposite ends of the
spectrum of possible structures: the *classical* and the *modern* structure. The
classical structure supposes the existence of formal relationships within a
hierarchical organization, which exists simply to maximize profits. Em-

ployees, who are characterized as being basically inefficient and antagonistic to management, are presumed to be motivated purely by monetary rewards. The classical idea views the imposition of pressure upon an alien workforce as being the best way to achieve the desired results.

The modern view of organizational structure views matters from a different perspective. The firm is seen as being a partnership or coalition of managers and employees who are not motivated solely by notions of profit and cash, but also by psychological and social needs. This view recognizes that individuals within an organization have different goals and levels of aspiration, and it is only by harnessing these to the particular situations facing the organization that an increased sense of commitment to the goals of the organization is achieved. The modern view incorporates the idea of *budgetary slack* representing a degree of padding introduced into budgets so as to guard against possible failure to attain targets. It is deemed necessary to do this because failure to attain budget levels is seen as a social stigma which affects the individual in such a way that it reduces aspiration levels, goals and, eventually, performance.

Slack exists within even the most efficient and well run organizations. It exists because human nature requires it to exist. It is argued that if individuals are given no room to manoeuvre within a budgetary constraint, then conflict will quickly arise between the individuals' personal goals and those of the firm. The type of organizational structure possessed by the firm, whether classical, modern or somewhere in between, will have a direct bearing on the behavioural questions we have raised.

Consider now the first of the two questions posed above: how tightly should budgets be set so as to encourage maximum performance? For example, if budgets are set at too high a level, individuals may become discouraged in their tasks and not attempt to meet targets; alternatively, if budgets are pitched at too low a level, individuals may become self-satisfied and inefficient, and thus perform below their real potential. Two types of budgets are frequently referred to in this context: ideal budgets and currently attainable budgets.

Ideal budgets are intended to act as a powerful incentive to performance by making no allowance for such mitigating factors as machine breakdowns, material shortages or labour strikes. In effect, they assume that the firm can operate at maximum capacity with maximum efficiency. Under normal operating conditions they are not likely to be achieved. Research has shown that ideal budgets are unlikely to represent the best form of motivation, if the employees view them as being unreasonable and unachievable.

Currently attainable budgets represent those which can reasonably be achieved under normal working conditions. They allow for normal breaks and suppose less than perfect efficiency. The problem for managers is to define 'reasonable achievement' and 'normal working conditions' in such a way that the standards set are tight enough to prevent inefficiency while at the same time generate a feeling of satisfaction on achievement. It is a difficult feat to accomplish. Aside from the technical problems involved, it requires from the management a thorough knowledge of the workforce, much previous experience in the area and, most of all, a great deal of common sense.

The research studies on budgeting and behaviour raise a potentially serious problem, to which we briefly referred earlier. It may be desirable to set the budget at a particular level in order to motivate the individual to achieve some other level, e.g. to set the budget slightly above reasonable expectations; such a budget may elicit maximum performance from the employee, but it will not be a suitable basis for planning what is likely to be achieved. Thus it may be inconsistent to use the same budget for both planning and motivational purposes. [. . .]

The second question we posed earlier was: what degree of employee participation in the budgeting process should be encouraged? There is now a considerable body of research showing that better performance can be expected from employees if they have some say in the construction of the budgets to be used to evaluate their performance (i.e. that participative budgets are more likely to succeed than are authoritative, imposed budgets). Indeed, common sense suggests that participation by individuals who have detailed knowledge of the particular problems associated with any given task is likely to increase the realism of budgets. But, as with all topics which involve the interaction of human relationships, the issues concerning the optimum degree of participation are complex and unsuitable for instant solutions. [. . .]

Note

1 *The Accounting Review* (1956) 'Report of the committee on cost concepts and standards', 1 April, p. 189.

7

Managing a delegated budget: three schools' experiences

Rosalind Levačić

This chapter presents three short case studies of how a primary school and two secondary schools in Cambridgeshire managed a delegated budget.[1] The research is based on LEA and school documents, observing meetings, and interviewing school and LEA staff.[2] It was undertaken in 1988 when Cambridgeshire had extended its original 1982 pilot scheme involving six secondary schools and one primary school to all secondary and eleven primary schools. The focus of the case study is on the internal school management of a delegated budget rather than on the authority's process of generating a general schools budget and distributing it to schools. The case study aims to give a preliminary indication of how schools go about the overall task of managing a budget and the associated real resources. In particular it focuses on two of the standard subtasks of budgeting outlined in Arnold and Hope (1989) – these are: *budget planning and preparation*; and *budgetary control*. The third task, that of budgetary evaluation, gets much less prominence because it was difficult to detect any formal evaluative process being fed back into resource allocation decisions, though some informal evaluative judgements were evident. The case study is also concerned with how the practice of local financial management (LFM) at a school is affected by existing management styles and attitudes and how these, in turn, are modified as a result of LFM. It must be borne in mind that the case studies are a snapshot of where schools had reached at a particular point in time operating an LFM scheme that was in some respects different from that required by the 1988 Act. Over the next few years schools' practices with respect to the new task of financial management are likely to evolve and change quite quickly.

Case I: Elmwood Primary School

Elmwood Primary School has over 300 pupils from rising 5 to 11, and a teaching complement of 12.5. In April 1988 it had completed two years in the local financial management pilot scheme for primary schools. The head had been appointed in the course of the first year of the school's participation in the scheme and had inherited a poorly managed budget. At the time the research was undertaken she had completed her first full annual budgetary cycle.

Budget preparation

In early March 1988 the school was notified of its 1988–9 budget, which would run from April. As the 1988–9 budget was based on historical

Table 7.1   Elmwood School Budget Allocation for 1988–9

Code	Narrative	Base budget 1988/9
0110	Teachers	181860
0112	Supply	2270
0120	Support staff	9660
0141	Caretakers	6910
0142	Cleaners	2710
		203410
1330	Electricity	1560
1340	Gas–mains	4200
1341	Gas cylinders	770
1351	Water charges	610
1360	Cleaning materials	270
1370	Window cleaning	70
1391	Refuse collection	310
1540	Rates	9010
1541	Sewerage rates	1030
		17830
2042	Cleaning equipment	100
2600	Capitation	8310
2780	Protective clothing	20
3110	Car allowances	360
4040	Advertising for staff	140
4120	Interview expenses	70
8285	Heating of pools	−220
	Total	230020

08/03/88

spending, the authority presented the school with a line-by-line budget in which each major budget head was allocated a specific sum. The format of this budget is shown in Table 7.1. So, for instance, the teaching budget was determined by the actual salaries of the teachers in post in January 1988 and by any additional vacancies to the teaching complement as determined by the authority.

Following notification of the budget, a meeting was held between a member of the authority's LFM team, who has accountancy training, and school representatives (in Elmwood's case the head and deputy). In 1988 the LFM central team consisted of five people. The three more junior members each had a group of schools to advise and monitor. Their role was much appreciated by the schools and, generally, the team member was seen by the school as representing their interests in budget negotiations. The purpose of the March meeting was to agree the school's budget line by line. One element of this involved some haggling over the amount allocated by the LEA to the school. For instance Elmwood argued that too little was being allowed for sewerage rates, since last year's expenditure was £1000 more than the amount allocated by the authority and the 1988–9 allocation was still £500 short of last year's rates. The LFM team member promised to take this matter up. Most budget head allocations were agreed to be accurate. Checking the budget allocation is an important task for the school; in this case it is done by the head using her considerable knowledge of the school's budget expenditures. She keeps her budget accounts on her own computer spreadsheet. The meeting also discussed what the school planned to spend under each of the budget heads in Table 7.1.

Under the Cambridgeshire scheme schools have been able to vire (within certain constraints) between budget heads and to carry forward savings (or deficits) from the previous financial year – in Elmwood's case, a saving of about £6000.

The next formal stage in preparing the budget occurred in April when a staff meeting was held to go through the budget. This preceded a meeting of the governors' finance subcommittee on the same evening in order to approve the budget. At both meetings the budget plans were presented and explained by the head in a relaxed and informal atmosphere. Decisions about budget allocations were not being made at these meetings; no conflicting alternatives were presented. The meetings ratified a consensus already arrived at concerning how to spend the £6000 carried over from the previous financial year. The head put forward the items in Table 7.2. In the event of a shortfall in money it was readily agreed that the under-5s were the first priority.

Deciding on budget priorities

The head is very clearly the budget manager; she has far and away the greatest knowledge of the budget and explained it to both staff and governors. The

Table 7.2   Allocation of previous year's budget underspending

LFM BIDS 1988/9		
Aim	To continue to give help especially to the under fives coming into school in September	2,000
Aim	To provide a boost to the practical maths curriculum (a) storage units for investigation material (central resource) (b) games and equipment for classrooms	1,000
Aim	To take forward our Science curriculum policy document and start to gather resources to implement the policy	1,000
Aim	To look at the Junior section language area and provide group readers, language books, Magic Circle Readers	1,000
Aim	To widen the range of reference books in the Library (Look first to areas which have the greatest need)	1,000
		6,000

Money may only amount to a saving of 4,500 since the gas bill was paid.
Future things we may vire money from during the year.
Water cocks for the toilets.
Electric hand dryers – rent or buy?

staff seemed quite happy with this situation. The head seeks to inform all staff of the main contents of the budget but feels that her staff are too busy with their teaching to become involved in the details of budgeting. She sees this as protecting them from excess work. The main grade staff have little knowledge of the LFM scheme and, with the exception of a union representative who dislikes the implications of the scheme, few strong feelings about it. However, staff with extra responsibilities, such as early years, special needs, or drama, who have obtained additional resources from the scheme, are much more in favour. The head and deputy are strong advocates of LFM.

The head, having recently moved to Elmwood from the headship of a smaller school, is actively engaged in further improving the school. She sees developing the staff, both individually and as a team, as a key element in her endeavours. She has definite policies of her own for improving the school, the chief one is admitting rising fives. All children in a year group have been given the opportunity to start school in September. For the younger ones this means morning attendance in the autumn term. One advantage of this policy is that it removes the disruption caused by staggered entry, when children had to change classes mid-year in order to make room for new entrants. Another is that all children have a similar length of schooling. LFM enabled Elmwood to operate a different admissions policy from the official area one of admission at statutory age. £2000 was vired from the teaching budget to employ a general assistant to work with the rising fives teacher. Money had also been spent equipping a classroom for rising fives. The educational benefits of the policy have been to settle children into school more successfully and therefore to enable them to progress more rapidly. It is felt that this is already occurring, hence the benefits will feed into the upper end of the school in due course. Thus the allocation of a large chunk of money to the rising fives was not questioned by other staff.

In selecting projects for funding out of savings the head relies on informal day-to-day discussions with staff, both individually and in groups, about the school's needs. It is generally agreed that splitting such sums up evenly amongst teaching areas on an annual basis would spread the money too thinly: it is better to select specific schemes and fund them properly, on the tacit understanding that each teaching area would get its turn. An active fund-raising PTA currently provides £4000 a year for items not funded from the school's budget.

Operational management – generating budget 'savings'

An important part of budget management is generating the 'savings' from particular budget heads which can then be spent on items with higher priority. In part such savings are fortuitous and in part deliberate. In the case of Elmwood a large chunk of their savings were fortuitous. This was certainly the case in 1986–7 when the total amounted to almost £12,000. This arose from historical budgeting. The previous head had been on grade 6, whereas the current one is on grade 5; the difference in cost accrued to the school under LFM – and was worth around £6000 in 1986–7 and £1900 in 1987–8. The supply budget was also underspent by £1700. To some extent this was fortuitous, but it also reflected a low absentee rate by committed staff. The other major saving in 1987–8 was on gas heating, partly due to a mild winter but also to deliberate efforts to economize, for instance by putting curtains in the hall. The electricity has been monitored and the tariff changed. Plans were in hand to monitor water usage and to install valves in the toilets to prevent continual flushing during the holidays. Different bids for window cleaning and refuse collection were considered. It was notable that it was in relation to premises issues that the governors (in the meeting observed) contributed most and offered advice based on their own experience. The caretaker is valued by the head and takes a very active interest in the school, particularly in running the premises more efficiently. Steps have also been taken to increase the revenue from letting the buildings. Schools are free to set their own rates for private users. The head is keen to encourage community use but also has an eye to the costs of keeping the premises open. She aims to get more lettings at the same time so as to spread the heating costs over more rentals and has put up the charge for the hall because of its heating costs.

Budgetary control

Once the budget plan has been agreed, it is reported to the authority's finance department which is responsible for operating a budget reporting system. This provides information on actual and expected expenditures on a monthly basis, which is essential for budgetary control to be exercised. A sample of the budget profile printout sent to schools is shown in Table 7.3.

The first column shows the amount the school has planned to spend for the whole financial year on each budget head. The second column is the expected expenditure to date. This is estimated by the LFM team as the month-by-month amount the school should spend given its annual plans. Arriving at these monthly estimates, known as the budget profile, involves making judgements about the future pattern of expenditure, such as adjusting the teacher budget for expected salary or national insurance increases and the fuel budget for anticipated price rises and seasonal temperature differences. The third column is the actual expenditure to date; the fourth column is the difference between expected and actual expenditure to date. It is this variation which is monitored by the budget manager. It alerts managers to specific areas of expenditure where positive or negative (underspending in this table) variances have occurred, so that explanations can be sought and, if necessary, action taken. There are a number of reasons for such variances. In a poorly operated reporting system variances will arise because actual expenditures have been miscoded to incorrect heads (or even schools), or the expected expenditure profile may have been wrongly estimated, so that while the actual total for the year is correct the allocation of this annual total to individual months is incorrect. Given that the reporting system is reasonably accurate, then the variance is due to the school's actual expenditure behaviour. So underspending on teachers and supply cover is known to be due to appointing a head on a lower salary than the previous one and to the low incidence of sick leave. Some underspending may be undesirable – such as staff failing to spend their capitation allowance. Underspending on gas was due to mild weather and careful use, but it was partially misleading since the current quarter's gas bill has not yet been presented and paid. This last consideration points to an inadequacy in the budget report in Table 7.3 – it does not inform the budget manager of committed expenditures. As this authority is responsible for paying the school's bills it records actual expenditure – committed expenditure is known only to the school and it is up to the school to keep a commitments account for its own budgetary control purposes.

In Elmwood the head also undertakes the administrative task of checking through the monthly budget statement. This requires her to check that the amount the authority reports the school as spending tallies with the school's own records. This task takes half a day per month but it enhances her knowledge of the budget. The day-by-day operational budget decisions, whereby the budget is controlled, are taken mainly by the head. She, for

Table 7.3 The monthly budget report

	Revised total budget for year £	Expected to date £	Actual to date £	Variation to date £
Employees				
0110 Full time teachers	178,164	162,802	160,876.20	1,925.80-
0112 Casual supply teachers	2,707	2,425	661.99	1,763.01-
0113 Repl tchrs on training	1,193	1,014	0.00	1,014.00-
0120 Support staff	10,479	9,569	9,396.10	172.90-
0141 Caretakers	7,095	6,403	6,954.43	551.43
0142 Cleaners	3,020	2,724	2,400.15	323.85-
	202,658	184,937	180,288.87	4,648.13-
Premises				
1330 Electricity	1,660	1,435	1,625.68	190.68
1340 Gas–mains	4,200	3,654	2,126.63	1,527.37-
1341 Gas–cylinders	770	648	361.86	286.14-
1351 Water charges	478	430	941.90	511.90
1360 Cleaning materials	560	500	139.57	360.43-
1370 Window cleaning	61	55	0.00	55.00-
1391 Refuse collection	323	292	309.23	17.23
1540 General rates	9,280	9,280	9,246.24	33.76-
1541 Sewerage rates	659	592	1,581.46	989.46
	17,991	16,886	16,332.57	553.43-
Supplies and services				
2600 Capitation allowances	18,940	14,659	13,890.36	768.64-
3110 Car allowances	344	311	173.98	137.02-
Establishment expenses				
4031 Internal printing			4.40-	4.40-
4040 Advertising for staff	125	113	75.38	37.62-
4120 Candidate expenses	64	58	0.00	58.00-
	189	171	70.98	100.02-
Total expenditure	240,122	216,964	210,756.76	6,207.24-
Income				
8285 Heating of pools	222-	222-	181.00-	41.00
8420 Casual lettings			413.75-	413.75-
8421 Ctkrs/clnrs etc fees			208.70-	208.70-
8422 Heat and light charge			45.30-	45.30-
8423 Special charges			5.00-	5.00-
	222-	222-	853.75-	631.75-
Net expenditure	239,900	216,742	209,903.01	6,838.99-

instance, decides when to provide supply cover for additional INSET (in-service training) activities. The deputy manages capitation items. Both she and her staff recognize that local financial management, for which she does the bulk of the managerial work (i.e. budget planning and decision making) and some of the administrative work, takes up a significant amount of time; she does not teach on a regular basis but instead provides cover herself when available. She spends time going round the school regularly and knows her pupils individually. She relies on a good school secretary who, by taking on the additional work involved in invoicing and coding expenditures and running school lettings, has lost her afternoon off without gaining extra pay.

Conclusion: the financial management process at Elmwood

A useful taxonomy of the key features of a school resource allocation system is provided by Simkins (1986). The key features relate to:

- Information. Is it gathered informally or formally by, for example, a process of making written bids for resources?
- Openness. Are decisions reached by:
    (i) the head or senior management team alone;
    (ii) bilateral negotiations between senior manager(s) on the one hand and other staff (such as heads of departments or curriculum co-ordinators) on the other;
    (iii) multilateral interaction and agreement amongst staff at various levels in the school (e.g. by heads of departments or all teaching staff collectively)?
- Criteria. Are the criteria used to decide on resource use incremental (a small adjustment from last year), judgemental, or formalized (e.g. judgements are reflected in a formula for allocating departmental allowances)?

Applying this taxonomy to Elmwood, it appears that information is gathered and disseminated informally by the head through bilateral and multilateral discussions. In making resource allocations judgemental criteria are applied and are subject to open and multilateral discussion. The priorities are determined largely by the head after she has consulted staff in order to ascertain their preferences and to persuade them to support her own. The head is a committed enthusiast for local financial management – 'you can switch resources around and put the emphasis where you think it belongs'.

Case 2: Oakwood School

Oakwood School, an 11–18 comprehensive with 1200 pupils and around 70 teachers, has been operating a delegated budget for six years. In March 1988 the school received its notification of next year's budget, determined for the first time by a formula. It received a one-line budget of £1,366,000; no breakdown amongst budget heads was provided.

Budget preparation

The process of budget preparation occurs in stages. Oakwood operates a formal annual budget planning cycle, into which are fed a number of subsidiary processes, such as bidding for departmental allowances. On notification of next year's budget total, the head, without assistance from the LFM team, prepares a draft budget, using a personal computer spreadsheet. This is presented to the heads of departments' committee for amendment and approval before being considered by the governors' finance committee for final approval and submission to the authority.

The 1988–9 draft budget is based on earlier policy decisions made by the heads of departments committee and governors. The budget is derived from the curriculum, which a few years ago was reorganized. These curriculum decisions concerned the range of subjects and options offered and the size of teaching groups, and thus determine the teaching and support staff complement. Specific aspects of the curriculum have been developed such as craft, design and technology (CDT) and graded tests, which the head considers would not have been possible without the additional resources provided by LFM. Currently the school is experiencing a 6 per cent fall in rolls, but in four years' time this trend will be reversed. The governors have agreed to maintain the teaching establishment at two posts in excess of the number required by the authority's now defunct pupil–teacher ratio. So in September 1988 the teaching establishment is to fall by just one. The amount allocated to capitation in the draft budget, which is £124,000, includes departmental allowances and these are an aggregation of the initial bids heads of departments have made for the coming financial year.

At the heads of departments' committee, the head goes through the draft budget, shown in Table 7.4. He presents the committee with a problem – planned expenditure exceeds the school's anticipated revenues for next year. Total net expenditure is £1,401,000 compared to the budget allocation of £1,366,000. Now, £40,000 is being carried over from last year; however, the head wants to retain a contingency fund by carrying forward £30,000 into 1989–90. No one demurs with this strategy, so there remains a need to cut planned spending by £25,000. The head already has a clear idea of how such savings could be made; the purpose of the meeting is for the heads of departments to establish priorities and make firm recommendations. This takes some time as there is a reluctance for individuals to make suggestions. At first the discussion turns to raising income from lettings, as the school has so far not pursued this actively. The member of staff who raised this issue finds himself leading a working party on income generation. The head considers that they cannot plan spending on the basis of very uncertain additional income; the search for £25,000 savings continues.

Table 7.4 Oakwood School: draft budget 1988–9

School expenditure and income financial year 1988/9 – budget = £1,366,000

Employees		estimate £
0110	Full-time/school part-time	1,050,000
0112	Supply	12,000
0114	Supply – INSET	3,000
0120	Administrative/professional/clerical	30,000
0124	Laboratory/technical/welfare/general	17,000
0141	Caretakers	25,000
0142	Cleaners	30,000
0179	Peripatetic teachers	4,000
	Total	1,171,000
Premises		
1320	Oil	13,000
1330	Electricity	12,000
1340	Gas-mains	6,000
1351	Water charges	4,400
1360	Cleaning materials	3,500
1370	Window cleaning	850
1391	Refuse collection	850
1540	General rates	65,000
1541	Sewerage rates	4,400
	Total	110,000
Supplies & services		
2600	Capitation allowances	124,000
	Total	124,000
Establishment expenses		
3110	Car allowances	600
4040	Advertising for staff	1,600
4110	Staff travel and subsistence	500
	Total	1,407,700
Income		6,700–
	Total expenditure	**1,401,000**
Budget	Brought forward from 87/88	40,000
	Suggested carry forward 89/90	30,000

Attention focuses on the supply budget, which was considerably underspent last year, and it is agreed to reduce this by £4000. Each item is looked at in turn. For instance, under caretakers, the head points out that although one of them is retiring, they already do a lot of overtime so that the establishment could not be reduced. Eventually it is agreed that the only other item which can give is capitation; the total for departmental allowances will be cut to 80 per cent of the initial bid. If, as the year proceeds, other budget heads are underspent, money can be vired into capitation. The head points out that without LFM capitation would be much less – around £68,000.

The head subsequently revises the budget along the lines agreed and presents it to the governors' finance subcommittee. This consists of seven governors, five of whom are present. The head leads them through the budget. He states that subsequent to the heads of departments' committee meeting he realized that a 20 per cent cut in the aggregate bid for departmental allowances was insufficient since it was not possible to cut other elements of capitation, such as exam fees. Hence departmental allowances had to be reduced further to get the capitation total down to £103,000. He will inform the heads of departments' committee of this at the next meeting. As they go through the budget the head supplies additional information in response to questions and discussion. While he evidently has the greatest knowledge of budgetary matters, especially regarding the effects of the formula on the school's budget allocation, three of the governors contribute knowledgeably to the discussion; two say nothing. Particular interest is taken in supplies and services. There is much discussion of the heating, which is being converted from oil to gas, and the money to be obtained from selling the school's stock of unused oil. The head clearly has a good working relationship with the governors; the budget before them is, in part, the outcome of earlier decisions agreed to by the governors, hence it is a matter of keeping themselves informed of the school's budgetary position. This committee meets about once a month to monitor the progress of the budget. At this stage no difficult choices have to be made; the budget is approved.

Subsidiary budgetary processes – determining departmental expenditures

In the more complex budgeting of a secondary school it is much easier than in the primary case to see how the total budget for the institution is built up from the subsidiary budgets of subunits, in this case subject departments and service areas. At Oakwood there are elements, albeit attenuated, of budget negotiation between subunit budget holders (heads of departments) and the overall budget manager (the head). However, while the heads of departments have collectively agreed with the head the aggregate of departmental expenditure, they do not collectively agree individual departmental budgets. This is conducted by means of bilateral negotiation between the individual head of department and the head. In the autumn term each head of department puts in a bid to the head and makes a case for each item on his or her shopping list. The head then decides within the total sum available how much to allocate to each department. He is anxious to see that whole projects get funded. The heads of departments interviewed were happy with this system, recognizing that it relied on them making realistic bids and on the head being able to make informed judgements about the bids and distributing the overall expenditure fairly. Departmental bids for expenditure falling on other budget heads, such as ancillary staff, would also depend for their success on convincing the head and, in cases where major commitments were being made, securing the agreement of the heads of departments' committee. Thus the humanities departments had secured an ancillary post to help with GCSE work.

Teachers without departmental responsibility secure resources through their departmental head. How the departments function internally in allocating their budgets is not a matter that concerns the head. One head of department has a formal system of securing written bids from his department to feed into his own bid to the head. LFM at Oakwood has had the effect of reinforcing an already strong departmental structure; the heads of departments are the direct line of information and control used by the head in allocating resources. Heads of year and deputy heads are not directly involved in budgeting and so feel somewhat remote from it; this remoteness is even more marked for main grade teachers, as the head himself recognizes. He has therefore placed one period a week on the timetable for departmental meetings, where minutes are taken and are passed to the headmaster.

It is widely felt that LFM has greatly enhanced the resources available to Oakwood. This message is constantly broadcast by the head who points to evidence of this on open display – such as the school coach, the computer laboratory, and the technical design centre; the CDT department has been actively built up through enhanced staffing and material resources. However, there are departments which feel less favoured and individuals who think that money should have been spent in other directions.

Decision-making structures and processes

As well as affecting the school materially, LFM has made a distinct impact on the decision-making structure of the school and hence on the relative influence of different post-holders. The head has been in post many years, so his management style is imprinted on the school. He, himself, recognized that the advent of local financial management, which he welcomed enthusiastically, would cause staff concern that his power would be further enhanced. He has therefore tried to share decision making with them. He decided to do this by using the heads of departments' committee as the forum for collectively agreeing budget decisions. A senior management team of head and deputies to manage the budget was not set up. The line management runs directly from the head to the heads of departments; the deputies are assigned roles which do not involve financial issues in any direct way. Thus the head undertakes the whole task of budget management himself, a task at which he is widely recognized as being highly capable. Though he does no teaching, this was also the case prior to LFM. The head's policy of sharing financial management with the heads of departments is perceived by most of the staff interviewed as having diminished the relative status of the heads-of-year committee and to have side-lined the deputies (now reduced from three to two). The head has responded to this by making each deputy responsible for a major management committee, one concerned with pastoral care and the other with academic staff support.

Conclusion

Information for budget decision making is largely gathered and disseminated through formal processes. The budget is derived from the curriculum structure, written bids for resources are made by heads of departments, department meetings are minuted, papers are prepared before committee meetings, and decisions are disseminated to the staff through further papers. The staff compendium includes detailed information on the budget, including incentive allowances and departmental resources. The criteria used to determine priorities are largely judgemental; there is no formula for allocating departmental allowances, but prior decisions about the curriculum are used to justify resource allocation priorities. Resource allocation decisions involve a combination of multilateral and bilateral interactions between the head and heads of departments, with the latter being relied upon to involve the rest of the teaching staff within the departmental nexus. There are different perceptions of the extent to which the head influences decision making at Oakwood. While formal structures have been created to involve teaching staff and governors in budget making, this by itself does not mean that the source of decision making is to be found in the collective membership of those committees and the interests they may represent.

Case 3: Beechwood Community College

Beechwood Community College has around 600 11-to-16-year-old pupils and 36 teachers. The governing body is responsible for both school and community education; thus its budgeting incorporates both aspects. Separate and combined budget figures are produced by the authority for the school and for community education. There are two budget holders – the warden for the school and the community education tutor. Beechwood, together with all the non-pilot secondary schools, entered Cambridgeshire's LFM scheme in 1986–7. The first year was a 'dry run': schools were allocated budgets and sent printouts, but had no new powers over spending decisions. 1987–8 was the first year in which the school was required to manage its own budget.

Budget management: letting things ride

The warden is not in favour of the LFM scheme. For him, financial management intrudes on the head's role as an educational leader. He spends as little time as possible on it and maintains a regular teaching commitment. He has a particular objection to formula funding because he believes that it cannot be sufficiently sensitive to the needs of individual schools, in relation to such matters as the actual salary costs of the staff, maintenance costs, or the amount spent on examination fees. He is concerned that local financial management will result in educational decisions being extensively dominated by financial considerations. So, for instance, when making a recent teaching appointment he did not inform the governors of the different cost implications of hiring the various candidates.

His tactic for 1987–8 was to do nothing with respect to the budget. The allocation by budget head given by the authority was not altered and no checking of monthly printouts was done by the school's financial secretary, since she had to give higher priority to other tasks. The major overspending of £6000 occurred on capitation, one important element of this being examination fees. Heating, cleaning and water charges were all slightly underspent but this was offset by higher sewerage charges than the authority had allowed for. Over £6000 was saved on teachers and £3500 on supply. The net result was that the school obtained an overall surplus of £5000 which was put into the 1988–9 budget. However, budget inactivity ceased at this point – decisions on how to spend the surplus in 1988–9 were made.

One aspect of the warden's disenchantment with LFM is that it has not been practised consistently. While it is proclaimed that schools are given the freedom to manage their own affairs, the authority has continued to allocate some resources in the old way. He has been frustrated by the difficulties placed in the way of his attempts to have his clerical staff regraded: the personnel department, concerned with comparability of jobs across the local authority, demanded the completion of extensive job grading questionnaires. (Other heads have experienced similar problems.) However, he did succeed in obtaining more money from the authority for examination fees in 1987, on the grounds that Beechwood had more than the average number of entries. What enthusiasts would regard as teething problems in an evolving scheme, is seen by the warden as constantly moving the goal posts, and thus reinforces his initial antipathy towards LFM.

Beginning to manage

Responsibility for LFM has been shared with the deputy head, who takes particular responsibility for it. She is, with reservations, favourably disposed towards it, and sees her task as coming to grips with managing the budget in the current financial year. She has already seen some of the advantages of flexibility that the scheme brings. For instance, Beechwood employed examination invigilators at £3.20 an hour to free teachers for other duties, which was appreciated by the staff. She sees the school now developing a much greater awareness of what things cost – heating needs monitoring and far more needs to be known about the additional costs of lettings. This is particularly important for a community college, which, as it is using its premises for both community education and private lettings, needs to know how costs should be apportioned between school, community education and private lettings so as to fix charges and course fees appropriately.

The deputy considers that the budget could be managed effectively by giving it an hour a week in her timetable for going through the budget with the financial secretary. She reckons that three days is required to prepare the budget, including consultations internally and with the LFM team. She represents the warden at the meetings held between groups of schools and the authority and thinks there is a lot to learn from other schools. She would welcome considerably more training.

The governors' finance subcommittee oversees and approves both the school and community education budgets. The governors are regarded as supportive, fostering good links between school and community. They accept senior management's guidance on budgetary matters. Although the school is experiencing falling rolls, the reduction in teachers (now nine fewer than several years ago) has proceeded smoothly so that with the advent of formula funding the school is not facing a budget deficit problem due to overstaffing.

The priorities for spending the £5000 surplus from 1987–8 are made by the senior management team of head and two deputies. This is done informally – there is no formal consultation of heads of departments or of staff through a committee structure. The head and deputies gather information about the staff's views on the school's spending needs through regular informal contact, and on this basis agree priorities. As yet, financial matters do not explicitly surface at staff meetings or at the staff council, which is a forum for all staff other than the senior management team to formulate views on matters of policy implementation. It was created in response to implementation in school of the 1987 Education Act (Teachers' Pay and Conditions). The staff have little knowledge of, or interest in, how the budget is spent. There seems to be general acceptance of both the current decision-making procedures and the outcome with respect to the allocation of last year's budget surplus. It has been decided to spend this on improving the college entrance, providing additional computers for school and community use, extra assistance in the library, and refurbishing a classroom for special needs.

One interesting development in response to LFM is that a formula has now been agreed for disbursing departmental allowances. This replaces the previous method of informal bids and bilateral negotiation between heads of departments and the warden, which was felt by some staff to penalize class-based subjects, such as English and maths, with large pupil numbers. The formula method was promoted by a head of department who, as a teacher–governor and a member of the finance subcommittee, takes a particular interest in financial matters. The formula allocates the departmental allowances on the basis of the number of pupil contact hours taught by the department; for consumables and equipment, art, science, music, home economics and CDT have a weighting of 2, and PE one of 1.5. Each department then decides how to spend its budget allocation.

At Beechwood, also, LFM is beginning to change the resource allocation process. While information is still gathered and shared informally, and judgemental criteria are important, the development of a formula for allocating departmental allowances is a significant step in formalizing judgements and in replacing bilateral negotiations between the warden and heads of departments by multilateral decision making. However, overall budget creation and, within it, the allocation of budget savings is still, at this stage, undertaken by senior management relying on informal consultation and qualitative judgements. As Beechwood is still in the early stages of adjusting to financial management, further changes in decision-making processes are likely to occur.

The community education budget

In 1976 adult education and the youth service in Cambridgeshire were brought together under community education. The community tutor at Beechwood is responsible for community education over his 'patch': a designated geographical area; he organizes courses and activities at Beechwood and at other premises. Community education has been experiencing a form of delegated budgeting over the last seven years. The community tutor is responsible for the community education part of Beechwood's budget. Under LFM there is virement not only between adult education and the youth service but between school and community education. (This will not be permitted in Local Management of Schools (LMS) schemes under the 1988 Act, since community education expenditure does not come out of the general schools budget. Community school governing bodies may receive earmarked funds for community education.) In practice, the school and community education budgets have been kept separate. If community education made a loss, the community tutor would need to ask the governors for a supplement from the school budget. He would be most reluctant to do this and so strives to maintain the community budget in surplus. The authority expects the college to provide basic education courses but otherwise does not stipulate what courses to run. The community tutor, warden and governors decide on the annual course provision and on the fees charged. Basic education courses and the youth service do not charge fees. Overall, community education must break even. The tutor sees his role becoming 'more of a supermarket manager and less of an educationist who considers the actual need for a particular course'. Courses in villages, which he sees fulfilling a valuable social function, have been cut back.

Beechwood has over the years managed to accumulate a surplus of £3000 in the community education part of its budget, to which £4000 was added in 1987–8. The tutor judges that 60 per cent of this surplus was due to deliberate managerial action, such as not appointing staff. The £1750 saved on staffing the youth service arose from being unable to appoint a youth leader for four months. Savings were made last year in anticipation of a lean time in the following year.

One important issue for community education arising from LFM is that of the charges for using school premises. Currently other schools are willing to let them use their premises without charge, while a fee has to be paid for the use of other premises such as village halls. Community education at Beechwood is charged by the authority 26 per cent of Beechwood's premises costs. This is a budget transfer, from the community education part of Beechwood's budget to its school budget. Cambridgeshire was still at this time trying to devise a more satisfactory system for charging for community education's use of school premises. In 1988 schools still received a recharge for community education usage of a fixed percentage of their premises costs – this fixed percentage being based on some estimate of the previous year's usage. There was little hard information for schools on the additional costs arising from community use of their premises to compare with the compensation received from the authority.

The effect of LFM in making community education costs more transparent and making schools liable to bear part of them has not been a welcome development for community educationists. It is making it more difficult to sustain activities for which the price charged to users is very low (even zero) in comparison to their costs. At Beechwood the governors' finance committee was concerned that, while the adult programme is self-supporting overall, the youth service budget did not appear viable. Community education prior to LFM already had considerable flexibility in that courses, venues and tutors could be changed relatively easily, and so its managers are less ready to appreciate the flexibility in resourcing that schools value from the LFM scheme. However, when a surplus is generated it is then possible to obtain additional resources. For instance the youth service had not had an equipment budget for many years. Budget savings in Beechwood's community education budget were to be spent on additional equipment for the youth service, and on telephone and computing for administrative purposes.

At Beechwood both the warden and the community tutor share the view that 'moving over to a commercial system from an educational system is a little bit of an anathema'.

Case studies: a review

The three cases studies were selected to give a contrast in types of school and in styles of management. It is not possible to generalize from such a small sample but certain issues are raised. Delegated budgeting does make staff in schools more conscious of the costs of using specific resources and of taking these costs into account in decision making. Some aspects of this are widely welcomed, while others, in particular taking account of the salary costs of individual teachers, are not.

A significant issue which emerges from the case studies is the relationship between a head's management style and the way in which financial management is undertaken. In terms of the headship style taxonomy adopted by Hall *et al.* (1988), the teacher–educator head is predisposed to minimize involvement with financial management. This is then taken up by a more enthusiastic deputy or, collectively, by heads of departments. In contrast, the chief–executive-style head welcomes the powers and responsibilities offered by financial delegation and takes on the additional role of budget officer which reinforces the chief-executive role. How the professional-leader head is likely to respond to financial delegation is less obvious. The case studies suggest that such heads may well respond with enthusiasm to financial delegation because of the enhanced ability it gives to pursue their educational aims. The case studies also give some indication of how the different styles of headship adapt in response to the demands and opportunities of financial management. It is difficult for the teacher–educator to ignore the impact of financial delegation, while the chief-executive style of head feels the need to devise ways of including staff in resource allocation decisions. The motivation for heads sharing, to differing degrees, the task of budget management can arise from diverse sources – the need to legitimize decisions, a genuine desire for participation, or from disinterest or lack of confidence in financial matters.

Whatever the management style, all schools face the problem of how to involve staff beyond the immediate circle of senior managers in budget decision making without misallocating staff time with lengthy consultation on the one hand, or making staff feel deliberately excluded from important decisions on the other. This is likely to be less of a problem in smaller schools where internal consultation and negotiation including all staff can occur more easily. Decision-making structures and the roles of specific post-holders in relation to financial management need to be determined. How is financial management to be shared out amongst the senior management team? Should there be a senior financial manager who does not perform pastoral or academic tasks? Should there be a governors' finance/resources sub-committee and a separate school committee covering the same ground, with either appointed or elected members drawn from the teaching staff or from all groups of school staff? An elected membership has the advantage over an appointed senior–middle management committee in giving greater opportunities for all staff to be involved if they so wish; but this advantage may be offset by weakened line-management linkages via the departments, with some areas of the school failing to become fully involved in the resource management of the whole school. A further alternative is a single finance/resources committee containing both governors and elected or appointed staff. This has the disadvantage compared to two committees of involving fewer people, given limitations on the effective size of committees, but may be favoured because it is better at bringing together staff and governors, and in preventing the staff side feeling that their decisions and concerns are not properly considered by the governors.

So as well as coming to grips with the technicalities of financial management, schools have to consider how their decision-making processes need to be adapted in the light of the new responsibilities and opportunities presented by financial delegation.

Notes

1 The schools have been given fictional names.
2 Excluding headteachers, nine staff were interviewed at Elmwood and Oakwood, and six at Beechwood.

References

Arnold, J. and Hope, T. (1989). 'The budgeting process' in R. Levačić (ed.) *Financial Management in Education*. Milton Keynes, Open University Press.

Hall, V., Mackay, H. and Morgan, C. (1988). 'Headteachers at work: practice and policy', in R. Glatter *et al.*, *Understanding School Management*. Milton Keynes, Open University Press.

Simkins, T. (1986). 'Patronage, markets and collegiality: reflections on the allocation of finance in secondary schools', *Education Management and Administration*, **14**(1).

Principles of financial management: the rational perspective

8

Local management of schools

Coopers & Lybrand

I Introduction

1.1 [. . .] As they affect schools, the main changes [in the Education Reform Act] are concerned with:

- the establishment of a National Curriculum;
- the provision for open enrolment;
- the greater delegation to schools of responsibility for financial and other aspects of management;
- the provision for grant-maintained schools.

1.2 The Government has presented these proposals as a package, designed to promote accountability and responsiveness of schools and their Local Education Authorities (LEAs) to their consumers. Although the four proposals form a package, this report is only concerned with the proposal to provide greater delegation to schools of management responsibilities.
[. . .]

1.5 The underlying philosophy of financial delegation to schools stems from the application of the principles of good management. Good management requires the identification of management units for which objectives can be set and resources allocated; the unit is then required to manage itself within those resources in a way which seeks to achieve the objectives; the performance of the unit is monitored and the unit is held to account for its performance and for its use of funds. These concepts are just as applicable in the public sector as they are in the private sector.
[. . .]

1.7   The moves to delegation do not imply that there are not some significant strengths in non-delegated arrangements. A high degree of centralization
is more effective at achieving economies of scale, there are specializations
which are better provided on a wider basis, central arrangements are econ-
omical in record keeping and information, and they leave the head teacher
more time for other things. [. . .] In a system of financial delegation some of
these advantages will be lost; a delegated scheme should be designed to
minimize the losses.

1.8   But there can be major gains from delegation. It will increase the
accountability of schools for providing value for money; it will give schools
the flexibility to respond directly and promptly to the needs of the school and
its pupils in a way which will increase the effectiveness and quality of the
services provided. Schools will have more incentive to seek efficiency and
economy in their use of their resources since they will be able to apply the
benefits of their good management to further improvements in their services.
[. . .]

1.9   Financial delegation has other advantages too. It encourages more
clarity of thought by the LEA about what it wants from its schools, it helps
increase schools' understanding of the pressures on and perspectives of the
LEA, and, equally important, vice versa; it can also make the job of head
teacher a more complete and satisfying one, once it is realized that there are
significant positive benefits to be gained from the opportunities which it
presents. [. . .]

1.12   [. . .] The change at school level is from administration (of centrally
determined programmes) to management (of local resources). What is
required is a fundamental change in the philosophy of the organization of
education. Thus the changes required in the culture and in the management
processes are much wider than purely financial and should be recognized as
such. [. . .]

5   The implications for schools

5.1   [. . .] The processes which will be required by schools to exercise their
new financial and managerial responsibilities and to link with the overall local
authority financial systems [. . .] are those of:

- management;
- planning and budgeting;
- financial control;
- management information;
- administration.

Management

5.2 The largest single change for schools will be in attitude and culture reflecting a shift from an environment in which centrally determined programmes are administered locally to one in which the provision of education is locally managed. The differences between administration and management are considerable and necessitate a change in role for staff, head teachers and governors. Some may be reluctant to accept these changes if they are perceived to interfere with, rather than support and enhance, the educational process. The success of the change will in large part depend upon the clarity with which management structures and processes are established.

5.3 Decision making will need to cover all aspects of school activities starting with the setting of objectives, through the preparation of detailed budgets and operating plans, the monitoring of progress and achievement, agreement of changes and finally an annual review of the year. The results of this process will need to be made available to the LEA; schools opting for grant-maintained status will need to go through the same set of processes but with the DES.

5.4 Heads and governors will need to decide what consultations there should be with teaching and non-teaching staff and with pupils. It will be important to ensure that any such consultation does not unduly slow down decision-making, nor reduce management flexibility.

5.5 Heads of department will need to be involved and, with the head teacher, will effectively form a management team for the school which will need to have recognized roles and processes for the conduct of business. This will include the need for discussion and evaluation of different proposals and options in order that heads and staff should be accountable for their decisions. This will all consume staff time: some will be able to be diverted from hitherto routine administration tasks which are no longer required (for example in detailed communication with the LEA). It is possible that in some schools, staff time will need to be diverted from teaching functions leading to a requirement for some additional teaching support.

5.6 The role of governors in school management will become much more direct and meaningful as they will now have real resources to control and responsibility for the selection for appointment (and dismissal) of staff. [. . .]

5.8 Decision making through a full and formal structure of the governing body will not allow the flexibility for prompt action which will be required to make the best use of resources. An LMS (Local Management of Schools] scheme should involve considerable delegation of powers and responsibilities to the head teacher, for which the Bill makes provision. A small governing body sub-committee might be appropriate, consisting of perhaps the chairman and two specialist members – one with a finance and one with a personnel background – meeting perhaps two or three times per term. Such a sub-committee would act as a safeguard for the head teacher and also as a filter for the full governing body on such matters as budget reviews, budget monitoring, and appointments. [. . .]

Planning and budgeting

5.11   [. . .] Each school will then be faced with the task of planning its operations to achieve its educational objectives within the constraints of cash limit and overall policies and guidelines set by the LEA. [. . .]

5.13   With a March end to the planning and budgeting process a typical planning timetable might be:

Before the end of September	– setting of educational strategy, objectives and planning targets
End September	– notification of provisional cash limit by LEA
October to December	– reappraisal of strategy and setting of detailed operational plans and budgets in the light of cash limit
January	– approval by governors
January/February	– ratification by LEA
March	– confirmation or adjustment by LEA of cash limit
	– adjustment by school of its budget in line with final cash limit

5.14   Schools will need to be able to respond quickly to changes in their resources which result from changes in pupil numbers. [. . .] This can partly be achieved through forecasting pupil numbers but the speed with which those forecasts may change as a result of falling rolls and open enrolment is such that it will be unrealistic to expect schools to prepare their budgets very far in advance of the start of their financial years. [. . .]

5.16   The operating plans and budgets developed at this stage should contain proposals with estimated costs for curriculum and extra-curricular development, administration and administrative systems, staff development and training, and building and grounds maintenance. Of importance at this stage would be a review of the ways in which continuing activities are carried out, with a view to ensuring the best use of resources and value for money, and to take account of clients' demands and needs. It will also be necessary to set targets against which performance can be measured.

Financial control

5.19 Once a school's operating plans and budgets have been agreed by the governing body, their execution will need to be controlled. This will involve regular (probably monthly) monitoring of actual and committed expenditure against expected expenditure derived from the annual budget, profiled as appropriate. Schools will also need to monitor activities and achievements in parallel with the budget. This can be done through a variety of means from reports by staff through to the use of performance indicators and unit costs. [. . .]

5.20 Inevitably, as the financial year progresses, problems will arise and opportunities will be identified which may be dealt with through modifications to the budget. Minor changes could be managed by the head in consultation with the chairman of governors or with the governing body sub-committee. Major changes, involving large amounts of budget or staffing matters may require a more formal approval process. [. . .]

Administration

5.27 Experience of delegation schemes to date suggests that LMS adds considerably to the administrative workload at the school level, a factor which emphasizes the need to lighten the administrative burden on schools in other respects. [. . .]

5.29 This raises a question about the ability of small schools to operate a scheme of local school management; if the only flexibility for resource reallocation is consumed by the costs of administering the system, local school management will have at best a neutral effect and at worst a detrimental one. [. . .]

5.31 [. . .] extra costs will be incurred, at least in the short term. It may be necessary for LEAs, and the DES, to recognize this as a necessary cost to be incurred in achieving better management and better education through the school system.

6 Information requirements

6.1 Information provision will lie at the heart of a successful LMS scheme. [. . .]

6.2 The forms of information for LMS and the way it is collected and communicated depend on the uses for which it is required. The management process for a school will follow a cycle of:

- strategic planning and objective setting;
- detailed operational planning of timetables and budgets;
- control and administration of the execution of the planned activities;
- monitoring of operations and feedback on variations in order to amend and update plans;
- reporting on performance.

The LEA and the wider community will both need to provide information for this process.

6.3 *Strategic planning* will follow an annual cycle matched to the local authority annual planning and budget cycle. It will require high level information from the LEA on policies, resources and workloads and also information from the community which the school is seeking to serve. Schools will need to generate information about the options available to them. This will cover staffing, curricula and any performance targets agreed with the LEA.

6.4 Detailed *operational planning* will be an exercise largely contained within the school, though the final form of the plan will need to be conveyed to the LEA under a few major budget headings so that the treasurer can consolidate the school's budgets into the overall local authority budget. Schools will need to set out their budgets in a standardized format to enable local authority treasurers to consolidate them consistently. [. . .]

6.5 The *execution of plans* will require much detailed information, but schools should not need high level accountancy skills to provide it. LEAs and local authorities will therefore need to provide administrative and accounting systems which remove as much as possible of the detail of financial adminis-tration and accounting from schools, leaving them the tasks of deciding on the use of resources, placing orders and monitoring the results. The in-termediate tasks of transaction processing and accounting should be done automatically as far as possible.

6.6 *Monitoring plans* and adjusting them as required will demand infor-mation not only on actual performance to date; [. . .] Schools will also need financial information, for example on commitments and on forecasts of likely results. This will require careful profiling of budgets, matched to each school's characteristics and plans. [. . .] The LEA will also require monitor-ing information which should be a subset of that which the school requires for its own management. [. . .]

6.16 LMS will inevitably require more management information to be available in schools.

9
Program budgeting: implications for secondary principals

Fred J. Brockmann

Budgeting by program is but one facet of a total PPBS (planning, programming, budgeting system) operation. In reality it may, but should *not* be, separated from efforts to formulate goals and objectives, assess alternative methods, and seek evaluative measures. These associated activities must be kept in mind at all times, even though they may not be formalized at the immediate inception of a new PPB System.

In the paragraphs that follow, a discussion of a particular application of program budgeting is provided. Examples of actual program budgeting forms are included along with a brief description of the impact of the new budget format upon the school district.

Program budgeting as part of a total system

In brief, program budgeting is an attempt to link all the allocations of resources needed to support a particular program. A *program* is defined as a combined set of activities directed toward achievement of a predetermined goal. Traditional budgeting techniques may or may not provide this effect. For example, you may choose to separate out the total costs for a program in reading, or in literature, or in any one of the traditional disciplines. Or you may prefer to channel funds into a program that is interdisciplinary in nature or is based on criteria other than the standard subject matter. Some schools may be more interested in channeling resources in an all out effort to solve immediate human relations problems, ecological difficulties, or drug issues. How one chooses to define programs in a program budget varies considerably from school to school.

Purposes of program budgeting

Program budgeting was instituted in Guilford, Connecticut for the basic purposes of: (1) improving communication about expenditures made in traditional programs because of severe budget cuts imposed earlier (2) providing a centralizing influence on programs to strengthen curriculum articulation both horizontally and vertically in a school district that had grown rapidly and promises continued growth, and (3) providing a means for meaningful discussion about educational objectives and evaluation.

[. . .]

How does program budgeting differ from traditional budgeting?

The basic differences between program budgeting and traditional budgeting at the secondary school level are summarized below:

1 *The Program Budget reflects an educational plan.* It is not merely an estimate of what will be needed to survive for next year. It implies knowledge of expectations to be realized from that plan. As such, curriculum development does not take place in the summer with hopes that somewhere, somehow, the financial resources can be found to implement the programs that have been put forth on paper.
2 *Planning by program is holistic rather than incremental.* The goal is for total program efforts to be achieved. What will the art program need to accomplish its curriculum objectives next year in terms of staff, textbooks, materials, equipment, supplies, library support, hardware, facilities, transportation, and equipment maintenance? Program chairmen are asked to think through the total budget implications of their plans for the following year. (In a different context, have you ever bought a kiln only to find out you don't have adequate electrical supply?)
3 *Planning by program focuses on the programs that are new as differentiated from programs that are continuing.* It emphasizes the multi-year impact of these new programs. New program additions are not 'slipped' into being. The short- and long-term implications of new programs are clearly identified for administration, for board of education, and for community.
4 *All programs affect all other programs in the unit.* Changes in science programs and math programs do affect each other. If you change program directions in English, what effects are encountered in the foreign language department? Program budgeting techniques allow for integration of effort when those efforts are clearly identified and articulated by all program leaders. All programs are reviewed by an advisory council made up of all building principals and all program chairmen.

[. . .]

5 *Incremental budgeting is eliminated.* Zero base budgeting is applied with the requirement that all requests be justified as if the program were to start from base zero with no resources. Present inventory, present priorities, and present resources dictate the allocative design, not the cost of the program increase based on a certain percentage over last year's allocation.

6 *Contingency funds will not be available next year.* This notion may be difficult to eliminate. Someone in the organization always believes that the principal or budget supervisor has additional hidden funds which will allow for instant implementation of 'new programs', 'new materials', 'new ideas'. But, too often, these 'new' ideas may not be carefully thought out as to their effects on the total unit, and should be considered not in isolation, but as part of the total educational plan [. . .]. Note that the unassigned portions in the budget are those items which cannot be realistically charged to one specific program before the fact. These are not contingency items. A good goal to shoot for here is to reserve one percent of your operating budget as an 'unassigned' category. You will note that Guilford did *not* meet this goal its first time through with program budgeting.

If the budget is not an estimate, but a specific, researched plan, greater generation of data is needed. Data will have to be organized in such a way that the complete program picture is available.

In Guilford, data are ordered into two classes (1) those that are needed to continue programs at existing levels, and (2) those that describe or support new programs.

A new program has been defined as those activities that expand or add to present offerings other than those expansions or additions needed because of additional students. All new courses are, therefore, planned for, budgeted for, and made visible – complete with their educational and fiscal implications.

The important point is that a new program is disapproved or approved with full knowledge and forethought by those responsible and accountable for the educational program.

Basis for program proposal analysis

The budget review [. . .] involves these basic questions:

1 *Is the new program consistent with established priorities?* Program budgeting requires an early identification of what areas or programs are most in need of strengthening. This process of collegial decision-making can take place simultaneously while developing your program structure (or chart of accounts).

An example of our program structure is shown in Table 9.1. The definition of this structure leads directly to informal program description analysis. Priority-setting naturally follows. Do we have an art program?

Table 9.1 Program budget summary for Guilford, Connecticut

Constructional Program	Certified personnel		Non-certified personnel		Books	Supplies	Equip.	Contracted other exp.	Total cost by Program
	No.	Cost	No.	Cost					
Language Arts	61.3	$ 594,363	.20	$ 1,000	$ 9,272	$ 5,530	$ 0	$ 1,635	$ 611,800
Social Studies	22.3	225,189	.30	1,300	5,497	1,914	0	782	234,682
Science	24.3	241,187		0	1,364	5,162	2,700	695	251,108
Mathematics	34.6	342,566		0	2,892	4,420	437	1,032	351,347
Health	4.0	43,208		0	1,061	142	30	50	44,491
Physical Education, Intramurals	7.7	79,284		0	0	2,853	1,000	50	83,187
Foreign Language	12.4	104,170		0	3,600	692	178	550	109,190
Art	6.4	58,510		0	130	6,515	60	120	65,335
Music	8.0	86,404		0	244	1,377	4,050	1,305	93,380
Industrial Arts	6.0	57,125		0	140	8,221	1,801	0	67,287
Business Education	4.0	45,605		0	596	2,728	975	1,710	51,614
Home Economics	3.0	29,020		0	526	2,101	350	166	32,163
Special Services	14.0	160,718	.87	3,315	0	3,000	1,999	66,522	235,554
Driver Education	Hrly	2,850		0	0	615	0	225	3,690
Dramatic Arts	Daily	0	1.36	10,000	0	50	0	0	10,050
Extra Curricular, Int. Sch.	Rated	12,681		0	0	0	4,196	6,863	23,740
Adult Education		9,300		0	0	0	0	0	9,300
Instructional Support		$2,092,180		$ 15,615	$25,322	$45,320	$17,776	$ 81,705	$2,277,918

Guidance	7.0	87,470	1.58	8,986	0	967	0	800	98,223
Health Service	1.0	16,380		0	0	500	51	300	17,231
Testing	0	0		0	0	2,400			2,400
Library	7.6	38,575	1.56	11,943	17,915	8,101	1,288	17,581	145,403
Building Administration	10.0	177,774	10.74	43,528	0	12,688	1,807	16,545	252,342
General Administration	2.0	41,000	4.00	29,222		4,100	800	11,512	86,634
Transportation	Hrly	750		0				172,440	173,190
Food Services		8,500	1.00	0					8,500
Custodial Cleaning		0	19.54	139,060		16,600			155,660
Building and Site Repair		0	2.00	16,288		2,150	751	41,900	61,089
Fixed charge and Utilities		0						287,433	287,433
Unassigned to Program		72,678	.77	4,347					77,025
	235.6	493,127	43.92	253,374	17,915	47,506	4,697	548,511	1,365,130
Total		$2,585,307	43.92	$268,989	$43,237	$92,826	$22,473	$630,216	$3,643,048

What does it contain? Should we break out costs for reading? or literature? or language arts? Can we? How do we presently evaluate these programs? How should we evaluate them? A program structure is a guide to lead you to an assessment of your deficiencies and strengths.

The structure becomes even more meaningful when you add flesh to the skeleton with cost data and later with goals, objectives, and evaluation criteria.

2 *What are you trying to accomplish in this program and what alternative methods have been considered?* If you are trying to increase individualized learning for students with perceptual handicaps, should you (1) hire additional teaching staff? (2) consider a series of programed software and hardware designed for remediating perceptual problems? (3) or add teacher aides to work on a one-to-one basis as differentiated staff under the supervision of the specially-trained reading personnel? As many alternatives as possible are considered, costed, and a decision is made on the basis of cost-benefit analysis. That is, the alternative is selected that will be most beneficial to the students relative to the amount of money put into the program. And that leads to the third basic question.

3 *Have evaluative criteria been established as part of the program proposal to assess the impact of this proposal in terms of desired pupil behavioral change?* This is one of the most difficult parts of developing PPBS. It involves searching for behavioral indicators that demonstrate pupil learning as a result of new program. In Guilford, we are still struggling with this facet, but now in our second year we are stressing the fact that good written objectives imply the evaluative measure, especially in the cognitive and psycho-motor domains.

After having developed a program budget, both new and maintenance (continuing), you are now ready to translate this into costs per program, per instructional unit, per pupil – information that is the beginning of a data bank of comparative information for the future.

More importantly, the new budget reflects a set of specific plans that can be discussed in depth and can gain support for educational dollars that are all too difficult to come by, both from within and without the educational system.

[. . .]

What problems or conflicts may develop?

Principals' involvements in program budgeting are not without difficulty. As most secondary principals are well aware, involvement can create conflict and ambiguity.

Role conflict between principals and program chairmen is not only possible, it is natural. Both view themselves as instructional leaders. But program chairmen, when viewed as advisers of staff capacity, can be a real asset to over-burdened building administrators at any level.

[. . .]

Another conflict is [. . .] that the establishment and coordination of district priorities, building priorities, and program priorities may be disparate. At the very least, the PPBS techniques bring such conflicts and disparities into the open where, with intelligence and persistence, these problems can be effectively dealt with and resolved.

A further conflict may develop in the demands on the principal's time from both the district and the building. With greater data generation and more extensive program description [. . .] there is an increased demand on the time of busy building principals. But if principals are to be involved as part of a management team, they must be willing to contribute to the over-all system effort.

What are the pay-offs?

By way of summary, and to end on a positive note, here is what program budgeting can do for your school:

1 Focus power of resources by program and thereby create observable changes in instructional activity in the classroom.
2 Enhance professionalism through involvement of all levels of staff and provide greater total knowledge of all programs.
3 Foster [. . .] intra-program cooperation [. . .].
4 Sensitize the staff to the realization of limited resources and therefore a consideration of alternatives at all levels for all programs.
5 Create awareness of basic planning questions such as
   • What are we trying to do?
   • Are there different ways to do it?
   • How much will it cost to do it?
   • How can we tell when we've done it?

And when all staff, principals, and classroom teachers start to think that way, the result should be a substantial improvement in the quality of education.

10

Zero-base budgeting for schools

Harry J. Hartley

[. . .]
A preface of caution, is that the overselling of innovations is a chronic problem in education. Some zero-base budgeting (ZBB) proponents promise more than they can deliver and underplay potential misuses of the concept, such as creating excessive paperwork and forms, reducing staff morale, and overemphasizing quantification in the evaluation of instructional programs. However, in the hands of a competent principal, ZBB can be used to improve budget planning, control of expenses, and justification of funds to support various program alternatives.

What is zero-base budgeting?

The primary purpose of ZBB is to exert greater control over budgets by requiring justification for every proposed expenditure, beginning theoretically from a base of zero. This represents a major shift from incremental budgeting (critics call it 'budget creep'), in which the budget focuses on increments, while the 'base' is given little scrutiny. With ZBB, program managers must start fresh each year by developing a rationale, objectives, evaluation criteria, and needed resources for alternate levels of service for each program.
[. . .]
The essential ingredients of ZBB are identified and defined below:

- *Decision Unit:* An organizational entity, activity, program or function that is usually the lowest level for which budget decisions are made; in a secondary school, this could be an academic department, such as math.

- *Decision Package:* A written justification (objectives, evaluation, alternate funding levels) that concisely describes budget implications for each decision unit in the school (see Figure 10.1 for an example).
- *Minimum Funding:* The lowest of several levels of funding required for each budget unit; generally, ZBB requires a program manager to submit at least two or three different levels of funding for each decision unit (or department), and one level must be *less than* the current spending level. Theoretically, the minimum level could be zero dollars, but in actual practice the minimum is usually expressed as a percentage of the current level (for example, 80 per cent of current appropriations for the math department).
- *Priority Ranking:* Ranking of individual decision packages and funding levels in order of importance so you can formulate overall budget priorities; each administrator is likely to use a unique 'mix' of criteria and ranking procedures (see Figure 10.2 for a list of ranking criteria).

How should ZBB be implemented in schools?

[. . .]

1 *Define decision units.* This requires principals to classify their buildings into programs, or cost centers, for budget purposes. A typical secondary school could have 20 or so decision units (such as art, athletics, pupil activities, administration) that would account for the entire budget of the building. Program managers are identified for each instructional and support program to ensure accountability.
2 *Identify funding levels.* Either the superintendent or principal should specify the levels of funding that will guide the budget preparation. For example, the principal might ask the math chairperson to submit decision packages based on three levels of funding:

- *preferred level* – perhaps a 10 per cent increase over current spending to allow for program improvements;

Figure 10.2 Criteria used in setting budget priorities

1 Subjective judgment	11 Staff seniority factors
2 Past practice	12 Collective bargaining provisions
3 Legal requirements	13 National curricular trends
4 Quality of program	14 Effect on matching funds
5 Test results	15 Non-instructional services
6 Number of students	16 Principle of least opposition
7 Parental pressures	17 Accreditation recommendations
8 Needs assessment	18 Other options available
9 Staff recommendations	19 Total program costs
10 School board priorities	20 Local political factors

[. . .]

BUDGET/ACCOUNT CODE: 52300　　　DECISION PACKAGE　　　DISTRICT PRIORITY NOS. ☒1

Decision Area Name ____ Mathematics ____ Prepared By ____ Forest Park High School ____ Date Prepared ____ March 15, 1979

Decision Unit (School/Department) ____ J. Sam Scott (Principal) ____ Approved By ____ C. Thomas Budlin (Asst. Superintendent)

Check One: ☒ Existing Decision Area　☐ New Decision Area
Check One: ☒ Curriculum & Instruction　☐ Management Services　☐ Auxiliary Services

Check – Criteria Code(s)

☐ A = Legal Requirements
☒ B = Contract Requirements
☒ C = Board Requirements
☐ D = Other: _____

Function or Purpose of Decision Area:
To develop competency in mathematical skills for individual students that meet their needs and interest. Mathematical skills are organized into the following major strands: Operations and properties, measurement, geometry, numeration, and interpreting data.

Description of Services Provided by Decision Area:
This area offers courses in basic math, consumer math, algebra, geometry, trigonometry, analysis, probability and statistics and calculus.

District Performance Standard(s):
80% of all students will master 80% of all the objectives.

Consequences if Existing Decision Area is eliminated: (Partial or All)
Students will not develop the mathematical skills needed, or some other area will have to absorb this function. If the upper courses were eliminated, students preparing for higher education would not develop the required competencies.

Reproduced with permission of R. Meade Abbott, Director of Business Services, School District No. 12, Adams County; Northglenn, Colo.

Zero-Base Budgeting

COST ANALYSIS

Existing Decision Area – Present Performance Level (Justification of all cost changes) 68% of all students enrolled in mathematics courses; 75% of all math students master 80% of the district math objectives.

PRESENT FISCAL YEAR			NEXT FISCAL YEAR			INCREASE (DECREASE) From Present Fiscal Year	RANKING Unit	Div.	Dist.
Salaries F.T.E.	8.25	$105,450	Salaries F.T.E.	8.25	$115,995				
Employment Benefit		17,927	Employment Benefit		19,179				
Purchasing Services		2,000	Purchasing Services		2,000				
Supplies & Materials		5,000	Supplies & Materials		5,500				
Capital Outlay		2,000	Capital Outlay		2,500				
TOTAL COST	8.25	$132,377	TOTAL COST	8.25	$145,714	0 $ + 13,337			

Alternative A:
a. Description: Add an additional teacher in basic math.
b. Justification: To lower the pupil/teacher ratio to 1/15 in order to give more individualized help.
c. Expected Performance Level: 80% of all math students will master 80% of the math objectives.

NEXT FISCAL YEAR			INCREASE (DECREASE) From Present Fiscal Year	RANKING Unit	Div.	Dist.
Salaries F.T.E.	9.25	$128,995				
Employment Benefit		21,929				
Purchasing Services		2,000				
Supplies & Materials		5,500				
Capital Outlay		2,500				
TOTAL COST	9.25	$160,924	1 $ + 28,547			

Alternative B:
a. Description: Reduce personnel to six teachers.
b. Justification: Lowest level possible of offering basic and intermediate mathematics.
c. Expected Performance Level: 50% of all students enrolled in math.

NEXT FISCAL YEAR			INCREASE (DECREASE) From Present Fiscal Year	RANKING Unit	Div.	Dist.
Salaries F.T.E.	6	$89,112				
Employment Benefit		1,515				
Purchasing Services		2,000				
Supplies & Materials		4,000				
Capital Outlay		500				
TOTAL COST	6	$97,127	(2.25) $ (35,250)			

Note: Use back for additional information or more detailed cost data if above space are too limiting.
SCHOOL DISTRICT NO. 12, ADAMS COUNTY, COL.

Figure 10.1 A decision package for math

- *maintenance level* – this represents a no-growth, or 'business-as-usual', budget that maintains the current level of service (plus a provision for salary increments and an inflation factor in supplies);
- *reduced level* – a minimum request that might represent 80 per cent of the current spending level (this usually involves a reduction in services based on reduced supplies, equipment and staff).

Each school must define precisely what constitutes 'minimum level funding' for each decision unit. In an austerity environment, some schools have defined minimum level to mean only those services which are absolutely required by law.

3 *Develop decision packages.* For each decision unit, prepare forms called decision packages that justify each of the several levels of funding. An example for a high school math program in Northglenn, Colo., is shown in Figure 10.1. Math was one of 19 areas for which decision packages were prepared in this school. Some schools select a pilot program first before developing decision packages in all areas.

4 *Rank decision packages.* You might develop several categories (essential, desired, marginal) in order to assign relative values to the competing decision packages. A 'ranking sheet' is then prepared by the principal in order to list the packages in priority order, identify costs and personnel for each, and specify the cumulative cost at each level in the ranking.

5 [. . .] The value of the ZBB process is to initiate a rigorous process for identifying potential savings at the program level on a more rational basis. As available financial resources are reduced, the lower priority decision packages are eliminated from the budget request. Conversely, in a happier world in which funding for education is increased, decision packages can be added to the budget based on their priority and the dollars available.

11

Costing educational practice

John Fielden and Philip Pearson

Knowing what something costs is the first stage in a weighing of its value against that cost. In education particularly, the outcomes, the benefits of an activity are not readily weighed and measured.

However, to say that educational outcomes cannot be quantified is not to say that decisions will not be made about the relative merits of different processes. Indeed such decisions must be made and if they are going to be made, with so many unquantifiable factors, there is surely merit in quantifying where we can, especially as, while there is no limit to the extent of educational aims, there are very definite limits to the material resources available. And we can quantify the costs, in terms of money, human effort and other resources which may not be so readily connected to monetary equivalents.

There is [. . .] no one absolute and correct way of costing. Equally, comparisons of costings of dissimilar activities do not tell us very much that is useful. But when we have two or more alternative ways towards the same educational aim, then if the same basic costing principles are adopted, the same elements included and excluded, conclusions can be drawn as to the relative costs of the different methods. It still remains necessary to assess, by non-quantitative methods, relative educational merits, and then to make decisions on the basis of *all* available information. [. . .]

Role of cost analysis

[. . .]

We suggest that a cost analysis will provide at least half the input to an educational decision. It should aim to summarize (not necessarily in money terms) the net resource implications of an educational activity over a period of time. [. . .] The conventional role of cost analysis is in assessing a possible change. There may be one or several alternatives to an existing situation. The perspective may be wholly in the future or may include some retrospection. The decision could be an investment one (should we go ahead with Scheme A at a cost of £x?), a reappraisal one (are we right to continue with B at a cost of £y?), or a review (were we right in retrospect to do C?).

In considering a change we must decide whether we are interested in its total resource implications or only in its extra cost. If we choose the former we have a harder task, but are able to provide data to any other organization that wishes to repeat the project or change themselves. The choice could depend on the purpose and location of the study. A cost analysis of a school for one authority could concentrate on extra costs only, since it could conclude that the change would never happen in that particular form anywhere else. The extraction of total and hidden costs would not therefore be justified.

Audiences

When a cost analysis is being planned one of the initial key decisions is the identification of the audience for the analysis. This affects the technical cost content, the format and the presentation of the study. [. . .]

Costs

Our objective in identifying the cost implications of an activity is to summarize the extent to which it is consuming or appropriating resources. The cost label which we use is an attempt to quantify or measure that consumption or appropriation. Sometimes the use is not measurable or we are forced to use a proxy for a precise allocation (we cannot, for example, say how much of the central administrative overheads relate specifically to one school).

We must initially distinguish between the basic 'resources' which are deployed in educational activities and the 'costs' of the activities. The latter are simply ways of expressing a measurement of the former. Most educational undertakings involve the use or consumption of the following resources:

- space in buildings
- equipment with a long life
- time of professional staff
- time of non-professional staff
- teaching materials and consumables
- consumable overheads (postage, telephones)
- other overheads (rates, insurance, etc).

[. . .]

Cost definitions

It is essential to clarify some cost definitions before we venture farther into a costing approach. Different audiences will have different perceptions of costs. They will interpret the cost of an activity differently according to the cost and budgetary conventions within which they operate. There is thus no such thing as an absolute cost and the cost labels or totals people attach to activities will rarely be transferable. There are, however, some commonly understood cost definitions and these we must now consider. [. . .]

Direct costs

These are the simplest to define; they are the costs which can be directly attributed to an activity. A new media centre will probably have its staff costs, equipment, supplies and consumables separately identified, budgeted for and controlled in the accounts. These will be its direct costs. [. . .]

Indirect costs

These as one might expect, are resources which cannot be clearly apportioned to an activity. Included in this category are the time of supporting staff and many types of overhead expenditure. In many costing exercises all costs of an organization are apportioned to each of its activities. A school, for example, might attempt to allocate *all* its costs among subjects. This is called 'absorption costing'. Direct costs such as teachers' salaries could be allocated easily, but indirect costs would have to be apportioned on a rational basis of some kind.

Marginal costs

These are the incremental costs of an activity or, put another way, the costs which would not have been incurred if the activity had not started. All the costs of an activity can be divided into either fixed or variable costs. Fixed costs do not alter when the scale of an activity changes (telephone rental is unaffected by an increase in pupil numbers). Variable costs do alter. Thus, marginal costs will be found among the variable categories of cost. Marginal costs are clearly influenced by organizational factors; what is marginal in one situation, where there is no unutilized capacity on a resource, may not be marginal in another. There are frequently large jumps in marginal cost. It could, for example, be feasible to accommodate twenty more students at a lecture session, but the addition of the twenty-first would require another hall and another member of staff. In this case the marginal cost of the twentieth is tiny, but the marginal cost of one more student is very great. [. . .]

Total cost

This means the total cost from the national (and sometimes the world) viewpoint. This definition of total cost differs from that used in commercial costing, where it means what we have earlier called absorption costing. Costs will be included which fall outside all the institutional or authority budgets. Precise definitions of the boundary of total cost vary, since some economists include some cost elements which others omit. We ourselves find it none too helpful to include concepts such as interest on capital employed or earnings forgone by students who could have been on the labour market. Total cost can be of real value, if sensibly defined, as it is the only objective all-embracing measure of cost that can be applied to a whole host of different accounting conventions.

Opportunity cost

This is worth defining, although it is on a different level to marginal and total cost, and is not always applicable in education. It relates to the concept of an alternative profitable use for the resources which are invested in an innovation. If money or time is spent in one area which could be productive in another area, the income or benefit that has been lost is the opportunity cost of going ahead with the activity. It is useful for appraising an investment in or extension of an innovation, but, since it fails to account for the relative qualitative outcomes of two alternative educational programmes, it must not be relied on as the sole basis for a decision.

Not all these definitions will be used in cost analyses and the principal ones met will be direct, marginal and total costs. In educational decision-making misunderstandings arise because of different perceptions of marginal cost and different conventions of costing. What is marginal from one viewpoint will not be marginal from another. A decision which has no impact on a departmental budget can have substantial resource implications on institutional budgets. [. . .]

Benefits and outcomes

It is not the function of the cost analyst to measure all educational benefits or qualitative changes. He must, however, be prepared to identify what has happened and to summarize the outcomes in those cases where they are measurable.

We believe that it is helpful to consider outcomes as falling into three different categories: those which are measurable and realizable, those which are measurable but cannot be realized and those which cannot be measured. A further classification applies to all three categories since outcomes can be both direct and indirect in their incidence. Let us now consider the three types.

Measurable and realizable outcomes of an educational activity could be cash income generated, cash expenditure saved and space or equipment no longer required. [. . .] There should be little difficulty identifying such outcomes since they are generally related to the direct costs of an activity.

More common are the *outcomes which are measurable but unrealizable*. Principal among these are fractions of staff time freed from one activity, which will always be reinvested by the individual concerned in another activity. In some cases space or equipment will be used less than before, but will not be freed entirely. One department may cut the use of a resource entirely, but another department will require it so that no realizable saving results. If less demand is put on indirect or support staff, the saving may be identifiable, but could only rarely be realized because of the small fractions of time involved.

Our third category, *immeasurable outcomes*, relates as one might expect to qualitative aspects. [. . .]

Measures and units

[. . .]

The data on use of resources will be collected in the most suitable basic unit; time, for example, could be measured in days, man-months or percentages of a man-year. Almost all these basic units will be capable of conversion into a financial figure. In some cases this may not be necessary since, if there are pluses and minuses in the same units, it may be possible to net them off first before considering a financial conversion. An activity may save one person's time, but add to the effort of his colleagues; the analyst needs to know the net total of these two impacts.

The stage in an analysis at which one carries out a conversion of basic units into money will depend largely on the audience for the analysis and their perceptions of cost. A head of department, for example, would far rather be told that an activity required 20 square metres of laboratory space than learn that its space costs were £300 per annum. Even in institutional decision-making it may be more valuable to talk of 1½ man-years for a senior lecturer than of £30,000 of staff time. [. . .]

A unit cost is sometimes preferred as a measure of resource impact. Cost per pupil, per student-hour or cost per film are useful ways of studying educational activities. Their principal value is that they are a limited link between inputs and outputs, even if only an intermediate measure. They also bring any economies of scale into account and can be used for relative comparisons between alternative ways of carrying out an activity. One disadvantage is that they can be misused. The most widely applicable unit cost measure for educational technology would be cost per student-hour. We used this measure in some of our studies of computer-assisted learning projects, but found it misleading and inapplicable in some cases. What unit cost could one find to describe the use of media to supplement a lecture presentation to undergraduates, for example? Is it realistic to consider student numbers in this case? Is the medium any more cost-effective because the lecture group numbers 80, than it is if only 25 attend?

In much educational decision-making cost per student per annum is a common measure. [. . .] It should not be forgotten, however, that the unit cost will alter as the number of pupils increases, depending on the way the costs are divided between fixed costs and costs which vary with pupil numbers. The use of an annual unit cost inevitably leads to comparisons with capitation rates or the total cost of educating a pupil. While such comparisons can be valuable we must not forget that the outcomes of the unit costs will be very different and will bring the decision-maker back to a value judgement in the end. [. . .]

Evaluating costs and outcomes

[. . .] The main criterion in considering whether any cost or outcome should be included in the analysis is whether it has a discernible effect on any resource at the level of decision-making considered. For example, if a special project team is recruited, then it will require accommodation, which has a real impact on the resource of space. It matters little in deciding whether to include space as a resource that the institution might have unused accommodation available: there has been a real resource change, even if it is only that there is less unused space than before; in other institutions or at other times space might be at a premium and therefore it should be included. By contrast, if the project is developed, for example, by existing academic staff in their personal research time, there is no impact on space as staff will generally use the same accommodation irrespective of their activity. Generally, the only resources which need not usually be considered for inclusion in the analysis are those which in normal cost accounting are derived purely on an allocation basis. The primary example of these is the allocation of an institution's administrative and service overheads; this type of cost rarely has a place in project appraisal, as it cannot reflect any discernible change in resources as a result of the project. There are exceptions to this where projects lead to definite and measurable extra work-loads on administrative staff. [. . .]

In a full economic analysis the cost of any item which is most relevant is the opportunity cost, that is the 'value' of the best alternative use to which the resource can be put; the 'worth' of savings, similarly, is the value of the use to which the savings can be put, or the amount that people or institutions are willing to pay for them. [. . .] All that can be done is, for example, to base the cost of time of existing staff on the salaries of the people concerned or to calculate the cost of computing time by apportioning the total cost of the computer department on the basis of processor time used. This approach is, at best, a fairly crude evaluation of the comparative value of different resources.

For this reason we recommend that such resource data be retained in terms of their primary units of measurement for as long as possible in the analysis. If it is necessary to translate their effects into financial terms, then this should form a fundamental break-point in the analysis and results should also be presented in terms of primary units so that a decision-maker can, if he wishes, make his own judgement on the relative value of the various resources. The analyst can sometimes help by making his own, subjective, judgement of how the true economic value of resources differs from that of their notional monetary value. [. . .]

Qualitative effects, in particular the educational 'enrichment benefits', need to be discussed. Any associated quantitative data, such as the number of students and the proportion of their contact time involved, should also be given and it might also be possible to summarize the results of any educational evaluation of the scheme, if this is not already separately available.

[. . .]

There is one interesting side effect of costing that is worthy of note. The main purpose is to arrive at the costs of an activity, yet in the process of doing so we also arrive at a clearer understanding of what the activity involves. We are forced to be clearer about what constitutes development work, about allocation of time, about all the implications of innovation. The same heightened awareness would come from the application of costing techniques to existing activities, and not only to teaching activities but to those non-teaching activities which seem to absorb an ever-increasing proportion of the available resources.

To do sensible costings is not easy or trivial, but when sensible costings are available they are one contribution to the taking of well-informed decisions.

12

A practical unit cost approach to budgeting and accountability in colleges

David Jones

In order to evaluate and monitor the college system, or any other organization for that matter, one needs to be able to deal with the following issues.

Firstly one should be able to describe the nature of the business in an objective way. In commercial terms this means being able to establish a clear definition of the product. [. . .] It is not enough just to produce a stirring statement of educational aims, and one's aspirations for the people graduating from the organization. If measurements are to be made, the product needs to be defined in tangible terms.

The second task is to be able to determine the extent to which one is able to achieve the product aim. In other words one should be able to quantify the output of the production process. [. . .] One problem in education is that many useful things go on which are not readily quantifiable.

The third area of concern is to establish the cost of the operation so that one can make some sort of measurement of the cost-effectiveness of the process by relating the extent of product success to the cost of achieving it. [. . .]

Any education system which seeks to make a meaningful measurement of cost-effectiveness must tackle this problem of measuring the output of the production process in educational terms which recognise the system as something other than just a body-counting one. Not only is it difficult to achieve some sort of consensus as to the aims of the educational process, there is some uncertainty as to who should determine those aims. [. . .] In vocational further education, objectives are somewhat clearer in definition than in the school and university sectors. [. . .] In cost-effectiveness terms, [. . .] the product needs to be defined in a manner that measures the extent to which the college qualifies people for employment. The vast majority of college students enrol for the purpose of getting such qualifications. [. . .]

This is not to say that activities that do not directly subscribe to the getting of qualifications are unimportant, but rather that if they consume resources, then in the present situation where students are turned away from some areas of work because of inadequate resources, there needs to be a conscious and properly justified decision to supplement the provision for those who are already enabled to secure qualifications. [. . .] The systems described [. . .] employ the measure of qualification rates as the indicator of college production. [. . .]

The over-all aim of the management task is to secure a better performance from the organization. The monitoring of performance through internal accountability systems is directed at revealing shortcomings in the operation so that remedial steps can be taken. For management to be able to identify appropriate remedies the college information system needs to be suitably detailed and directed so that it signposts the likely source or sources of a problem.

Value for money in theory

The major operating cost of running a course is that required for the payment of the teaching staff. Other costs are associated with non-teaching staff, equipment, materials, and a variety of other types of expenditure.

Teaching costs far outweigh any of the others and the performance of the educational process in cost-effective terms is usually identified as some sort of relation between the staff hours used and the number of students who benefit from that attention. The techniques described here are based on the notion that one can define for any particular course an optimum condition of operation which will, in general, lead to the best performance for a given investment.

In focusing attention on the level of staffing investment one can define the cost of running a course as the number of hours used to teach it over the year. The product leading from that investment is the number of passes resulting from some form of assessment. One can then calculate the unit cost, that is the cost of one pass, in the following terms:

$$\text{unit cost} = \frac{\text{course length in weeks} \times \text{hours taught/week}}{\text{number presented for assessment} \times \text{pass rate}}$$

The operational aim of management is to minimise the unit cost.

Unlike other types of productivity measurement, such as student to staff ratio and average class size, this one indicates that there is an optimum mode of operation. Because it incorporates an assessment of the quality of the educational process the measurement acknowledges that there is a limit to the investment level below which further economies would be counter-productive. [. . .]

One can [. . .] define an optimum level for the two major cost parameters of a course as follows.

The optimum course population is the maximum number of students that acceptable educational practice allows, or which is limited by the capacity of available accommodation or safe practice if that is lower. The optimum number of teaching hours for the course is the fewest number of hours allowed by acceptable educational practice to lead to the target pass rate. The target pass rate is that determined as appropriate for the course and considered to be a proper aspiration for professional performance.

One can then derive an optimum value for unit cost, which is a description of the minimum unit cost that one can reasonably be expected to attain, as follows:

$$\text{optimum unit cost} = \frac{\begin{array}{c}\text{optimum course length in weeks}\\ \times \text{optimum hours taught per week}\end{array}}{\begin{array}{c}\text{optimum or locally limited population}\\ \times \text{target pass rate}\end{array}}$$

The incorporation of a quality term in the measurement brings the approach into line with good commercial practice where it is recognized that beyond a certain point cost-cutting is counter-productive insofar as it leads to excessive losses at quality control and correspondingly fewer marketable products. The absence of this ingredient in SSR measurements, for example, endangers the educational process because there is no inbuilt protection against excessive economy. It allows the investment to be reduced in accordance with the funds made available to the organization without regard to the educational consequences of that strategy. The SSR type of measurement does not suggest a target for performance but requires some arbitrary objective to be set, such as the national average, which has no logical substance. [. . .]

The college principal has two major roles in the system. Firstly, he must allocate budgets to enable the line manager, or head of department, a reasonable prospect for achieving production targets. Secondly, he must ensure that the system responds in a positive way to any shortcomings in the production process revealed by the accountability system which relates actual cost performance to the target that is set for each course. [. . .]

Accountability procedures

Optimum unit cost measurements

The procedures outlined in the following pages lay great importance on the need to involve all staff in the professional task of setting targets and measuring actual performance against them. It will be seen that not only is this involvement represented by meaningful consultation but that the mechanisms of accountability are accomplished by teachers assessing the work of those in other parts of the college so that there is a sense of corporate responsibility for the performance of the college.

At the root of the accountability procedure is the acceptance that for a given student and staff input to a course the success of that course can be measured in terms of the number of students who successfully pass through an assessment process. In many cases the assessment is accepted as being the externally set examination that leads to certification. [. . .]

Every year's course programme must have a defined performance target. It is part of the professional responsibility of teachers to establish at the outset of a teaching programme the criteria which will establish whether or not the year's effort has been a success. This requires that the objectives of the course are clearly defined in terms which can be assessed. Secondly, it requires that for each programme a target is identified which indicates for a theoretically optimized course the proportion of students who would be expected to achieve success at the assessment stage. For example, a City and Guilds course of one year's duration would very likely have the objective defined as the achievement of the City and Guilds certificate for that course. It could then be decided that for a course which has an optimum input of students and staff hours the target for the course should be to achieve the national average pass rate for that course. [. . .]

It should be emphasized that these are matters for the college to determine or, more specifically, for the principal to agree with a head of department in deciding whether to make a budget investment in a particular proposal. A college with a high demand for, say, an 'A' level course may choose to be especially selective and aim for a pass rate beyond the national average.

[. . .]

Some courses, for example special programmes for youngsters from ESN schools, present special difficulties but are not excused from the procedure. No member of staff should expect to be able to embark upon a year's work with the considerable investment that it entails and the far-reaching implications for each student without carefully defining the aims of the enterprise. In this example with ESN youngsters individual student aims can be defined in terms which relate specific skills acquisition to be accomplished by the end of the year. [. . .]

Agreements about optimum performance parameters are established through negotiation between the principal and each head of department individually. As well as determining target pass rates the negotiation also leads to an agreement about the optimum population and teaching hour investment for each course. The expectation is that the head of department will have consulted subject and course specialists before representations are made to the principal. [. . .] During these debates, which may be attended by other staff at the invitation of the principal or head of department, fundamental issues relating to the educational process are discussed as one explores the most efficient ways of transferring information, thoughtful habits and skills to students. Not only are inter-personal transfers of concern, but attention is focused on the range of audio visual and practical aids as contributors to increased cost-effectiveness. [. . .]

The procedure is time consuming and one has little hope of covering the work of a medium sized department in less than half a day together with a possible adjournment for the HoD to repair to the department for further consultations with colleagues. Once the task is completed, however, it forms a stable information bank for the foreseeable future. In each subsequent year there is a routine review which confirms the criteria already established, or changes them in the light of experience or because of changing conditions and adds to the bank for new courses. [. . .]

Measuring performance

The performance of each course is measured after the results of assessment are available, usually at the beginning of the new academic session. The data recorded for each course includes the number enrolled, the number entered for assessment, pass rate, and the teaching hours invested in the course. The data is tabulated as shown in Table 12.1, where the results are shown for a selection of full time and part time courses across the college. The table also records the enrolment for the new session and, for each course, the optimum operating parameters for a single group. [. . .]

Account is taken of every hour of teaching in the college, that is, there must be a justification for every part of the course-based teaching salary budget.

The penultimate column shows the actual unit cost, that is, the teaching hours used for each successful student with the optimum value shown in each case for comparison. The final column, described as the percentage variation, indicates the difference between the actual and the optimum teaching hours per pass expressed as a percentage of the optimum value, and it is this figure that measures cost-effectiveness and therefore indicates the performance of that course. [. . .]

The major internal guardian of the educational performance of the college is seen as the academic board, whether or not it is advisory to the principal. The function of the board in this regard is carried out by a standing committee called the Student Assessment Committee which reports and makes recommendations to the board. The Student Assessment Committee has representatives from each teaching department and these, according to the rules, must be below head of department status. The board is free to elect the chairman of the committee but it invariably decides that the post should be filled by the principal. The Student Assessment Committee is the direct monitor of each department's performance at the level of individual student performance. [. . .]

Monitoring the department

[. . .] As one moves up the hierarchy of accountability the account becomes less detailed. At the course to head of department interface the concern is with

Table 12.1 Measuring unit cost performance

Course title	Year of course	Enrolments		Course success rate %/Number entered	Optimum pass rate %/Optimum class size	Actual/Optimum		% variation
		84/5	85/6			Course hours per week	Course hours per pass	
Department of Business and Office Arts								
BTEC National Diploma	1	35	31	97/29	90/20	53/26	68/52	+31
	2	18	24	89/18	84/20	32.50/26	73/56	+30
BTEC General Diploma	1	34	19	82/29	77/20	52/25	78/58	+34
BTEC National Certificate	1	37	55	86/21	90/20	14/7	28/14	+100
	2	27	22	69/16	85/20	8.50/7	28/15	+86
Shorthand 50 wpm+	2/3	39	26	44/34	64/20	4/2	10/6	+71
Typewriting I/II	2	39	30	69/29	62/20	4/2	7/6	+24
Department of Computing, Science and Mathematics								
Physics 'A' Level	1	15	14	77/13	90/18	5.50/5.50	20/12	+61
	2	8	10	100/10	64/18	5.50/5.50	20/17	+15
Department of Hotel Catering and Hairdressing								
Basic Cookery for the Hotel & Catering Industry	1	31	42	76/29	76/18	34/15	55/39	+41
C & G 707/1 Food Service	1	31	32	74/31	68/18	12/6	19/18	+4
Department of Electrical and Electronic Engineering								
BTEC Diploma in Electrical/Electronic Engineering								
Theory (14 units)	1	28	28	89/21×14	90/15	60/30	8/6	+44
Theory (11 units)	2	34	16	33/27	85/15	60/30	240/85	+182

individual students. The link between the head and the principal concerns itself with course details and the major representation of this account is that described earlier and illustrated by Table 12.1 where the performance of each course is compared with optimum circumstances. Each department prepares a comprehensive form of Table 12.1 for presentation to the principal. This takes the form of a computer read-out and is available in September or October. [. . .] The results for each department are scrutinized by the Student Assessment Committee in order to select those courses which warrant a more detailed account from the department because of evident unsatisfactory performance. In practice this is almost a routine process based on the following approach.

One of the important operational advantages of this unit cost method is that, in regarding the actual cost of the successful student as the important criterion, it is not concerned with the arrangements made by the department manager to secure a satisfactory unit cost. There is consequently no need for an initial scrutiny of class sizes, pass rates, drop-out rates and teaching hours because these factors are not at issue if the unit cost is acceptably low. If, for example, the head of department has managed to accommodate a small group by a judicious manipulation of course combinations or other techniques then, as long as he achieves a satisfactory unit cost outcome, this is not of concern to the auditor of that department's business. The unit cost approach therefore allows the safe delegation of a wide range of organizational powers to heads of department.

The criterion for performance is the percentage variation in the last column of Table 12.1. The question then is to determine the boundary value of this variation for an indication of satisfactory performance. The argument goes as follows.

Taking the situation of a full time course which consumes 27 teaching hours per week for 36 weeks in the year and which has an optimum class size of 18 and a national average pass rate of 70 per cent then, if all other things are equal, one might consider an unsatisfactory situation as having developed if the population falls to, say, 13. This would represent a percentage variation of +38.5.

Taking the same situation, then if other factors corresponded to the optimum situation but the pass rate were 50 per cent instead of 70 per cent, the percentage variation would be 40.

These two cases may be thought to describe a reasonable limit and we therefore use a percentage variation of 40 as the boundary between satisfactory and unsatisfactory performance for this first sift by the Student Assessment Committee. A college may of course establish its own criterion for satisfactory performance and this may be allowed to vary for different parts of the college operation.

The procedure then is to ask each department to attend to each course in the department which exhibits a percentage variation of 40 or more and to make two statements in each case. Firstly, the department is required to explain why the variation is apparently unsatisfactory. In many cases the Table itself identifies the nature of the problem but this in turn requires some elaboration. Why is the class size so small, or the pass rate so low, or the taught hours so lavish? Secondly, the department is asked to indicate what steps it intends to take to ensure, as far as possible, that a satisfactory situation will be restored during the next cycle.

The college is effectively requiring an explanation of, and a justification for, inefficient use of resources. [. . .] The committee delivers to the academic board a formal report which directly relates the matters aired by departments and adds its own thoughts which result from its deliberations.

The adoption of the report by the academic board, or some modification agreed by the board, formally records an expected course of action by departments and, perhaps, other sections of the college directed to secure an improved performance. In this way the involvement of every sector of the college in the business of providing the best service possible for its students and the community is brought within the professional scrutiny of the whole college. This gives a real sense of corporate responsibility.

The annual report

The ultimate stage of accountability is that between the organization and its shareholders. In the case of the college the shareholders can be identified with the elected members of the local authority, the governors, the parents of students, the employers of students, the public at large and the students themselves. To be on the safe side we recognize an obligation to be accountable to all of these and the principal's Annual Report which is published each November is available to them after it has been formally received by the governors.

The report represents an account of the work of the previous session, a reflection on the current situation and an indication of likely developments into the future. [. . .] The statistics which are presented are reduced to the minimum required to reveal the main management indicators of college performance and, as far as possible, are based on measurements already needed for other purposes. A major account is that represented by the data illustrated in Table 12.1. This table is presented for every course in every department in the college other than special short courses with independent financial arrangements. Department reports will comment on particular courses where the statistics reveal some difficulty or where the performance is particularly noteworthy. [. . .] The report is received at the autumn meeting of the governing board and it is then customary for the governors to set aside a special evening meeting to discuss it. Heads of department and the chief administrative officer are invited to attend. This provides an opportunity for senior staff to make direct observations to governors and join in discussions about future developments and existing difficulties. It also provides an opportunity for governors to call the principal to account for any aspect of the college operation in a context which impresses upon the management team the significance of the chain of accountability referred to earlier.

In all of the machinations described in these processes of accountability it is important to recognize that statistics themselves do not condemn out of hand, nor do they provide solutions. They are the tools of the monitoring process which point the manager to the questions that need to be asked if the organization is to respond in a positive way in seeking to improve its performance.

There can be no dispute about the responsibility of a publicly funded organization to give such an account of its affairs. The revelations demanded by the report are not always pleasant and it is important that its structure is constant from year to year so that selective reporting is not allowed to focus only on the pleasurable. [. . .]

This annual process obliges each member of the college management team to face up to the situation that he or she manages. The manager is compelled to review the performance of the team and to make a conscious effort to review current practices and future plans. [. . .] Perhaps the most important advantage to be gained by this vehicle of professional accountability is that it persuades those whose task it is to make policy and resource decisions at a higher level, that they can support the college confident in the knowledge that they know what is going on and in the expectation that the fruits of any investment will be required to be properly reported by those who will then be most strongly motivated to succeed.

This link between performance and investment based on perceptions that lead to objective and sensible measurements and in terms which are understood by and acceptable to the practitioners in the system is of critical importance if there is to be a meaningful drive towards increased value for money. The system described here provides such an interaction and there follows an account of that part of it which determines the way in which the budgets for teaching staff and consumables are dealt with in the college. [. . .]

Handling the teaching staff budget

Planning the budget

[. . .]

The annual teaching budget is, in the main, committed in September with the enrolment of students onto the new prospectus of courses. The budget is identified in the spring so that the college has several months to plan for the next academic year within the boundaries allowed by the budget. By the time the budget is announced the college has an early indication of the level of interest in its full time courses. [. . .]

The aim in the spring is to provide each head of department with as firm as possible an indication of what the budget is going to allow the department to provide in the new session. The head can then plan the affairs of the department in terms of accommodation, allocating materials and equipment budgets, modifying course promotion and publicity activities as appropriate and amending enrolment strategy as demanded by the constraints of his or her share. It is especially important that this earliest possible planning be seen as an opportunity to give an indication to staff of their likely teaching commitment for the new session so that they can, in turn, set about planning their work and preparing their new courses as the demands of the current session allow.

Having established a base of information in regard to the optimum operating conditions of different courses for the accountability system, one has a valuable tool for determining the proper distribution of the teaching budget.

As a first stage in the process each department is required to establish its proposed list of courses for the new session. The list must include all courses other than those dealt with under other funding arrangements and which are often mounted at comparatively short notice. The head of department is then required to provide alongside each course an estimate of the likely enrolment and the department's bid for a number of teaching hours to accommodate the course.

In practice the whole procedure is conducted on computer-based spreadsheets with the principal and head of department each having their own records of information for the department. The layout of the information is similar to that shown in Table 12.2 which illustrates the final stage in the procedure. The courses are listed in the first column and include those for all modes of attendance. This list is the same as that used for the accountability system illustrated in Table 12.1. The next two columns show the same optimum performance information already negotiated for the accountability system and the fourth column, which shows the optimum hours per student, represents the unit staffing cost of a student on that course if it operates under optimum conditions.

The appropriate investment for a given enrolment is then determined by multiplying the optimum unit cost by the number of students on the course. At the planning stage this number is an estimate based on the level of applications at that time, historical trends and any other factors that might influence such trends. At this stage in the proceedings columns five and six in Table 12.2 are entitled Planned Number of Students and Planned Teaching Hours/Week respectively and planning data is entered in these columns.

The seventh column indicates the result of multiplying the planned number of students by the optimum teaching hours per student and therefore represents the ideal investment for that plan of operation. The final column shows, as a percentage, the difference between the proposed investment for the course compared with the optimum. The spreadsheet keeps a running total of the proposed and the optimised teaching hours and computes the over-all percentage difference between the two and this is entitled the 'Balance' in the Diagram.

Table 12.2 The department staff budget form, North West Kent College of Technology Course Accounting Form

DEPARTMENT:
HOTEL, CATERING AND HAIRDRESSING
SESSION 1985/86

Course	Optimum No. of Students x	Optimum Teaching Hrs/Wk y	Proposed Budget 422.50 — Optimum Hrs/Stud = Unit Cost U=y/x	Actual No. of Students N	Optimised Budget 366.41 — Actual Teaching Hrs/Wk H	Optimum Investment I=N×U	% Overall Balance 15.31 — Balance (H−I)/I×100 %
Full-Time							
City & Guilds 705							
General Catering 1A	18.00	32.50	1.81	16.00	32.50	28.89	12.50
General Catering 1B	18.00	32.50	1.81	16.00	32.50	28.89	12.50
General Catering 1C	18.00	27.00	1.50	16.00	27.00	24.00	12.50
General Catering 1D	18.00	27.00	1.50	17.00	27.00	25.50	5.88
Professional Cookery	18.00	20.25	1.12	8.00	17.25	9.00	91.67
(with PTD 706/1)	18.00	6.75	0.37	18.00	6.75	6.75	0.00
Advanced Food & Beverage							
Service 2A	18.00	23.00	1.28	15.00	23.00	19.17	20.00
Food Service 707/2	18.00	6.00	0.33	17.00	4.00	5.61	−28.70
Service 2B	18.00	27.00	1.50	15.00	27.00	22.50	20.00
Professional Cookery year 2	18.00	26.00	1.44	18.00	26.00	26.00	0.00
Accommodation Operations & Hotel Reception year 1/2	18.00	16.50	0.92	16.00	16.50	14.67	12.50

[. . .]

The stage is then set for establishing a negotiated budget. The department's proposals, course by course, are scrutinized and the principal agrees an investment for each course taking account of the balance between optimum and proposed investment as well as the total balance for the department.

[. . .]

Should the balance appear to be excessive then the negotiation revolves around the department's ability to reduce the number of teaching hours by amalgamating, perhaps partly, with other courses; by combining, perhaps in part, the first and second year of two-year courses; by the design of modular schemes which allow the mixing of students from different courses or part and full time students or, perhaps, by agreeing that with such a reduction in student numbers the course may be accommodated with fewer teaching hours. [. . .]

During the negotiations especial attention is paid to the results of the previous accountability survey and the principal will need tangible evidence that the strictures of the academic board are receiving attention as a condition for continued investment in certain courses. A provisional agreement is eventually reached for the department as a whole. The proviso is that the plans will stand so long as the college budget is capable of meeting the total cost when all departments have been seen.

In practice the principal's computation leads to a total count of teaching hours required across the college and by evaluating the teaching hours available from the full time establishment together with the teaching budget, it can soon be established whether the total resource can accommodate the college's plans.

In fact one allows a percentage overshoot of planned, as compared with budgeted, hours in the sure knowledge that not all plans will materialize in September. The amount to be allowed depends on local circumstances but it is important to arrange affairs so that any likely slack in the budget is identified early enough for more provision to be made in the planned prospectus of courses.

[. . .]

The final part of this stage in the system is to confirm each department plan in the light of the college budget. What is effectively established is a contract between the principal and the head of department which declares that a specified investment for a course will be forthcoming provided the department delivers appropriate students in numbers regarded as justifying that investment.

Applying the budget

September is a time for rapid teaching budget decisions in colleges. As students appear plans are either confirmed or require rapid modification. If the initial plans underestimated the actual demand that materialises, a head of department will want a speedy response to a request for additional budget to allow for extra groups of students. If the numbers fall short of those expected it is important that the budget thereby released is immediately made available to other parts of the college. [. . .]

As soon as the first wave of part time and full time enrolments has been established, the head of department enters the actual enrolments on the spreadsheet illustrated in Table 12.2, in place of the previously entered planning figures. If the enrolments match the plans, the contract with the principal assures the department of the teaching hours already agreed. In those cases where the enrolment cannot claim to have earned the conditionally allotted teaching budget, the head endeavours to devise a teaching strategy which will minimise the teaching cost and thereby reduce the balance to acceptable proportions. [. . .] The negotiations are again conducted directly on the computer spreadsheet so that both parties can see the immediately calculated effect of any strategy and then determine whether it is adequate to provide an acceptable balance.

Throughout these negotiations the principal keeps an eye on the over-all college situation which is shown on a summary sheet as illustrated in Table 12.3. This enables him to monitor the over-all budget and to compare the investment data for each department. A final copy of this sheet is made available to each head of department. It is important to achieve a situation where any significant departures from the over-all college balance can be explained.

Table 12.3 shows that in this case the over-all balance for the college is around 13 per cent. Experience suggests that up to 15 per cent describes a reasonable level for normally acceptable performance. [. . .]

Table 12.3   The college staff budget summary, North West Kent College of Technology Course Accounting Form

COLLEGE SUMMARY			SESSION: *1985/86*
Departments	*Proposed budget*	*Optimized budget*	*Over-all balance %*
Automobile and Production Engineering	473.75	425.15	11.43
Business and Office Arts	601.00	519.22	15.75
Computing, Science and Mathematics	240.50	212.35	13.26
Electrical and Electronic Engineering	414.75	382.35	8.47
General Vocational Education	321.75	288.99	11.34
Hotel, Catering and Hairdressing	422.50	366.41	15.31
Mechanical Technology	118.75	92.73	28.06
TOTALS	2593.00	2287.20	13.37

[. . .] The important point is that the computer does not determine the outcome of the process but serves as a management tool which provides the range and detail of information necessary to make properly considered decisions.

[. . .] At the proposal, the agreed plan and the September implementation stages, the department records the teaching hours required for its courses according to the department which is to provide them. It also indicates the student enrolments expected or achieved according to the type of course, and the teaching hours are distinguished between those accommodated by full time staff and those served through part time contracts. For cross referencing purposes the department also indicates the hours it has agreed to provide as service work for other departments.

[. . .]

One can then readily compute the teaching demands to be made on each department, including service work, and then, by subtracting the teaching commitment of full time staff, establish the required pool of part time contracted hours that remain. This provides a budget limit for that department.

[. . .]

Handling the consumables budget

The consumables budget is the one within colleges that is used to purchase books, stationery, materials and smaller items of equipment. [. . .]

The consumables budget is a particularly sensitive issue in colleges. Its distribution is within the control of the principal and it is difficult to establish a uniformly objective method of determining its proper allocation. The educational health of a department and its prospects for development can be very dependent on the extent of its consumables allocation. [. . .] Keeping track of these changes in terms of budget response is not easy and the traditional hunch basis for allocating the budget is no longer acceptable. There is no simple formula based on full time equivalent student numbers or other types of head count which can be regarded as fair for the determination of the distribution whether one is concerned with that between departments or between colleges at the local authority level.

It is particularly important, therefore, in order to secure a proper development of activity across the college and also to safeguard the morale of staff, that a mechanism be developed for the distribution of the consumables budget which is not only fair in the operational sense but is also seen to be fair by the practitioners whose performance is dependent on its support. [. . .]

For the purposes of this system the consumables equipment limit is described as items which have a new cost of less than £500. Two types of equipment purchase came into consideration. Firstly, developing areas of work require the purchase of new equipment. For example, if the college moves into hairdressing courses for the first time, there is a stocking up need within the consumables budget. Secondly, there is a need continuously to replenish used stock as items reach the end of their useful lives or become obsolete.

The system described here is based on establishing the consumables cost which attaches to the student taken as a unit. More precisely it is the cost of a single student on a course which operates under optimum conditions. These optimum conditions are taken as the same as those which apply under the earlier staffing budget sections so that the course population and the hours for which it is taught are already defined. [. . .]

The optimum consumables unit cost for a course is then defined as the materials cost per student over a year to enable the course to run satisfactorily but at the minimum level of funding and with an optimum class size, together with the share per student of the cost of replacement of non-capital equipment to allow a satisfactory level of operation at minimum cost and with optimum class size.

[. . .]

Each head of department is required to evaluate the optimum unit cost for each of the courses run in the department and all courses must be covered other than those run under special funding arrangements. It is important that every effort is applied to make an objective evaluation and not to make some sort of per capita calculation on the basis of previous budgets.

Different techniques are used for determining the materials and the equipment part of the cost. There is little choice with materials other than to require the lecturer to calculate the need in going through a year's teaching programme. This can be done by estimating the requirements of an optimum sized group and calculating the cost per student or it may be easier to consider the needs of an individual student. Whichever method is used the head of department finally determines the official submission for the department and a provisional list is agreed through discussion with the principal.

Since this is such a sensitive management concern and the determination of the unit materials cost is very much a matter of personal judgement, it is felt necessary to introduce an external auditor at this stage. The submission of each head of department is scrutinized by the auditor who needs to be satisfied by the head that the estimate is a proper one. It is important that the auditor is fully conversant with the range of college courses and has the professional respect of the heads. In the procedure described here, the services of a highly regarded retired vice principal were employed. His brief was to spend as long on the enquiry as was required to lead to a satisfactory conclusion.

The technique used for determining the equipment part of the cost must ensure that each department follows the same procedure. As a first step it is necessary to establish for each item of equipment in the department having a replacement value of less than £500, its estimated total useful life under normal operating conditions and the cost of replacing it.

Instead of trying to establish a precise lifetime for each item it is considered satisfactory for a department to select the nearest from a limited set of lifetimes, say three, five, seven and ten years. In this case items having a lifetime of more than 10 years are disregarded; and an item with a lifetime of less than one year is treated as a material and is included in the first part.

Each item of equipment is identified with a unit of specialist accommodation. One can then calculate for each room the cost per hour per optimum student of replacing the equipment or, in effect, a rental charge for the room. The use of specialist accommodation by each course leads to an aggregate of rents and this forms the basis for determining the unit equipment cost for that course. The approach is as follows.

One supposes that a room is available for 30 hours per week for 36 weeks and that it is used to capacity when booked for 80 per cent of that time to allow for setting up and clearing away equipment and for general maintenance. Suppose the room has associated with it £E1 of equipment with lifetime L1 years, and £E2 of lifetime L2 years and £E3 of lifetime L3 years. Then, if the optimum number of students for that room is N, the cost per student hour for the equipment in that room is:

$$[(E_1/L_1 + E_2/L_2 + E_3/L_3)/0.8 \times 30 \times 36 \times N.]$$

Each room in the college is allocated a hire charge on this basis and an equipment unit cost for each course can then be evaluated. It follows from this approach that workshops or other practical rooms which are used more intensely than 80 per cent of 30 hours per week for 36 weeks a year earn a bonus replacement element if they accommodate optimum student numbers. Departments which allow rooms to be under-utilized are penalized through a diminished replacement budget.

[. . .]

The data is then transferred to a second spreadsheet illustrated in Table 12.4. This lists every course run by the department together with an indication of the rooms used by each course and the time spent on practical work in each of these rooms expressed as hours per week and the number of weeks per year. Departments are only allowed to claim rental for a room when it is genuinely used for practical work and not when it is used for normal classroom teaching.

The optimum number of students is entered in each case, and the materials cost per student derived from the separate exercise is also included. All that remains is to enter the actual number of students on each course and the computer then calculates the cost of the course. As a first stage the cost per student in optimum conditions is calculated and this value is shown in the penultimate column. This is then multiplied by the actual number of students to give the cost of the course. It follows that a course which does not attract the optimum enrolment leads to a reduced budget share for the department. Using the letters shown at the column headings in Table 12.4 the calculation is as follows:

$$[\text{cost of course} = [(C \times H \times W)/X + M] \times N]$$

Table 12.4 The department consumables costing form, North West Kent College of Technology Department: Computing, Science and Maths   Course BSAE Costing Form   Total Course Cost: 15,495.79

Course	Actual enrolment N	Facility	Hours used per week H	Weeks used per year W	Equipment cost per hour £ C	Optimum no. of students X	Materials per student £ M	Cost per student £	Actual cost of course £
'O' Levels									
Physics	24	Phy L	6	36	1.81	18	2	23.72	569.28
Chem	18	Ch L	3	36	1.59	16	25	35.73	643.18
Biology	11	Bio L	3	36	1.51	18	12	21.06	231.66
Hum Bio	33	Bio L	6	36	1.51	18	4	22.12	729.96
Maths	58	Cl R		36	0.00	18	4	4.00	232.00
Geog	17	Cl R		36	0.00	20	3	3.00	51.00
Stats	13	Cl R	1	36	0.10	18	5	5.20	67.60
Com Stud	28	CS 133	6	36	3.29	16	6	50.42	1411.62
'A' Levels									
Phys 1	14	Phy L	3	36	1.81	18	10	20.86	292.04
Phys 2	10	Phy L	3	36	1.81	18	10	20.86	208.60
Chem 1	10	Ch L	3	36	1.59	16	45	55.73	557.33
Chem 2	9	Ch L	3	36	1.59	16	45	55.73	501.59

10	Biol 1	Bio L	3	36	1.51	18	23	32.06	320.60
10	Biol 2	Bio L	3	36	1.51	18	45	54.06	540.6
28	P Math 1	Cl R		36	0.00	20	8	8.00	224.00
5	P Math 2	Cl R		36	0.00	20	8	8.00	40.00
29	CPA	Cl R		36	0.00	20	4	4.00	116.00
	BTEC Dip								
22	Com Stud 1	CS P A	15	36	2.01	16	12	79.84	1756.43
22	BOA Serv	Cl R					3.25	3.25	71.50
22	GVE Serv	Cl R					5	5.00	110.00
	BTEC Dip								
10	Com Stud 2	CS P A	10	36	2.01	16	12	57.23	572.25
	BTEC Dip								
10	Com Stud 2	CS Apr	6	36	3.47	16	0	46.84	468.45
16	NCC T/H 1	CS Apr	20	9	3.47	16	41	80.04	1280.60

The spreadsheet provides a total for the department and this can be regarded as the proper notional consumables budget for that enrolment distribution.

The completion of the measurements for all courses in the college leads to a startling variation in unit costs even for courses having the same mode of attendance. Some examples of costs for a range of full time courses are illustrated in Table 12.5. The final column shows that individual optimum student costs vary from around £25 per year for a student on a BTEC National Diploma in Business Studies course or a three subject 'A' level course, to more than £300 per year for a student on a mechanical engineering craft course.

The fifteen-fold range illustrated by the table amply justifies the need for the sort of detailed costing employed by this system. It follows that any method of allocation that is directly related to an over-all head count would be grossly misguided and it seems highly unlikely that the distribution resulting from this careful assessment would also emerge from guesswork based on hunches.

Allocating the budget

The college consumables budget is required to cover other areas of expenditure as well as the direct cost of running courses. The general administration of the college depends on this budget for materials and some items of equipment. Although the needs of administration are influenced by the nature and extent of the student population there is not the same sort of straightforward relationship as with courses. [. . .] The college system requires some over-all estimate of each of the library and audio visual aids budgets based on what can be afforded in the light of the total college budget.

Another factor to be considered is that budgets based on current student activities do not pay regard to the cost of developing new courses and sections of work. The system therefore requires that a part of the college budget be set aside for such developments and this can be described as a special project fund.

The allocation of budgets between departments can now proceed, and the method used is illustrated in Table 12.6. This shows a computer spreadsheet with the departments listed in the first column. The second column shows the consumables allocation including both the materials and equipment elements determined in the ways described earlier. The third and fourth columns show the materials and the equipment components separately. The over-all college allocation is shown below at £183,000 which is much less than the over-all requirement of departments without including the other sections of expenditure. When what are considered to be appropriate sums are set aside for the audio visual aids section, the library, administration and special projects, the remaining figure of £146,000 barely covers the equipment replacement need without attending to materials costs.

It is here that the manager establishes the policy for distribution. In this

Table 12.5 A selection of full-time student consumables costs, North West Kent College of technology
Selection of full-time Courses 1985/86   Course BSAE Costing Form

Department and course	Facility	Hours used per week H	Weeks used per year W	Equipment cost per hour £ C	Optimum no. of students X	Materials per student £ M	Cost per student £	Total cost per student £
AUTO & PROD ENG								
Mech Prod Craft	Wk 12 P	30.00	20	3.91	15	178.00	334.00	334
Motor Vehicle Craft	Veh Sh M	10.50	36	2.77	15	105.00	174.80	175
BUS & OFFICE ARTS								
BTEC Nat Dip	CS 232	3.00	36	2.31	20	12.95	25.42	25
Legal Secs	Typ Rm	12.00	36	2.12	20	16.80	62.59	
	Rm 104	3.00	36	3.21	20	0.00	17.33	
	Rm 105	2.00	36	5.02	20	0.00	18.07	
	Rm 106	2.00	36	2.78	20	0.00	10.01	
	Rm 108	1.00	36	3.47	20	0.00	6.25	114
COMP SC & MATHS								
'A' Physics	Phy Lab	3.00	36	1.81	18	10.00	20.86	
'A' Chemistry	Ch Lab	3.00	36	1.59	16	45.00	55.73	
'A' Pure Maths	Cl Rm	3.50	36	0.00	20	8.00	8.00	85
GEN VOC EDUC'N								
'A' English	Cl Rm	5.50	36	0.00	20	6.00	6.00	
'A' Sociology	Cl Rm	5.50	36	0.00	20	13.00	13.00	
'A' History	Cl Rm	5.50	36	0.00	20	8.00	8.00	27
HOT CAT & HAIR								
Gen Catering	37 Kit	10.00	36	6.29	18	68.00	193.80	
	Tr Rest	4.50	36	3.08	18	0.00	27.72	
	Acc Ops	4.00	36	0.87	18		6.96	
	Sc Lab	1.00	36	1.55	18	6.00	9.10	238
MECH TECHNOLOGY								
BTEC Diploma	Mc Shop	2.75	36	4.68	18	86.43	112.17	
	Mechs M	2.20	36	1.31	18	6.65	12.41	
	Therm L	2.00	36	1.54	18	4.50	10.66	
	CAD/CAM	1.75	36	1.98	18	6.30	13.23	148

Table 12.6   The allocation of the consumables budget, North West Kent College
of Technology
BSA&E allocation 1985/1986

Department	BSA&E X Total	BSA&E Y Materials	BSA&E X − Y Equipment	(X − Y)/3 = Z	Share Z + Y	Allocation £
APE	50,560	30,530	20,030	6,677	37,207	37,981
BOA	51,289	1,097	50,192	16,731	17,828	18,199
CSM	15,496	5,927	9,569	3,190	9,117	9,306
EEE	56,486	22,243	34,243	11,414	33,657	34,358
GVE	13,638	8,673	4,965	1,655	10,328	10,543
HCH	37,654	18,462	19,192	6,397	24,859	25,377
MT	13,309	8,388	4,921	1,640	10,028	10,237
TOTALS	238,432	95,320	143,112	47,704	143,024	146,000
	AVA	ALLOC				7,000
	LIBRARY	ALLOC				8,000
	ADMIN	ALLOC				12,000
	SPECIAL PROJECT	ALLOC				10,000
		TOTAL COLLEGE BSA&E				183,000
		DEPT BSA&E ALLOC				146,000

case it is argued that because the nature of the system requires departments to identify the minimum materials need, this component must be fully involved in the final outcome. In order to achieve an over-all distribution compatible with the college budget one can then afford only around one-third of the equipment replacement need. The college budget is therefore distributed in proportion to each department's requirement defined as its calculated materials budget together with one-third of its equipment needs. [. . .]

Once the initial set of unit costs has been evaluated the data only needs a simple annual review with, perhaps, a more strenuous overhaul every three or four years. [. . .] The annual review is intended to take care of any exceptional cost variations and to incorporate fresh data for any new courses.

[. . .] Each department is allocated 60 per cent of a year's budget based on the enrolment for the session coinciding with the beginning of the financial year. When the new enrolment arrives in September the budgets are recalculated and the total budget for each department is evaluated as one-third of the spring total together with two-thirds of the September total and heads are allowed to spend up to this limit. The 60 per cent factor would normally take care of any changes in enrolment going from one year to the next. If very dramatic swings are anticipated it may be prudent to adjust this figure downwards.

Another matter concerns service work. The system delivers to the department the budget appropriate to its courses even though some of the work and associated expense may attach to a servicing department. The initial allocation of budget must therefore be modified to take service work into account. The cost of service work is agreed by the two departments involved when the unit costs are established. It simply remains for the two heads to authorize notes of transfer of budget and these are lodged with the administration section so that each head's budget can be suitably adjusted. This arrangement reinforces the perception that service work is a direct transaction between the departments and the parent department can expect the delivery of satisfactory service in exchange for a tangible quantity of resource. [. . .]

It is worth noting that the equipment replacement mechanism can readily be applied to the allocation of technician hours across the college. Technician requirements can be determined on the basis of the number of hours of practical work required for a course, together with the population of the class, compared with the optimum capacity of the accommodation. Different types of practical work require different levels of technician assistance because of varying degrees of associated preparation, clearing up, stock control, hazardous conditions, class attention and so on. One therefore needs to determine loading factors which take this variation into account. [. . .]

The system described here is applicable generally in colleges. The individual college is free to determine how the unit costs should be handled, what emphasis to give the materials and the equipment components and how to split the budget between academic years. The important feature is that proper recognition is given to the wide variation in properly justified needs in going from one course to another. Once established, the system can be operated with speed while, at the same time, providing the principal with a broad scope for varying over-all budget policy in response to changing circumstances. [. . .]

Conclusion

The educational process is concerned with the interaction between the individual learner and the teaching organization. Any system which purports to measure the cost-effectiveness of this process must have regard for this individual experience in qualitative as well as quantitative terms. Systems which treat the individual learner as a notional fraction of a statistical unit immediately dispense with a concern for the quality of the process as it affects the student.

[. . .]

The systems described here attend to two basic needs of the members of an educational organization if they are to respond in a positive and professional way to exhortations to improve the cost-effectiveness of the service they deliver. Firstly, the practitioner must be convinced that the basis upon which the budget is distributed is a fair one. The demand here is not for a bottomless purse but an expectation that, especially when funds are in short supply, the division is based on techniques that properly relate to practice. When there are cuts the teacher must be assured that the privations of his part of the college are not to be endured in order to sustain more affluent practices elsewhere. Secondly, if measurements of cost-effectiveness are to provide the motivation required to induce improved performance, they must be seen to be relevant and generate an analysis that leads to credible conclusions for the practitioner.

13

Programme budgeting for colleges

Derek Birch

In a fully developed budgeting system there is a package of inter-related budgets. These are constructed in line with (a) the organization structure and managerial responsibilities; and (b) the organization's major products and services – its 'programmes'. In this chapter we explore how this may be achieved for a college.

The majority of budgets are currently drawn up by expenditure head. There is some movement away from this format towards responsibility budgets where the responsibilities are for clusters of resources organized in academic and non-academic departments. For example, the 'common framework for analysis' (matrix analysis) recommended by CIPFA (1988) involves firstly, a 'subjective analysis' which classifies expenditures by type (e.g. academic staff costs, rates, electricity) and income by course (e.g. sales, fees); and, secondly, an 'objective analysis' which assigns expenditures to cost centres such as academic departments, the library and central administration (see Figure 13.1). However, this arrangement still does not relate inputs to the products and services produced and provided by the college. This can only be achieved with 'programme budgeting'.

The concept of a programme budget

The first step in developing programme budgets is to view [. . .] all colleges [. . .] as a matrix with students grouped in courses on one axis, and lecturers and other resources grouped in academic departments on the other. Courses typically receive instruction from more than one department, and departments provide instruction to more than one course. The 'academic matrix' (Figure 13.2) relates the curriculum or course structure of the college to

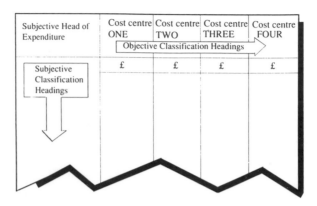

Subjective Head of Expenditure	Cost centre ONE	Cost centre TWO	Cost centre THREE	Cost centre FOUR
	Objective Classification Headings			
Subjective Classification Headings	£	£	£	£

Exhibit 19			Academic Cost Centre			Other Cost Centres					
CIPFA ' MATRIX ANALYSIS '	CONTROL TOTAL	Business & General Education	Services	Technol- ogy	Central Admin	Buildings & Premises	Grounds & Playing Fields	Central Learning Resources	Central Computer Facilities	Welfare Services
REF EXPENDITURE TO SET AGAINST COST CENTRES	a	b	c	d	e	f	g	h	i	j
1a Employees - Operational - Full time and associate teachers										
1b - Part time (hourly) teachers										
1c - Support										
1d - Other Employees										
2 Premises related expenses										
3 Transport related expenses										
4 Supplies and services										
GROSS EXPENDITURE ON RESOURCES FOR COST CENTRES										
INCOME TO SET AGAINST COST CENTRES										
5 Customer and client receipts - sales										
6 Fees and charges - general										
7 Fees and charges - full cost courses										
8 Research and consultancy										
TOTAL INCOME TO SET AGAINST COST CENTRES										
NET EXPENDITURES TO SET AGAINST COST CENTRES										
OTHER EXPENDITURE										
9 Agency and contracted services										
10 Central Departmental and Technical Support Services										
11 Capital financing transactions										
TOTAL OTHER EXPENDITURE										
OTHER INCOME										
12 Government Grants										
13 Other Grants, Reimbursments etc										
14 Fees and charges - except full cost courses										
TOTAL OTHER INCOME										
NET COST OF OTHER SERVICES										
15 Refectories										
16 Student hostels/accommodation										
17 Other trading activities										
TOTAL NET COST OF OTHER SERVICES										
NET EXPENDITURE OF INSTITUTION										

Source: **Financial information system for institutions of higher and further education in the maintained sector: Manual of Guidance** (Revised edition 1988)CIPFA.

Figure 13.1 CIPFA 'matrix analysis'

the department or academic organization structure through measures of instructional interaction such as student hours.

Given a forecast of enrolments, the 'academic matrix' may be used to calculate the workloads induced in academic departments by course. Departmental resources may then be distributed to courses in proportion to those induced workloads to form programme budgets.

For example, in Figure 13.3 a set of enrolment projections or targets have been used to multiply through the matrix of student hours from Figure 13.2 to produce the total student hour workload induced by each course in each department. The workload induced in a given department by a course represents a percentage of the total workload of that department. We can then distribute the predicted direct costs of a department to each of the courses receiving instruction from that department in proportion to this workload. For example, 73 per cent of the cost of the business studies department is distributed to the business studies diploma course, 10 per cent to the pre-nursing certificate and 17 per cent to the computer studies diploma.

Figure 13.4 illustrates two views of an instructional budget. On the one hand, we have the direct departmental costs (i.e. the responsibility centre budgets) totalling £75,000; and, on the other hand, the programme budgets (£31,150 business studies diploma, £30,500 pre-nursing certificate, and £13,350 computer studies diploma) also totalling £75,000. The direct departmental costs have been distributed to the programme budgets by an analysis of the predicted student hours (see Figure 13.3).

In sum there are four steps leading to a programme budget for teaching activities:

(i) set admissions policies (i.e. target enrolments) or otherwise forecast enrolments to the various courses/programmes;
(ii) determine for each academic department the total student hours a given mix of students from different courses/programmes will require of it;

Departments	Courses			
	Business studies diploma	Pre- nursing certificate	Computer studies diploma	
Business studies	450	60	210	720
Maths & Computing	150	300	300	750
General studies	150	360	90	600
	750	720	600	

Figure 13.2 Matrix of average student hours

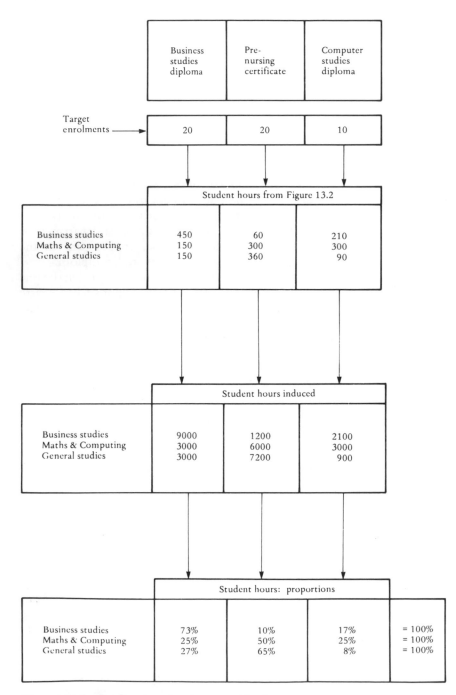

Figure 13.3 Predicted student hour workloads

Figure 13.4 Two views of an instructional budget (£)

Department *direct costs*	Responsibility *centre budget*	Programme Budget		
		Business studies diploma	*Pre- nursing certificate*	*Computer studies diploma*
Business Studies				
• academic staff	20,000			
• other staff	4,000			
• other costs	1,000	73%	10%	17%
	25,000	18,250	2,500	4,250
Maths & Computing				
• academic staff	18,000			
• other staff	10,000			
• other costs	2,000	25%	50%	25%
	30,000	7,500	15,000	7,500
General Studies				
• academic staff	14,000			
• other staff	4,000			
• other costs	2,000	27%	65%	8%
	20,000	5,400	13,000	1,600
		31,150	30,500	13,350
	75,000		75,000	

(iii) calculate the academic and support staff, 'supplies and services', and 'transport related' costs (i.e. the direct costs) associated with servicing the required number of student hours in each department;

(iv) distribute the department costs to the various courses/programmes it servicies in proportion to the flow of student hours from the department to the courses/programmes.

In the examples above the predicted pattern of student hours has been used to distribute estimated expenditures from the academic departments to the courses/programmes. There are other possibilities. For example, full time equivalent (FTE) students might be used or, indeed, the distribution could be achieved on the basis of 'negotiation' if neither student hours nor FTE students were thought sufficiently to reflect the flow of resources from departments into courses/programmes.

Throughout the examples three academic departments have been used. In reality what has been called an academic department might be any cost centre that can be identified and which provides instruction. It could be a discipline group, a department, or a division or school comprising several departments, or even the whole college. The level of aggregation chosen will depend upon the data available and upon the use to be made of the budget.

Estimating academic department costs

The matrix of predicted student hours (Figure 13.2) may also be used to budget for direct department costs. The logic of the calculation is set out in Figure 13.5. It includes various planning parameters such as:

- average class size (ACS) or maximum class size;
- average lecturer hours (ALH);
- the rank distribution of academic staff;
- salary schedules for academic staff;
- support staff ratios and associated salary costs;
- expense formulae.

These parameters are in addition to the average student hours (ASH) which underpins the logic of Figure 13.2. The effect of changing these planning parameters can be tested either by using dedicated software or by using spreadsheets.

The projected department cost per student hour is derived in Figure 13.5 by dividing the total instructional cost of each department by the total student hours. If cost comparisons between departments are required, they are most appropriately made using cost per student hour or cost per FTE student since this eliminates the effects of differences in size between departments.

Planning with programme budgets

Planning may be seen as an interactive process (Figure 13.6). The first two steps are (1) forecasting enrolments (broken down by programme area, level and mode of attendance if necessary); and (2) describing how the various academic departments will be operated. These data can then be input to a simulation model or spreadsheet as the basis for calculating the average annual cost per student in a programme (Step 3). Once the average annual costs have been calculated the total direct programme costs may be derived as a function of the number of students and the average annual cost per student (Step 4).

When using a programme budget to negotiate with the LEA (or other funding agency) or when planning for internal resource allocation, colleges should focus first upon the mix of students and types of programmes offered. If the projected programme costs exceed the available resources, they may be

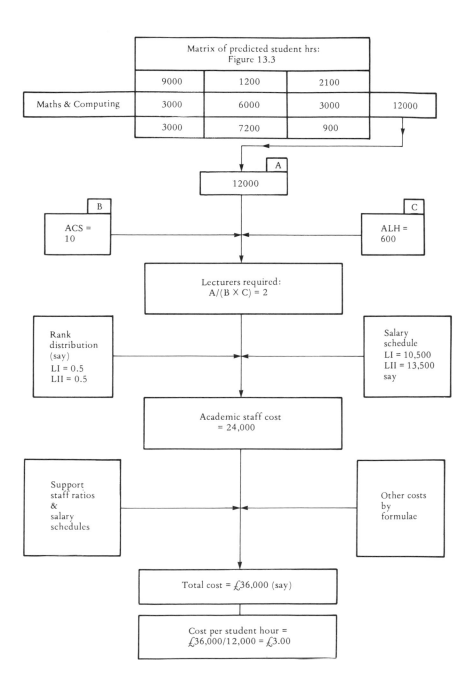

Figure 13.5 The logic of academic department budgets

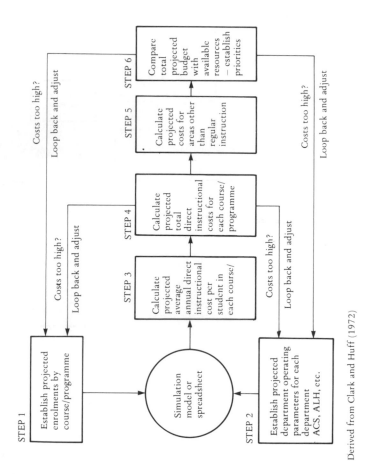

Derived from Clark and Huff (1972)

Figure 13.6 Planning with an instructional programme budget

reduced either by decreasing the enrolment (and hence the academic staff and other resources required); or by adjusting parameters such as average student hours, average class size, support staff ratios etc.

Once the direct programme costs have been established, the levels of support for other activities, including consultancy, research, and support programmes such as the library, etc., need to be specified (Step 5). In many cases the planning process will focus concurrently upon the teaching programmes and upon the central services required to support them. This might be achieved by basic estimating equations of the following form:

$$\left[Y = a + \sum_{i=1}^{n} b_i X_i \right]$$

where Y = the budget entitlement of the cost centre under consideration;
      a = the fixed costs of the cost centre under consideration (i.e. the basic cost of running the unit no matter what the level of activity);
      b_i = the variable unit of resource associated with X_1; and
      X_i = the indicator of activity such as enrolments, student hours, FTE students, class contact hours, FTE lecturers, FTE non-academic staff etc.

So that the budget for libraries, for example might read as:

[£50,000 + (£2 × FTE students) + (£5 × FTE lecturers).]

Planning requires that priorities be established so that in cases where resources are insufficient to fund all the courses at the desired level, feasible choices can be made (Step 6). [. . .] Without these priorities, it becomes difficult to plan meaningfully. Rather the tendency might be to make adjustments where cuts are least difficult or painful. In which case there is a danger that insufficient consideration will be given to the effects such adjustments have upon the mission and purposes of the college.

Distributing units of resource to departments

Under formula funding LEAs will give colleges a set sum per FTE student according to the course/programme on which the student is enrolled [. . .] This unit of resource should reflect the actual costs of provision; it might also include some 'steer' to reflect LEA and/or national policies. In any event the weighted unit of resource would vary from programme area to programme area.

A college may choose to arrange its internal resource allocation on a different basis. If it chooses to follow the logic of the unit of resource, however, it can use the 'academic matrix' to distribute the resources from programme areas to departments. Figure 13.7 demonstrates how this might be done.

In this case the units of resource are (say) £1,600 per FTE student for the business studies diploma, £1,500 per FTE student for the pre-nursing certificate and £1,300 per FTE student for the computer studies diploma. We are assuming that the enrolments to all these courses are full time students. The £32,000 allocated to the business studies diploma, for example, is distributed to the departments in proportion to the student hours of instruction they provide to that course. So the business studies department received 60 per cent of £32,000; mathematics and science 20 per cent of £32,000; and general studies 20 per cent of £32,000. If the enrolments had included part time students it would have been necessary, first, to convert the matrix of student hours to a matrix of FTE students.

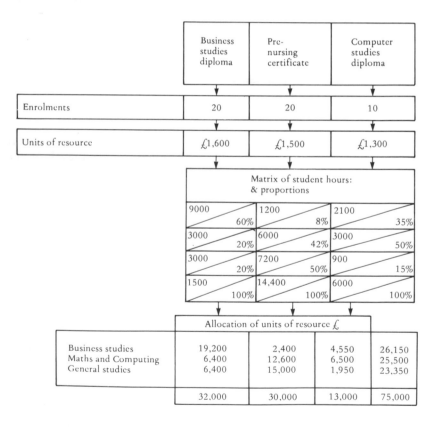

Figure 13.7   Resource allocation using 'units of resource'

If the budgets derived in this way do not meet departmental needs, and it is not possible to adjust their modes of operation in the short run, then the results of the procedure will have to be ameliorated. It may be considered still worthwhile to go through the process in order to highlight the messages contained in the units of resource. [. . .]

References

CIPFA (1988). *Financial Information Systems for Institutions of Higher and Further Education in the Maintained Sector: Manual of Guidance.* Chartered Institute of Public Finance and Accountancy.
Clark, D. G. and Huff, R. A. (1972). *Instructional Program Budgeting in Higher Education*, Boulder, Colorado, National Center for Higher Education Management Systems.

14

Formula funding for schools and colleges

Rosalind Levačić

The 1988 Education Reform Act requires LEAs to devise and use formulae for determining the budgets of colleges and all schools, except special schools, even if their budget is not delegated to the governing body. The Act also requires the LEA to consult governors, heads and principals over the specification of its scheme of financial delegation and the associated college or school formula. Primary and secondary schools must be resourced by the same basic formula, while a separate formula applies to the further education sector.

The legislation and the two supporting DES circulars on local management (1988a, b) set out firm guidelines regarding the permitted features of the school and college formulae. Within these restrictions LEAs have discretion to design their own school and college formulae in accordance with local policies and locally perceived needs. LEAs' formulae (together with other features of their financial delegation schemes) had to be submitted to the secretary of state for his approval by September 1989 with a view to the formula being operational for April 1990. While school and college managers may quite naturally feel that learning how to manage a delegated budget is a major priority, it is important for them to understand the basis of the formula which determines their institution's budget. Only if this is fully understood can local managers ensure that:

(i) they are able to maximize the institution's income, if they so wish, by engaging fully in those activities which bring in money;
(ii) are well informed about the effects on their institution's budget of the various parts of the formula and so are in a good position to press for changes in the formula that would benefit their institution and its students, as well as others in a similar position.

It is important to bear in mind that a resource allocation formula is the outcome of a complex policy-making process and is a reflection of both the central government's and the local authority's aims for the education service. Now that LEAs can no longer use detailed control of school and college resources as the means of implementing their educational policies, they need to design the resource allocation formula so that it reflects, as far as is possible within the DES guidelines, their educational policies. The purpose of this chapter is to outline the basic features of the school and college resource allocation formulae and to examine how these can be used to reflect educational policies. First the basic structures or templates that are required for the formulae are examined. The next section of the chapter discusses how certain broad policy objectives can be served through the design of the formulae.

The formula template

The basic requirements of the school and college formulae are similar. One starts from the LEA's *general budget*. For schools this is all the expenditure, including capital expenditure, planned for the coming financial year on primary, secondary and special schools and pupils in them. A general budget is similarly defined for further education. The LEA then subtracts from the general budget all expenditure it is retaining centrally. Some items are '*mandatory exceptions*' (these the LEA is not permitted to delegate); other items retained centrally will come from the list of '*discretionary exceptions*' which the LEA can choose whether or not to delegate, provided the total does not exceed 7 per cent (10 per cent in the first three years) of the general budget.[1] For FE the excepted items should not exceed 15 per cent of the general colleges budget.[2] What remains after deducting the excepted items from the general budget is called the *aggregated budget* and it is this that is distributed to schools or colleges by means of the formula. The amount thus distributed to each institution is known as its *budget share*, which is to be spent by the governors as they see fit for the purposes of the school or college. In addition, the LEA may transfer some of the money for excepted items to the institution as *earmarked* funds; i.e. this money can only be spent for the purpose designated by the LEA, or by central government in the case of categorical grants such as Education Support Grant or TVEI funds. LEAs are specifically encouraged to allocate earmarked funds to colleges.

The key requirements for the schools formula, set out in Circular 7/88 are:

- The formula should be based on an assessment of schools' 'objective needs', rather than on historic patterns of expenditure;
- At least 75 per cent of the LEA's total aggregated schools budget should be allocated on the basis of the numbers and ages of pupils at each school, while different subject cost weightings may be used for sixth form pupils;

- The remaining 25 per cent may be used within the formula to allocate money according to factors that affect the needs of individual schools and which may vary from school to school. The formula should include at least two specific factors:
  (i) the additional costs of pupils with special educational needs;
  (ii) the additional costs in small schools of maintaining a curriculum comparable to that available in larger schools, where the LEA considers that appropriate.

Other special factors which LEAs may include are differences in the socio-economic characteristics of pupils and the type and condition of school premises, as these will lead to differences in maintenance, cleaning and heating costs.

- The basic rules of the formula should be simple, clear and predictable 'so that governors, teachers, parents and the community can understand how it operates'.
- Budgets should not be affected by a school's budget deficit or surplus from the previous year.
- Schools may be protected from large year-to-year budget cuts (probably in excess of 3–5 per cent).
- Schools should be charged the actual salaries and on-costs (employers' National Insurance and pension contributions) of the teachers employed in them, not a notional charge based on the LEA average cost for teachers. However, for small schools with less than ten teachers (excluding head and deputy) the formula can be adjusted to allow for actual salary costs.

The main elements of the college formula are similar:

- The bulk of the colleges' budgets should be determined by student number allocations, which are set by the LEA (after submission of all FE college plans and joint consultation between the colleges and the LEA) and are based on the colleges' current enrolment performance plus evidence of future changes in demand.
- How much money a particular student allocation attracts depends on:
  (i) The type of course programme. Circular 9/88 envisages courses being grouped for funding purposes into just a few broad programme areas, distinguished by differences in their costs;
  (ii) The level of work – LEAs have discretion to weight this.
  (iii) Special needs – these are likely to need an additional weighting.
  (iv) The mode of student attendance. The formula will state how much money part-time students compared to full-time students attract. Thus total student number allocations refers to the number of full-time equivalent (FTE) places.
- The formula may take account of factors which differentially affect the costs of different colleges. Two factors are singled out:
  (i) premises costs;

(ii) size.
- There should be a presumption in favour of simplicity.

College funding is considerably more complex than that of schools because of the variety and significance of sources of income other than the budget share allocated by the formula. In addition to earmarked funds, the Polytechnic and Colleges Funding Council finances HE courses in FE colleges and colleges should 'be free to determine the fees for cost-recovery courses commissioned by outside organizations' (9/88, para. 3.68). A further issue for LEAs and colleges to resolve is whether the college budget is set net or gross of course fees from foreign students and those living outside the authority's boundaries.

The school and college formulae have certain key features in common. Both are designed to give institutions a strong financial incentive to attract students. Both require the LEA to determine the relative weight to give to pupils/students who differ by age, course, special needs, or mode of attendance. LEAs must now explicitly state the relative sums of money they wish to spend on different kinds of students. Both formulae give a certain amount of flexibility in allowing the average student cost at various institutions to differ because of the characteristics of the institution – in particular its size and premises. However, one thing should be made clear. Though an LEA formula may give an institution a particular sum of money for a given type of student, an institution with a delegated budget is not obliged to spend the exact amount on that type of student. All it needs to do is perform sufficiently well in the LEA's evaluation of its work. While the LEA can signal its priorities via its stated objectives, its resource allocation weightings and its evaluation procedures, the whole rationale of financial delegation is to give institutions considerable discretion in determining their own resource use.

To see how formula construction is linked to the promotion of policy objectives it is useful to consider the school and college formula separately and in more detail. Turning first to schools, Figure 14.1 contains the template of a formula model based on the Audit Commission's (1988b) advice to LEAs.

The formula is split into two distinct parts. The first part, which can be called the '*age-weighted pupil allowance*' is common to all schools (though for some the numbers of pupils in each age band will be zero). All schools should have the same grant per pupil in a specific age band. The total of all schools' age-weighted pupil allowances must be at least 75 per cent of the aggregated schools budget. The second part of the formula consists of various *specific allowances*. Not all schools will qualify for these additional allowances, which in total must not exceed 25 per cent of the aggregated budget. Most of these additional specific allowances should also be determined by a sub-formula, so that they are consistently applied across schools. If a formula is not capable of being derived, as for some elements of maintenance, then some general principles need to be used – for example, survey information on the state of

Figure 14.1   Template of the schools' budget share determination formula

---

A school's budget   =
[grant per pupil in age band 1] × [number of pupils in age band 1]
        +
[grant per pupil in age band 2] × [number of pupils in age band 2]   Minimum
        +   75% aggregated
....   budget
        +
[grant per pupil in age band *n*] × [number of pupils in age band *n*]
        +
[special needs pupil grant(s)] × [number of special needs pupils]
        +
socio-economic factors allowance
        +
small schools curriculum allowance   Maximum
        +   25% aggregated
small schools special salary cost allowance   budget
        +
additional maintenance and premises cost allowances
        +
budget change protection allowances (transitional and steady state)

---

the school building and cost estimates of the work required to bring it up to certain defined standards.

Any formula contains two sets of elements or components. One set are the *variables*; these are the actual items in the formula such as the number of pupils in a given age band or in a particular category of special needs, or the size of the school in net square feet. The second set of components are the *coefficients*, which are numbers attached to each variable. For example, the grant paid per pupil in a given age band (e.g. £900 for each pupil in age band 11–13, or 33 pence per square foot of floor area). The DES guidelines put constraints on both the variables that can be included and on the size of the coefficients, but leave some flexibility. For instance, the LEA can choose its own pupil age bands and the relative size of the coefficients attached to each age band.

Similarly for the college formula, LEAs are free to establish which course programme divisions to use and the size of the weights or coefficients to attach to each course programme. An example of one LEA's college formula (not yet approved) is given in Figure 14.2.

This particular authority was following the guidelines in choosing a broad set of only three course programme weights, based on those used in the DES Annual Monitoring Survey. This can be justified in the absence of detailed information on the relative costs of courses. However, some other authorities might wish to have a more detailed subdivision of course

Figure 14.2 Example of a college formula

The budget for each college will comprise three elements.

Element A (around 9%)
A fixed sum representing the administrative overheads of a Group 4 college. (This includes the costs of principal, vice principal, 4 heads of department and other key staff.)

Element B (around 17%)
The bulk of this fixed element covers premises and central administration and is initially to be based on historic costs. Specific grants will be included here.

Element C (around 74%)
This will be allocated on the basis of planned full-time equivalent student numbers, weighted by category of work.

Weights for modes of attendance:

Full-time	1.0
Sandwich	0.75
Block release	0.3
Part-time day/evening release	0.3
Part-time day/evening not released	0.3
Evening only	0.075

These weights are used by the DES for calculating rate (revenue) support grant. In addition the part-time FTE totals are increased by 10% to take account of the extra costs of part-time relative to full-time students.

Weights for course programmes:

Classroom	1.0
Practical	1.5
High-cost practical	1.8

Special needs students may be weighted in addition between 2 and 4.

Mitigation
No college will face in any year a more than 3% budget reduction.

---

programmes which they feel more closely reflects information on relative course costs, such as that provided by Jones in Chapter 12.

Once the basic formula template in terms of the variables to be included and the relative weights on the coefficients is established for an authority, this could remain unchanged from one year to the next. In any case, only 'non-significant' changes can be made without having to resubmit the formula for DES approval. However, what will always change from year to year (given inflation at least) is the absolute size of each of the coefficients. For example, the grant per age-weighted pupil will rise in line with increases in the aggregated schools budget. Additionally, authorities are likely to adjust the relative size of the coefficients in the light of experience with how the formulae affect schools and colleges.

General principles for formula design

In a well-designed formula the variables and coefficients have a rational basis for being selected. This derives from the underlying policy objectives for the education service and from the overall budgetary constraint set by the need to balance the demands of education against those of the other services and the ability to finance these through the community charge, central government grants, the business rate, and capital receipts.

Whatever may be the specific policy objectives, there are certain standard normative criteria against which public policy is commonly evaluated. These criteria are effectiveness, efficiency, equity, responsiveness and accountability.[3] Thus the overarching question is: 'How can a budget allocation formula be constructed so that it promotes effectiveness, efficiency, equity, responsiveness and accountability?' An important part of the policy determination process is to interpret what these criteria mean in specific instances, especially when it is often not possible to satisfy all the criteria at once. The following discussion focuses in particular on the criteria of effectiveness, efficiency and equity.

Effectiveness and efficiency

Effectiveness and efficiency are criteria much used by public-sector auditors, such as the Audit Commission, when evaluating the resource allocation practices of public-sector agencies. Effectiveness is defined as the extent to which a programme meets its objectives. These objectives are politically determined and are usually expressed in broad and qualitative terms, as are the government's objectives for education, set out in the annual Expenditure White Paper:

> The Government's principal aims for schools are to improve standards of achievement for all pupils across the curriculum, to widen the choice available to parents for the education of their children and to enable schools to respond effectively to what parents and the community require of them, thus securing the best possible return from the substantial investment of resources.

(HM Treasury, 1988)

The public-sector audit approach to assessing effectiveness, requires the broad policy aims to be translated into appropriate operational criteria. These are specific and measurable objectives or targets – such as increasing the proportion of the age group with five or more GCSEs or the proportion who enter post-compulsory education. *Effectiveness* can then be assessed as the difference between the desired targets set for the operational objectives (often called performance indicators) and the actual outcomes achieved. Effectiveness by itself takes no account of the value of the resources consumed in achieving the operational objectives. This is why efficiency is required as a separate criterion. *Efficiency* is the ratio between the measured outcomes of a programme and the inputs used to produce those outcomes and may be measured in physical units (e.g. teaching hours per examination pass, or units of energy consumed to heat a building of given size) or in money terms. An efficient programme is one that uses least resources to achieve a given outcome, but it will not be effective if it fails to achieve outcomes that are desired. An *efficient and effective* programme is one where the objectives are achieved with the least possible use of resources.

The effectiveness of a funding formula will depend on the extent to which the formula delivers central government and local authority aims for education. To the extent that these differ there will be differing judgements as to the degree of effectiveness achieved, especially when it is difficult to devise operational targets that are widely accepted as being adequate reflections of an agreed set of broad aims. However, the general principle that an effective formula should provide adequate funding to enable each school or college to undertake the tasks expected of it should command a wide consensus.

It is going to be very difficult to judge the relationship between a funding formula and the resulting educational outcomes. Problems arise first in clarifying what tasks are expected of schools and colleges (and which interests – central, local, institutional, or customer – should determine them) and in deciding what is an adequate sum of money for undertaking these tasks. In determining what variables should enter the formula and what values should be attached to the coefficients, the authority has to take an explicit view on what should be the recurrent costs of educating to a 'required standard' students of diferent ages, with different special needs, attending different courses at different institutions. The DES stipulation that school budgets should be cash-limited and subject to little revision during the financial year, makes a correct initial assessment of each institution's needs all the more important to ensure the adequacy of the budget shares.

How then are the appropriate variables and the sizes of their co-efficients, in particular the grant per age-weighted pupil or per student allocation, to be determined? One approach to this problem, advocated by accountants and operations researchers, is to estimate the 'standard cost' of educating a mainstream student in a given age band in a school or college of efficient size (usually deemed to be six or more forms of entry for secondary schools or more than ten forms in the primary sector). The standard cost is built up by considering each item of expenditure in the budget line by line – i.e. teachers, supply cover, ancillary staff, caretaking, cleaning, energy, water, maintenance, examination fees, telephones, postage, travel allow-ances, books, equipment, materials, and so forth. The physical quantities of each input that a school or college is deemed to need depend on LEA and central government policy assumptions. For example, teaching staff numbers are determined by LEA policy with respect to the curriculum, average class size and teacher contact hours, as well as by the institution's enrolment. Curriculum-led staffing – advocated by the Audit Commission (1986) – is the method whereby the number, specialisms and grades and incentive allowances of the teaching and support staff are determined by the curriculum. Expenditure on books, equipment, materials and stationery would also be determined by the requirements of the different areas of the curriculum. Some of the physical quantities are derived from known policies, others have to be discovered from current practice, for example, the average number of GCSE examination entries per pupil or the number of telephone extensions per school. Standard expenditure on energy would be estimated from known technical information on the kilowatt-hours required to achieve specific temperatures in particular sizes and types of building. A formula allocation of a heating budget would be based on physical data and forecast energy prices, not on past heating bills. Costs of cleaning premises and of routine maintenance of buildings and grounds can be estimated by specifying in detail the work to be done and costing it per square foot or metre as is now done in meeting the legal requirements that authorities invite tenders for such work from in-house and private contractors.

In this way the standard costs of a school (or college) of efficient size for its sector would be built up. The total costs of the various inputs used at such a school (excluding those resources still centrally provided by the LEA) for educating pupils in a given age band are then divided by the number of such pupils to obtain the standard unit cost per pupil in that age group. Table 1 illustrates how these estimates would be set out and summed to arrive at the standard cost per pupil in a given age group. The columns contain the major types of resource input which appear as budget heads in schools' budgets. These would have been broken down into finer detail in order to arrive at the figures such as those presented in the table. For example, teacher costs would be derived from a curriculum-led staffing model.

The standard cost per pupil would be distributed to schools as the age-weighted pupil grant. The remaining 25 per cent maximum of the aggregate budget can be allocated by means of the additional non-pupil-related allowances set out in Figure 14.1. Some of these allowances would be standardized and so apply equally to every school qualifying for them, such as special needs pupil allowances and any allowances for socio-economic characteristics. The curriculum protection for small schools is also standardized in

Table 14.1   An example of contributions to the standard cost per pupil (£)

Age group of pupil	Teaching staff costs	EMBS	Teaching support staff	Premises costs	Administration costs	Total cost in school of standard size
8–11 years	800	40	20	120	20	1000
12–14 years	1000	50	25	130	25	1230
15–16 years	1400	60	30	130	25	1645

Note: EMBS = equipment, materials, books and stationery. The figures are illustrative only.

relation to the size of the school. However, allowances for specific features of the premises (such as size, condition, number of sites) and for actual teacher costs in schools with ten or fewer teachers are school-specific.

The logic of the 'standard-cost' approach is that the total budget for each school is determined 'bottom-up' as a summation of the various cost elements. Following through this logic, the LEAs aggregated schools budget would be a summation of the individual schools' total direct costs. However, in practice LEA budgets are not generated in this manner and are not likely to be because of the political requirement to control overall expenditure.

In complete contrast to the standard-cost approach to determining the size of the age-weighted pupil grants and other allowances, is what might be termed the 'top-down' approach. The authority decides in the normal way on a general schools budget. This is the usual compromise between the need to control the total authority budget in order to limit rate or community-charge increases, and the pressures to maintain or even improve local authority services. This is incremental budgeting; last year's budgets are adjusted in the light of changes in needs (e.g. in pupil numbers), in marginal policy changes (e.g. in the average pupil–teacher ratios), and forecast price increases (e.g. teachers' salaries). Having arrived at the general schools budget (and FE budget), the next step is to subtract the centrally retained portion and then to divide the remaining aggregated budgets for schools and further education into budget shares for each institution. In the case of schools an explicit decision would be taken on the weights to be given to pupils of each age, plus an additional percentage for special needs pupils. Then the 75 per cent minimum (or more) of the aggregate budget allocated according to the number and ages of pupils is divided by the total number of pupil units in all the authority's schools. The result, which may be termed '*the basic pupil grant*' is the grant per pupil in the age band weighted by one (i.e. the least-cost age band). Each school's budget is then its number of age-weighted pupil units times the grant per pupil unit.

There are several advantages to the top-down approach. It is cheap on information because it does not pretend to provide a rational costed basis for the amount allocated for each pupil unit. The relative cost weightings for different kinds of pupils are used to distribute the cake (the aggregated schools budget): they are not used to determine the actual size of the cake as a summation of the pupil grants or other allowances, as in the standard-cost approach. The top-down approach avoids line-by-line haggling between institutions and the authority since no figures exist for how much is being allocated to the institution for expenditure on each input for each type of pupil.

From the point of view of educationists, the standard-cost approach may be preferred because it provides ammunition to argue that education should be allocated more money in order to cover its standard costs. Its disadvantage is that it is data-greedy and so expensive to operate, though the use of a standard software programme could eventually cut costs. It scores on accountability in so far as it provides an explicit and reasoned account of the authority's unit costs, but the extent of the detail means that only a few specialists will fully understand it. The many coefficients embedded within the standard-cost calculations reflect at best explicit judgements about required resource-use based on technical evidence and a consensus about good educational practice. Inevitably some will be arbitrary or based on dubiously reliable statistical regressions of historical expenditure data.[4]

It is doubtful if the standard-cost approach to generating school and college budgets at the LEA level is politically feasible. Local authority members and officers would find that it opened the way to continual haggling with school and college interests over what are the correct standard-cost figures and thus put undesirable upward pressure on local authority expenditure. Past experience of implementing planned programme budgeting system (PPBS) – particularly in the USA where this was tried in the 1970s – indicates that rational budgeting systems get subverted by political realities. If this is the case then simpler budgeting systems which rely on rough rules of thumb are in practice more efficient because they use up less manpower and computer time and, in the end, achieve about the same degree of rationality as a subverted PPBS system. Hence we are likely to see local authority budgets generated and distributed by some combination of the incremental top-down approach and the standard-cost bottom-up approach. Since budget generation and budget distribution are distinct processes (see Howard, Chapter 5), a standard-cost approach could be used to generate relative weights for the different variables in the allocation formula, while the usual incremental approach remained in use for generating the general schools and college budgets.

Whatever combination of approaches to determining the funding formula is used, there is likely to be a discrepancy between the budgets individual institutions get under formula funding and what they would have got had budgets continued to be allocated largely in relation to historical costs. The key question is whether these budget discrepancies reveal inefficiency in resource use by those institutions which suffer budget cuts in per capita funding or whether they reflect unavoidably high standard unit costs due to specific characteristics of the students or of the institution's size and buildings. One advantage of estimating the standard cost of each institution (provided this is done reasonably accurately) is that the budget thereby determined provides – by definition – the resources that the institution needs to perform its educational tasks given that it is run efficiently. Thus formula funding, provided that it finances each institution according to its standard costs, will force institutions with actual costs in excess of their standard costs to become more efficient. Increased efficiency in the allocation of a given amount of resources between institutions should increase the effectiveness with which this given quantity is used.

It is clear that the DES's insistence that a large proportion of the budget is determined by age-weighted pupil units (or student allocations) is intended to make institutions responsive to their clients by requiring them to attract sufficient students in order to cover total costs. In this way educational institutions are being made to render accountability to the market and not just to education professionals or political representatives.

Equity

The equity of any method of budget determination, whether it be formula-driven or historical, is necessarily a matter of judgement about what is fair and just. Nevertheless such judgements can be based on commonly used principles of equity. One important distinction is that between horizontal equity, which is the principle that each individual (or institution) in like circumstances should receive the same treatment, and vertical equity, whereby individuals (and institutions) with different characteristics should be treated in ways which take account of and compensate for such differences (see Musgrave and Musgrave, 1984, p. 232). Horizontal equity implies that each student should benefit from the same amount of public expenditure. Hence differences in per capita expenditure are inequitable, especially within the same LEA where they cannot be justified by the principle of local government autonomy. There is considerable evidence (Hough, 1981; Audit Commission 1984 and 1986) that such differences have persisted under historically based resource-allocation procedures. Vertical equity justifies differences in per capita education expenditure if they result from differences in the characteristics of students which are judged to require differences in per capita expenditure in order for all students to reach a common minimum level of attainment. Vertical equity also applies to differences in per capita costs which arise from the characteristics of particular institutions, such as their size or type of building. The fear that formula funding will 'unfairly' penalize institutions with unavoidably high costs in relation to their student numbers has been frequently voiced.

However, the DES guidelines lean strongly towards horizontal equity in the importance given to age-weighted pupils and student course allocations, plus the insistence that, except for very small schools, the budget share must be based on average LEA teacher costs, while the institution is charged its actual teacher costs. The DES is clearly unsympathetic to the inclusion of a 'multiplicity of factors' in the formula, as would happen if a good number of vertical equity considerations were taken into account. This 'will make the formula less intelligible without necessarily making it more equitable' (7/88, para. 104). LEAs can use the allowances in the 25 per cent of the aggregated budget that need not be distributed according to age-weighted pupils, to take account of vertical equity factors. The guidelines recommend two vertical equity factors, special needs and a small schools curriculum protection allowance, for inclusion in the schools' formula, and premises and size for inclusion in the college formula. Additional vertical equity factors are now explicitly permitted in Circular 7/88: 'LEAs will be free to take into account any other factors, such as the incidence of social deprivation amongst pupils in different schools and the distribution of gifted pupils' (7/88, para. 115). Many LEAs have in the past adjusted the allocation of school resources to take account of social deprivation. One way is the use of Section 11 grants for pupils from immigrant communities. These will remain centrally allocated as they need to be accounted for to the Home Office. However, under formula funding, LEAs will no longer be able to use informal and ad hoc information as the basis for diverting extra resources to socially deprived pupils. Some quantified measure of pupils' social deprivation is now required.

An easily available, but rather rough, measure of social priority used by Cambridgeshire in its 1988–9 formula is the number of free meals.[5] This measure will become even more unsatisfactory with the removal of family credit recipients from entitlement to free meals. The most sophisticated scheme adopted in the UK has been ILEA's Alternative Use of Resources. This required considerable research effort to collect data for measuring the educational priority needs of each school. Indices used were free meals, family size, one-parent family, parental occupation, pupil behaviour and mobility, fluency in English, and ethnic origins. From 1981 the weight attached to each index was determined by the extent to which it was found by regression analysis to be related to educational measures, in particular, verbal reasoning scores. Possible measures of educational priority which are less costly to collect than ILEA's but less crude than free meals are tests of ability (which may be more generally collected with the coming of national testing) or pupils' socio-economic status derived from the socio-economic classification given to the ward in which they live by the Registrar General's analysis of census data. Information on parents' occupations or education may be regarded as too sensitive to collect.

Another aspect of equity is the judgement that it is inequitable for an institution to have to adjust very rapidly to resource cuts, especially if others are receiving unaccustomed largesse. This point of view has won some response from the DES, which will permit a four-year adjustment period during which schools and colleges may be protected from large year-to-year budget cuts by being funded partially on a historical basis. Long-term protection from rapid budget change (in excess of 5 per cent is suggested in the guidelines) is also permissible.

The use of standard costing would promote horizontal equity by helping to ensure that like pupils have similar amounts of resources allocated to them. If standard-cost estimates can adequately reflect unavoidable differences (i.e. those not due to inefficiency) in institution-specific costs and can encompass differences in student-related costs due to special needs, then vertical equity can be promoted as well. If costs can be appropriately assessed then equity objectives can coincide with those of effectiveness and efficiency, since it will be known how much of the budget is allocated according to estimates of what is required for efficient operation and how much because of specific vertical equity considerations. In practice, the key policy and technical problems are to determine what differences in institutional or student-related costs are justified either on efficiency or equity grounds, and which are not.

The value of explicit normative criteria

The application of explicit normative criteria does not, of course, given unequivocal guidance to budget formula construction. As is usual with multiple objectives, the criteria when applied may be mutually inconsistent and so a balance has to be struck between them. For instance, allocating budgets so as to promote efficiency in resource use by institutions may be judged to have effects which are not equitable (because of adjustment problems); or producing an elaborate formula to promote equity may make the resource allocation process less accountable because it is not easily understood. It is therefore necessary to make judgements concerning the relative weights to be given to the various criteria in specific circumstances.

Preferences for the degree of balance depend on people's values and interests. The usefulness of explicit and widely used normative criteria in such circumstances is to disentangle self-interested arguments from those based on values, since the normative principles of efficiency, effectiveness, equity, responsiveness, accountability, and their interpretation, are underpinned by values. The criteria also enable one to clarify what predictions are being made about the likely effects of particular decision rules and how these predicted effects relate to the basic principles underlying policy objectives. Issues in relation to financial delegation tend rapidly to fragment into points of detail, which are often quite contentious because they affect interests differentially. Reference to general principles helps in reaching agreed and consistent solutions to specific problems.

Notes

1 School meals, severance costs, governors' insurance and transitional exceptions are not included in the 10 per cent (7 per cent) limit.
2 Certain mandatory excepted items – capital expenditure, staff severance costs, specific grants and governors' insurance – do not count towards the 15 per cent.
3 A more detailed discussion of these criteria is given in Levačić (1989).
4 Coopers & Lybrand point out some of the difficulties:

> In an ideal world it would be possible, through detailed surveys and analysis, to determine the expenditure required to achieve a given standard of temperature, light and state of repair for each school's configuration. In practice, however, such calculations would be extremely time consuming to perform and the results would be unreliable and probably contentious. However, the alternative of basing allocations on historical spending is equally unreliable since it would not adequately

reflect differing historical standards of provision or quality of management, nor fluctuations in ambient temperatures or repairs required which affect the need to spend.

5 Each free meal is worth 50p (Cambridgeshire, 1987).

References

Audit Commission (1984). *Aspects of Non-Teaching Costs in Secondary Schools.* London, HMSO.

Audit Commission (1986). *Towards Better Management of Secondary Education.* London, HMSO.

Audit Commission (1988a). *Delegation of Management Authority to Schools.* London, HMSO.

Audit Commission (1988b). *Local Management of Schools: a Note to LEAs.* Bristol, Audit Commission.

Cambridgeshire County Council (1987), *LFM Distribution of Resources on a Pupil Unit Basis.* Education Resources Sub-Committee, October Minutes, Appendix 1.

Coopers & Lybrand (1988). *Local Management of Schools: a Report to the DES.* HMSO.

Department of Education and Science, and Welsh Office (1987). Joint Efficiency Study, *Managing Colleges Efficiently*, HMSO.

Department of Education and Science (1988a). *Education Reform Act: Local Management of Schools.* Circular No. 7/88.

Department of Education and Science (1988b). *Education Reform Act: Local Management of Further and Higher Education Colleges: Planning and Delegation Schemes and Articles of Government.* Circular No. 9/88.

Further Education Staff College (1986a). *Joint Efficiency Study of NAFE: Matched Pairs Case Studies.* vol. 19, no. 11.

Further Education Staff College (1986b). *Joint Efficiency Study of NAFE: Non-Teacher Costs.* vol. 19, no. 12.

HM Treasury (1988). *The Government's Expenditure Plans 1988–89 to 1990–91.* Cm 288–II, London, HMSO.

Hough, J. R. (1981). *A Study of School Costs.* Windsor, Berks, NFER-Nelson.

Inner London Education Authority (1982). *Educational Priority Indices – a New Perspective.* RS858/82.

Inner London Education Authority (1983). *The Effect of the 1983 Educational Priority Indices on the Allocation of AUR.* RS 899/83.

Inner London Education Authority (1987). *1987 Educational Priority Indices: Changes in the Characteristics of the School Pupil Population between 1985 and 1987.* RS 1124/87.

Levačić, R. (1989). 'Rules and formulae for allocating and spending delegated budgets: a consideration of general principles', *Education Management and Administration.* vol. 17, no. 4.

Musgrave, R. A. and Musgrave, P. B. (1984). *Public Finance Theory and Practice*, New York, McGraw-Hill.

The political and organizational context

15

Budgeting as a political and organizational process in educational institutions

Tim Simkins

Introduction

A major thrust of the 1988 Education Reform Act is to give greater autonomy in resource management to educational institutions. For schools and colleges of further education this thrust is embodied in the requirement that LEAs develop plans to delegate the main responsibility for managing finance and staff to the institutions themselves; for public-sector institutions of higher education autonomy in resource management is part of the broader move-ment to corporate status. These developments bring to centre-stage the question of how institutions should utilize these expanded powers of re-source management; and this chapter explores these questions with respect to institutions of post-compulsory education.

A rational model

The case for granting institutions greater financial autonomy is based on the argument that resources are likely to be managed most effectively and efficiently if those who are responsible for delivering a service to the client are given maximum discretion to deploy and redeploy resources in response to their perception of local needs and circumstances. Coopers & Lybrand, in their advice to the DES state the position clearly: (see Chapter 8, Section 1.5). Their statement – and indeed most arguments for greater financial autonomy for schools and colleges – contains both normative and empirical assump-tions. In normative terms, it is assumed that management is primarily about harnessing resources for the achievement of clearly specified goals. Empiri-cally, it is assumed that financial autonomy will cause this to occur. In other words, the underlying model of decision making is one in which those responsible for managing resources both *should* and *will* act in a rational way.

This emphasis on rationality in resource management is part of a wider concern about obtaining 'value for money' in education in a context where resource availability is increasingly constrained. For colleges of further education, the initial work of the Audit Commission (1985), which was critical of the value for money obtained from resources in this sector, was succeeded by the 'Joint Efficiency Study' undertaken by the government and the Local Authority Associations (DES/Welsh Office, 1987). The rationale of the latter study was quite clear: 'All organisations reliant on public resources need to be able to measure their *efficiency* (the relationship of inputs to outputs) and *effectiveness* (the extent to which their objectives are achieved), and to show that they are giving value for money' (p. 13). Consequently the study aimed 'to identify and recommend principles of good practice' (p. 1) which are now embodied in a manual of guidance (Birch, 1988).

What exactly does such a rational approach imply for the budgeting process? Its implications can be encapsulated in three key principles. First, the budgetary process should encompass a comprehensive view of the organiz-ation with all budgetary decisions reflecting organization-wide objectives and priorities and an awareness of the longer-term implications of particular resource commitments. This implies the need for a strategic plan which provides a framework for the budgeting process and an information system, perhaps designed on 'programme budgeting' lines, which enables managers to relate key organizational results to the costs of producing them.

Second, the process should embody a thorough consideration of alternative patterns of expenditure, and in particular an awareness of the opportunity costs of particular expenditure decisions in terms of the sac-rificed alternatives which they imply. This means that budgeting should involve an adequate consideration of options, including some 'zero-basing' which admits the possibility of major cutbacks in some areas to facilitate the growth of others.

Thirdly, the budget which is produced should represent an optimal allocation of resources in terms of the organization's objectives. This means that there should be some ongoing evaluation of the performance of the organization's subunits in terms of their effectiveness and efficiency in achieving objectives at acceptable cost, and the outcomes of this evaluation, perhaps expressed in terms of explicit performance indicators, should be used to help in the process of budgeting.

The case for making both management in general and budgeting in particular more rational is a strong one, especially at a time when educational institutions are faced by increasing demands on scarce resources. By empha-sizing the importance of relating resources to desired ends and by considering what options are forgone when a particular pattern of resource use is chosen, it provides a clear framework for thinking systematically about resource management. It is not surprising, therefore, that the rational approach to resource management has been the subject of much advocacy and a wealth of literature over the last twenty-five years (e.g. Lyden and Miller, 1982).

Yet, to argue for rationality is not necessarily to ensure its occurrence. Indeed, despite their repeated advocacy, rational approaches do not seem to have replaced traditional methods of budgeting, with their subjective accounting, incremental choice and comparatively short time horizons (Wildavsky, 1978). The findings of the Audit Commission, the Joint Efficiency Study and the Jarratt Report on universities (CVCP, 1985) all suggest that this is probably at least as true of educational institutions as of other organizations in the public sector and elsewhere. Why is this?

A starting point for analysis must be the assumptions underlying the rational approach. Organizations are assumed to have goals which are generally agreed and accepted by those within them and which provide a basis for action. The rational approach therefore becomes intrinsically problematic where goals are ambiguous, contested, or conflicting, or where the relationship between means and ends is unclear. In such circumstances other models of budgeting may offer better explanations of reality. The most significant of these is the political model.

The political dimension of budgeting

The key questions addressed by the political perspective relate to the power bases of organizational members and the strategies and tactics that they use to influence budgetary decisions. Such an approach does not treat disagreement or conflict over values or objectives as problematic; it treats them as axiomatic. And where such conflict exists it is likely to be expressed, at least in part, through competition for resources, since it is the obtaining of such resources which provides the basis for participants to develop programmes of activity which embody their values and further their interests and, in addition, provides organizational legitimation for the activities they are engaged in. Indeed this is the focus of one definition of political behaviour: 'Political behaviour is defined as behaviour by individuals, or, in collective terms, by sub-units, within an organization that makes a claim against the resource sharing system of an organisation' (Pettigrew, 1973, p. 17). Pettigrew is using the term 'resource' here in a very broad sense, but clearly the budgeting process would appear to fit into this scheme very well. For example, Wildavsky (1968, p. 193) conceives of budgets

> as attempts to allocate financial resources through political processes. If politics is regarded as conflict over whose preferences are to prevail in the determination of policy, then the budget records the outcomes of this struggle. If one asks who gets what the (public or private) organisation has to give, then the answers for a moment in time are recorded in the budget. If organisations are viewed as political coalitions, budgets

are mechanisms through which subunits bargain over conflicting goals, make side-payments, and try to motivate one another to accomplish their objectives.

This perspective leads us to focus on three variables which are potentially relevant to an analysis of budgetary processes. The first is differences in values and interests among organizational participants. These may be differences among individuals; but the political model places particular emphasis upon differences among groups, especially formal groups such as subunits or departments within organizations. In further and higher education there may be a number of bases for subgroup differentiation. The most common is likely to relate to disciplines, especially as faculties or departments are typically disciplined-based. Thus a political perspective would regard it as perfectly natural for members of a science department and a humanities department in a college to have different views about the relative importance of their subjects in the curriculum and therefore to work to compete for scarce resources to enhance the effectiveness of their own teaching and, incidentally, the status of their departments.

Other bases for differentiation may exist alongside more traditional discipline-based ones. For example, as external demands on institutions become more varied, differentiation may arise around alternative views on how the college's work should be legitimated:

> If staff were interviewed on the various legitimations, they would express different and possibly irreconcilable priorities and principles. Staff who view an FE college as a local community resource would give higher priority to requests from local groups and to developing close links with local businesses, schools and citizens of all ages. Staff who view the college as a channel for compensation to disadvantaged groups who lose out in others areas might stress courses for the unemployed and ethnic minority groups, and downgrade GCE work as being available elsewhere. Staff who view colleges in a more entrepreneurial light might advocate elaborate marketing exercises to attract self-financing course or advanced level work, and dismiss low-level basic skills courses.
>
> (Cavanagh, 1983, p. 58)

It would be surprising if these conflicting perspectives did not express themselves in competing demands for resources, which are likely to express in potentially conflicting statements about the nature of the college's 'mission' and the priorities which this implies.

The second key variable is the power that individuals and groups can bring to bear upon the decision-making process of the organization. There are many classifications of sources of power. One (Handy, 1976, Ch. 5) suggests that an individual's power within an organization may arise from position, either formal or informal, within the organization, from expertise, from personality, from possession of key resources, or from an ability to use physical sanctions to influence decisions. Institutions of post-compulsory education typically exhibit complex power structures which comprise both 'hierarchical' and 'collegial' elements. Thus formal hierarchies of senior management teams, heads of departments and section heads or course leaders coexist with academic boards, faculty boards and similar groupings whose composition and *de jure* powers are defined by the Articles and Instruments of Government. The *de facto* distribution of power within such systems, however, is often complex and difficult to discern. Ebbutt and Brown (1978), for example argue that power in the FE college: 'does not . . . lie within the governing body, which is primarily a "rubber stamp" for decisions taken elsewhere, nor with the academic board as such, which is a battleground for competing interests rather than a power centre in its own right. Power is shared between the principal and heads of department' (p. 16). Cavanagh (1983) argues that this is too simple a view, and it may be the case that in some institutions there is an 'involuted hierarchy' (Noble and Pym, 1970) with the locus of power appearing to recede from whichever position it is viewed. Nevertheless, as far as budgeting is concerned, it is normally the case that the key power centres within college will be faculties, departments, or other organizational subgroups which compete for resources (or the representatives of such subgroups, such as heads of department) on the one hand, and the principal or senior management team who are responsible for managing the budgetary process on the other. As Ebbutt and Brown argue, whereas the former 'may have particular interests to defend, the principal's interest is the college' (1978, p. 10).

Various factors have been suggested which affect the power of subunits within educational organizations. One is the ability of the subunit to control critical contingencies for the organization, through, for example, its ability to mobilize external resources and to meet the needs of key external stakeholders (Hickson *et al.*, 1971). A second is the degree of cohesiveness of the subunit. For example, Beyer and Lodahl (1976) argued that high levels of 'paradigm development' in a discipline such as science or engineering will lead to greater departmental consensus about goals and means of goal attainment which in turn will reduce internal conflict, facilitate coalition formation and hence strengthen the department in any contest for power. Finally, there is general argument that access to decision-making structures and the ability to use these effectively is important. Thus Noble and Pym (1970) identified 'system relevant' (as opposed to academic or subject) expertise as a crucial factor in the power relations of a university, with membership of overlapping committees, boundary-spanning functions, and knowledge of the possible reactions of a wide range of staff giving the holder a key advantage in influencing decision-making processes.

The last factor, while clearly a possible source of power differentiation between subunits, is even more obviously a major source of power of the principal and other senior managers within institutions. Indeed, in the

budgetary process, such formal positions are likely to be particularly important because they will embody the legitimate right to be involved in (and often
to structure) the process and perhaps to take particular decisions, and also
because they provide the opportunity to control information flows through
'gatekeeping' activities. Membership (often chairmanship), usually *ex officio*,
of major committees, together with a wide variety of relationships with
external stakeholders, provides a power base which is likely to be at least as
potent as the formal authority attached to position.

The final variable in a political analysis concerns the processes through
which power is brought to bear on the decision-making situation. A range of
strategies are possible, but in the budgeting situation emphasis is likely to be
upon the use of persuasion through the marshalling of expertise and the
control of information, or upon the use of bargaining and exchange strategies
to reach acceptable compromises on resource allocation. It will often be the
case that: 'A department's share of scarce resources depends upon the skills of
its advocates in the use of essentially political tactics – such as knowing how
much to bid for, how far to pad estimates, how far to over/underspend, how
to "read" the political climate, how to generate and utilise public support'
(Greenwood *et al.*, 1980, p. 29).

Those in control of the budget, will have strategies at their disposal too,
however. These include:

- structuring the activities, timetable and responsibilities of other
  persons in the budget process;
- retaining authority for establishing planning assumptions and
  budget preparation guidelines;
- controlling access to information about important elements of
  budgeting, such as past performance of subunits, budget guidelines,
  expectations of influential persons and one's own priorities;
- retaining large discretionary accounts or accounts such as travel and
  equipment so that 'favours' may be given;
- retaining authority for budget control so that mid-year and end-of
  year transfers among accounts may be made easily and obscurely.

(Tonn, 1978, p. 580)

According to the political perspective, it is the effectiveness with which these
strategies are used which is a major determinant of budgetary outcomes.
Such an approach has been little applied to date to decision making in general
in education, let alone to budgeting; but it clearly has great potential for
enhancing our understanding in this area.

The approaches compared

It may be useful at this point to consider more systematically the differences
between the 'rational' and the 'political' approaches to budgeting. These are

set out in Table 15.1. From a budgeting perspective a 'rational' organization will have clear goals which are either arrived at by consensus or are effectively imposed within the organization, and the basic budgetary problem may be seen as establishing structures and processes which provide a framework for effective planning and rational choice in the sense described earlier. There will be an emphasis on the 'technical' dimension of resource allocation problems with substantial information inputs to the budgetary process provided by appropriate experts, probably using programme budget frameworks and zero-base reviews. Since the prime purpose of the budget is to achieve the optimal use of the organization's resources in terms of its overall objectives, the budgetary process is likely to concentrate power at the centre and, in addition, to give considerable power to those individuals and groups who, probably on the basis of defined expertise, control both the structures of the budgetary process and the gathering and processing of the information which it requires. Furthermore, the process is likely to be a top-down one, with

Table 15.1   The rational and political approaches to budgeting

	[Rational]	[Political]
Overall focus	The whole organization; goals and priorities	Key subunits and individuals; differences in values and interests
Structural emphasis	Centralized; integrating mechanisms	Decentralized; differentiation among subunits and hence power distribution important
Role of information	Wide parameters of review and comprehensive search (e.g. planning, programming, budgeting system (PPBS) and zero-based budgeting (ZBB)); importance of neutral technical expertise	Narrow parameters of review and strategic use of information; gatekeeping roles and partial use of expertise
Budgeting processes	Top-down; emphasis on rationality and analysis	Bottom-up; emphasis on bargaining strategies and tactics
Definition of acceptable decisions	Economic optimization	Political viability
Assessment of outcomes	Cost-effectiveness; efficiency	Distribution of gains and losses

overall objectives and priorities established at the centre providing the broad basis for allocations within the organization. Finally, since the key organizing idea for the budgetary process – indeed for the whole organization – is objectives, there will be an explicit attempt to evaluate performance in terms of the efficiency and effectiveness with which these objectives are achieved.

In contrast, a 'political' organization will exhibit a very different kind of budgetary process. Since overall organizational objectives are nonexistent, controversial, or unimportant, the prime concern of budgeting will be to produce a pattern of resource allocation which can command a sufficient degree of acceptability given the distribution of power and influence which exists. Budgeting will be clearly perceived as a political bargaining process, and therefore there will be an emphasis on the political skills of the actors involved – both those who compete for resources in the budgetary arena and those at the centre who hold the ring – and on the strategies and tactics each uses to influence the process. In this context information will be used selectively and strategically to influence decisions rather than comprehensively and rationally to identify optimum decisions. The budgetary process will be a bottom-up one with spending departments making bids for resources which those at the centre attempt to balance within the resources available. Power is likely to be dispersed among the participants in the process, perhaps quite unevenly, and the distribution of resources which finally emerges will reflect this dispersal. Finally, since there are no clear organizational goals, evaluation of performance in any objective sense is not possible and the emphasis of the process will be upon the political viability of decisions reached and upon control and accountability.

It should be clear by now that the two approaches embody different 'ideal type' models of the organization, and that few organizations are likely to correspond to either model in every respect. This is particularly true of educational organizations. Although the management rhetoric may reflect many assumptions of rationality, the problems of defining and agreeing objectives and the general lack of understanding of the technology which relates means to ends makes the effective application of rational ideas to decision making in educational institutions very difficult. These difficulties are exacerbated when the implications of the rational model for centralization of decision making are set against the values and ideals of autonomy and personal service to students which are embodied in the concept of professionalism which most teachers espouse. For these reasons, it is almost a commonplace now to argue that institutions of further and higher education are best conceptualized as political systems (Baldridge, 1971; Dufty, 1976; Cavanagh, 1983), or even as organized anarchies (Cohen and March, 1974; Enderud, 1980), rather than as rational organizations reflecting a bureaucratic or collegial consensus.

There is some confirmation of this view from empirical studies. Thus in a study of the University of Illinois, subunit power was found to be an important factor in determining budgetary allocations (Pfeffer and Salancik,

1974; Salancik and Pfeffer, 1974), a finding replicated in later studies of a state university system in the USA (Pfeffer and Moore, 1980) and of the University of Montreal (Hardy, 1988). In another study, of the University of Minnesota, budgeting was found to be incremental, '. . . but less so during times of relative resource scarcity when sub-unit power seemed to be an important determinant of changes in relative allocations' (Hills and Mahoney, 1978).

Such studies, however, do not imply that budgeting is a completely political process. This is not surprising: the sense of professionalism and common ideals about the educational process held by lecturers are likely to modify any tendency for them to perceive their colleges, or indeed for their colleges to operate, entirely as collections of feudal baronies defending their fiefs. Thus, while 'yearnings for corporate rationality may be illusory' (Davies and Morgan, 1983, p. 160), a budgetary process that is excessively political is likely to be unacceptable in most institutions as it will import a high degree of conflict and potential instability into the organization and possibly endanger its long-run survival. In the real world some middle way must be sought.

Budgeting as an organizational process

Budgetary systems, therefore, need to balance a number of potentially conflicting demands. Certainly they must attempt to:

(a) ensure the effective and efficient deployment of resources (an implication of the rational approach); and
(b) contain conflict and maintain a viable coalition among powerful individuals and groups whose values and interests may differ (an implication of the political approach).

In addition, however, they must attempt to:

(c) ensure that budgetary decisions are made within the limits of time and information at the disposal of managers;
(d) maintain a reasonably stable resource environment for those working within the organization even though the environment within which the organization is operating may be uncertain and rapidly changing; and
(e) ensure that those within the system who are responsible for managing resources can be held accountable for their performance in this role.

Such competing demands mean that budget making needs to be seen as an integral part of the process through which managers attempt to adapt the organization in the light of their perception of the multiple pressures arising from within and without. Budget making is a recurrent task and therefore needs to be understood as an organizational process which involves regular problem-solving routines and decision-making structures. The prime functions of such routines and structures are to introduce a degree of predictability and stability into the budgetary process without which the complexities of budget preparation would become unmanageable, and also to reduce to a manageable level the conflict which is inherent in budgeting. In so doing, however, they establish a set of constraints which often goes unchallenged or even unrecognized. An understanding of the constraining power of organizational processes, therefore, is an important complement to the more 'active' conceptions of budgeting embodied in the rational and political models.

Budgetary decision-making structures and routines will vary among organizations, but we can identify a number of issues of common concern. The first relates to roles and relationships. Who is involved in the budgetary process and how is such involvement structured? Often such involvement is quite tightly regulated with only a few individuals being closely involved and hence having access to relevant information. Typically, however, especially in large organizations, a good deal of negotiation may be involved. We have already noted that institutions of post-compulsory education typically comprise both management hierarchies and representative committee structures. Budgetary negotiations, therefore, may take place bilaterally within the hierarchy between a budgeter (typically a senior manager) and various budgetees (mainly heads of department) with the budgetees themselves being kept apart and ignorant of the content of other bilateral interactions. Alternatively, budgetary decisions may be taken collectively by heads of the major departments and others in committee. Or there may be some mixture of the two.

The method chosen, however, can vary considerably, depending on the general culture of the organization and the perspective of those who control the budgetary process. If the emphasis is on departmental competition, involvement in budgeting is likely to be structured around separate negotiating relationships between each department and senior managers with the final allocations being decided and imposed by the latter. Such allocations may reflect the relative political weight of the bidders or senior managers' assessment of bids in the light of their views about organizational goals and priorities. A more consensual perspective, on the other hand, might involve more genuine participation through the establishment of committee structures which include heads or representatives of subunits in order to attempt to achieve budgetary agreements which are widely acceptable and which budgetees feel they 'own'. Again, however, consensus might emerge through political bargaining and compromise, or as a result of all participants, including key subordinates, taking an organization-wide rather than a partial view of the budgetary process. These possibilities are outlined in Figure 15.1.

A second issue concerns the ways in which the information necessary for budgetary decisions is obtained and how it is kept to manageable proportions. The most common way of doing this is 'incrementalism', an

Figure 15.1   Types of budget negotiation

		Nature of process	
		Separate centre–subordinate negotiations	Agreement by centre and subordinates in committee
Underlying assumptions of system	*Rational*	Outcome determined by objectives and priorities imposed by centre	Outcome determined by objectives and priorities agreed by participants in committee
	Political	Outcome determined by centre's perception of relative influence of subordinates	Outcome determined by relative influence of participants in committee

approach best encapsulated in Wildavsky's statement that in most organiz-ations 'the largest determining factor of the size and content of this year's budget is last year's budget' (Wildavsky, 1974, p. 13). Those responsible for producing a budget in any complex organization operate under severe constraints of time and administrative resources. To cope with these within a context where objectives are unclear or conflicting, requires the development and use of relatively simple strategems if a budget which 'works' is to be produced in the time which is available. What sorts of strategems do budget makers in fact use? Empirical studies of governmental budgeting both in Britain and the United States suggest that a number of approaches are quite common. These include (Danziger, 1978, Ch. 7):

(a) taking the previous year's levels of expenditure as *prima facie* valid, i.e. the 'base' of expenditure goes largely unchallenged from year to year so that budgetary choices arc in effect focussed on changes at the margin;
(b) focusing attention on changes from the previous year's allocation on specific items, rather than on comparisons of expenditure levels between services, i.e. little attempt is made to compare the value of expenditure between areas of activity, which are likely to have differing objectives and incommensurable outcomes;
(c) focusing on amounts of money to be spent rather than on indicators of the real levels of activity or performance in different areas; and
(d) centring analysis on concrete detail, i.e. looking at specific expenditure items rather than at broad policy alternatives or value choices.

Such budgetary approaches are probably quite as common in institutions of post-compulsory education as elsewhere. Yet they are rarely adequate when an organization is operating within a dynamic situation and perhaps faces a hostile resource environment. The narrow historical perspective which such approaches embody makes response to changing internal needs and external demands both slow and uncertain. Two alternative approaches are possible, both of which imply a movement closer to the 'rational' ideal.

One is formula budgeting which attempts to relate resource allocations to some quantified assessment of need. Such formulae typically relate resource allocations to some measure of workload, such as student numbers or taught hours, often weighted to take account of such factors as differential subject costs. Formulae are quite widely used for resource allocation in education and they are likely to be increasingly used in the future. Their use seems to increase as one moves up the resource allocation hierarchy or as one moves from small organizations to large ones: Rourke and Brookes (1966, Ch. 4) call this the 'ladder of objectivity'. The reason for this is that the use of formulae becomes more necessary as those responsible for resource allocation become more remote from the activities to be funded and hence less able to marshal the information necessary to make judgements among a wide variety of competing claims. In higher education, public-sector colleges and polytechnics have been funded largely by formula for some years; while in further education, whereas incremental funding based on historical costs seems to be the norm currently, LEAs will be required under the 1988 Education Reform Act to determine college budgets mainly by formula (for examples of the use of formulae in further education see Whitbread *et al.*, 1988). Since there is some evidence (e.g. Pratt and Gill, 1986) that the use of formulae *within* institutions often follows their use in allocating resources *to* institutions, it seems likely that formula funding within further education colleges may soon be quite common.

The second alternative to traditional, incremental budgeting rules is some kind of zero-based approach (Pyhrr, 1977; Suver and Brown, 1977), which involves the regular review of all areas of expenditure and the possibility of significant reductions, or even discontinuation, of programmes in order that others deemed to be of higher value or priority can be developed. Such an approach – potentially involving a radical departure from traditional ways of doing things – may be based primarily upon qualitative judgements or it may incorporate the use of performance indicators. The value of such indicators and the ways in which they might be developed has been an area of major debate in recent years with respect to both further education colleges (DES/Welsh Office, 1987; Theodossin, 1988) and institutions of higher education (Sizer, 1982; Cave *et al.*, 1988).

Formula and zero-based approaches to the management of budgetary information are often characterized as 'technical' (i.e. rational) budgeting approaches which can be contrasted with more 'political' approaches which involve qualitative judgements arising from negotiation. This is clearly not the case, however. Any quantification – be it a formula or a set of performance indicators – involves value judgements, and where decisions are determined by numbers it is the power to influence these which becomes important rather than the power to influence resource allocations directly. Davies and Morgan (1983) found this clearly to be the case where formulae were used in higher education.

Thus it is through the design and management of budgeting processes that the tensions between 'rational' and 'political' pressures on the budgeting are resolved.

The role of leadership in budgeting

The design of budgetary processes which can resolve the tension between the 'rational' and 'political' elements in organizational choice is not easy. For example, Fielden argues that 'quantitative/qualitative' allocation criteria and 'dictatorial/participative' decision processes are two separate spectra of budgeting systems which can be related, but not in an obvious way.

> A hurried analysis might suggest that institutions with firm, almost dictatorial leadership preferred quantitative formula-based approaches to resource allocation or that the participative style automatically ensured a qualitative bias in decision-making. Observation, however, suggests exactly the opposite. Highly participative groups find it difficult or impossible to reach consensus about the quality of competing bids and tend therefore to welcome such quantitative aids as can be accepted as fair to all. The principles of 'equal misery' and across the broad cuts typify this style. In contrast, the powerful director or vice chancellor can protect the weak departments, where he identifies some concealed potential, at the cost of a numerically better endowed department. Away from the bluster of a competitive committee room most senior academic staff will recognise the need for a leadership prepared to take difficult value judgements.
>
> (Fielden, 1982, p. 177)

Organizational leaders clearly play a central role in establishing an institution's budgetary style, and in doing this they must take account of a complex set of internal and external pressures. Internally, the 'micro-politics' of the organization are clearly critical. Two variables are important here. One will be the relative importance of the managerial hierarchy and of the 'collegial' committee system in determining how budgetary decisions are made; the other will be the degree to which power is centralized with the principal, director or vice-chancellor and his or her close colleagues or dispersed among heads of department or committees. It is difficult to generalize here, and systematic evidence is scanty. However, while there is some power dispersal in all institutions of post-compulsory education, power is probably more dispersed and less hierarchically based in universities than in colleges of further education, with polytechnics and colleges of higher education falling somewhere between the two.

Where power is dispersed, conditions favour the development of budgetary approaches which contain conflict. Incrementalist budgeting is a classic way of doing this, because its historical basis means that allocations will tend to reflect existing power structures and decisions based on 'equal benefit or misery' can be justified by collegial rhetoric. Formula-based approaches may also contain conflict because they can be justified as 'fair'; but they have the additional advantage for senior managers of providing an opportunity to 'manage unobtrusively' by using 'high-leverage minor actions to produce major effects – to let the system go where it wants to go with only minor interventions that make it go where it should' (Cohen and March, 1974, pp. 212–13). Indeed, such approaches can be quite effective in shifting the emphasis of resource allocation in the longer term while containing conflict and maintaining a relatively stable internal resource environment. Like incrementalist approaches, however, they may not enable the institution to respond adequately to the pressures of an increasingly turbulent and threatening environment.

A consideration of the implications of these pressures immediately indicates a paradox identified by Levin (1978). On the one hand, increasing resource scarcity should mean that the resource allocation process becomes more political, as Davies and Morgan (1983, pp. 164–5) suggest with respect to universities:

> One can witness in many British institutions the interplay of interest groups as a manifestation of the apparent divisiveness which contraction or expected contraction induces. For example, high cost faculties are pitted against low-cost faculties; high staff–student ratio faculties against low ones; younger faculty members against older ones; academic purists against those who are market-oriented; departments against the centre; unions against management. These tendencies are greatly exacerbated as a result of contraction, and intensified territorial defence is the result.

Yet the needs of the situation are just the opposite. At times of external threat, greater emphasis needs to be given to the development of processes of resource management which enhance the chances of organizational survival, even if this means giving less emphasis to the 'political' concern of maintaining the widest possible internal organizational coalition.

It is this paradox which provides perhaps the greatest challenge of organizational leaders. Evidence suggests that their responses will be conditioned partly by the degree of contraction and instability faced by an institution (Davies and Morgan, 1983, pp. 153–7) and partly by its culture, management style and recent experience (Pratt and Gill, 1986). In most cases, however, it is likely to mean the abandonment, at least to some degree, of the unobtrusive style and the development of budgetary processes which give a much more explicit emphasis to the 'strategic' context within which 'operational' budgeting decisions are made. Such processes will need to use rational budgeting concepts to make options more explicit, while at the same time using political strategies to build consensus around feasible budgetary outcomes. In other words, *rationality* must be built in to the budgetary process in ways which use *organizational procedures* to manage actively the *political* tensions which will almost inevitably be generated by difficult choices. This will not be easy, but it will be essential for organizational survival.

References

Audit Commission (1985). *Obtaining Better Value from Further Education*. London, HMSO.

Baldridge, J. V. (1971). *Power and Conflict in the University*. New York, Wiley.

Beyer, J. M. and Lodahl, T. M. (1976). 'A comparative study of patterns of influence in the United States and English Universities', *Administrative Science Quarterly*, 21(1), 104–29.

Birch, D. (1988). *Managing Resources in Further Education: a Handbook for College Managers*. Bristol, Further Education Staff College.

Cavanagh, D. (1983). *Power Relations in the FE College*. Department of Education Management, Sheffield City Polytechnic (Sheffield Papers in Education Management No. 33).

Cave, M., Hanney, S., Kogan, M. and Trevett, G. (1988). *The Use of Performance Indicators in Higher Education: a Critical Analysis of Developing Practice*, London, Jessica Kingsley.

Cohen, M. D. and March, J. G. (1974). *Leadership and Ambiguity: the American College President*. New York, McGraw-Hill.

Committee of Vice Chancellors and Principals (CVCP) (1985). *Report of the Steering Committee for Efficiency Studies in Universities* (The Jarratt Report). London, CVCP.

Coopers and Lybrand Associates (1988). *Local Management of Schools: a report to the Department of Education and Science*. Department of Education and Science.

Danziger, J. N. (1978). *Making Budgets*. Newbury Park, Calif., Sage.

Davies, J. L. and Morgan, A. W. (1983). 'Management of higher education institutions in a period of contraction and uncertainty', in O. Boyd-Barrett *et al.* (eds), *Approaches to Post-School Management*. London, Harper & Row.

Department of Education and Science/Welsh Office (1987). *Managing Colleges Efficiently*. London, HMSO.

Dufty, N. F. (1976). 'Some notes on resource allocation in tertiary institutions', *Journal of Educational Administration*, 14(2), 220–35.

Ebbutt, K. and Brown, R. (1978). 'The structure of power in the FE college', *Journal of Further and Higher Education*, 2(3), 3–17.

Enderud, H. (1980). 'Administrative leadership in organised anarchies', *International Journal of Institutional Management in Higher Education*, 4(3), 235–53.

Fielden, J. (1982). 'Strategies for survival', in A. Morris and J. Sizer (eds), *Resources and Higher Education*. London, Society for Research into Higher Education.

Greenwood, R., Hinings, S., Ranson, S. and Walsh, K. (1980). 'Incremental budget-
    ing and the assumption of growth: the experience of local government', in
    M. Wright (ed.), *Public Spending Decisions: Growth and Restraint in the 1970s.*
    London, Allen & Unwin.
Handy, C. (1976). *Understanding Organisations.* London, Penguin.
Hardy, C. (1988). 'The rational approach to budget cuts: one university's experience',
    Higher Education, 17, 151–73.
Hickson, D. J., Hinings, C. R., Lee, C. A., Schneck, R. E. and Pennings, J. M.
    (1971). 'A strategic contingencies theory of intraorganisational power',
    Administrative Science Quarterly, 16(2), 216–29.
Hills, F. S. and Mahoney, T. A. (1978). 'University budgets and organisational
    decision making', *Administrative Science Quarterly,* 23(3), 454–65.
Levin, C. H. (1978). 'Organisational decline and cutback management', *Public
    Administration Review,* 38(4), 316–25.
Lyden, F. J. and Miller, E. G. (1982). *Public Budgeting: Program Planning and Im-
    plementation,* 4th ed. Englewood Cliffs, NJ, Prentice-Hall.
Noble, T. and Pym, B. (1970). 'Collegial authority and the receding locus of power',
    British Journal of Sociology, 21(4), 431–45.
Pettigrew, A. (1973). *The Politics of Organisational Decision-Making.* London,
    Tavistock.
Pfeffer, J. (1977). 'Power and resource allocation in organisations', in B. M. Staw and
    G. R. Salancik (eds), *New Directions in Organisational Behaviour.* Chicago, St
    Clair Press.
Pfeffer, J. and Moore, W. L. (1980). 'Power in university budgeting: a replication and
    extension', *Administrative Science Quarterly,* 25(4), 637–53.
Pfeffer, J. and Salancik, G. R. (1974). 'Organisational decision-making as a political
    process: the case of a university budget', *Administrative Science Quarterly,* 19(2),
    135–51.
Pratt, J. and Gill, J. (1986). *Responses to Financial Constraint in Institutions of Higher
    Education in the Public Sector: a joint research report by North East London Polytechnic
    and Sheffield City Polytechnic.* London, Department of Education and Science.
Pyhrr, P. A. (1977). 'The zero-base approach to government budgeting', *Public
    Administration Review,* 37(1), 1–8.
Rourke, F. and Brookes, G. (1966). *The Managerial Revolution in Higher Education.*
    Baltimore, Johns Hopkins University Press.
Salancik, G. R. and Pfeffer, J. (1974). 'The bases and uses of power in organisational
    decision making: the case of a university', *Administrative Science Quarterly,*
    19(4), 453–73.
Sizer, J. (1982). 'Assessing institutional performance and progress', in L. Wagner
    (ed.), *Agenda for Institutional Change in Higher Education.* London, Society for
    Research into Higher Education.
Suver, J. O. and Brown, R. L. (1977). 'Where does zero-base budgeting work?',
    Harvard Business Review, 55(6), 76–84.
Theodossin, E. (1988). 'Performance indicators: theory and practice', *Coombe Lodge
    Report,* 20(1).
Tonn, J. C. (1978). 'Political behaviour in higher education budgeting', *Journal of
    Higher Education,* 49(6), 575–87.
Whitbread, D. *et al.* (1988). 'Resource allocation: formula-based budgeting models',
    Coombe Lodge Report, 20(6).

Wildavsky, A. (1968). 'Budgeting as a political process', in Sills, D. L. (ed.), *International Encyclopaedia of the Social Sciences*, Vol. 2, New York, Crowell, Collier and Macmillan.

Wildavsky, A. (1974). *The Politics of the Budgetary Process*, 2nd ed. Boston, Little, Brown and Co.

Wildavsky, A. (1978). 'A budget for all seasons? Why the traditional budget lasts', *Public Administration Review*, 38(6), 501–9.

16

The changed role of the Local Education Authority under financial delegation

Derek Esp

The Education Act of 1902 brought education into the mainstream of local government. The term local education authority (LEA) gained common currency and 315 LEAs were responsible for the public education service up to the 1944 Education Act. This major legislation reduced the number of LEAs to 147 but gave them the seamless robe of responsibility for primary, secondary and further education. The education service in England and Wales was seen as a national service locally administered. In practice local education authorities were able to expand their services and their influence on schools and colleges. The reorganization of local government in 1974 further reduced the number of LEAs to 104 in England and Wales. By that time, however, LEAs had become the driving force behind the expansion and development of the education service. They had evolved as monopoly producers of state education services.

The acceptance of the LEA as universal provider or monopoly producer remained unquestioned until the mid-1970s. The criticism that the education service had failed to maintain 'standards', a growing demand for consumer influence on education, and some widely reported allegations of 'political interference' in schools helped to provide encouragement to those who wished to question the dominant role of the LEA. 'The accuracy of the charges that linked a supposed decline in standards to the secretive and unresponsive nature of the system was questionable; but this was less important than their political effect' (McNay and Ozga, 1985, p. 237). The most enthusiastic opponents of LEA monopoly see the new reforms as a first step towards reducing the role of the LEA to 'an agency whose sole business is to transfer funds so that no pupil is without a school place' (Lawlor, 1988, p. 5).

The changes brought about by the Education Reform Act 1988 reflect philosof .1y which is sceptical of medium- or large-scale planning in the public sector. It is assumed that improved standards in schools and a responsive education service will only be achieved through consumer choice in the market-place. The LEAs' monopoly of the public education service is broken by the creation of grant maintained schools and city technology colleges (CTC). LEAs lose power to central government with the creation of a National Curriculum and schools have delegation of financial and other managerial decisions which release them from detailed day-by-day LEA control. Many people see these new measures as a threat to the traditional monopoly producer role of the LEA. It is necessary therefore to consider the development of local financial management (LFM) as a major strategy for shifting power from the LEA to the consumer and from a single monopoly producer to a number of individual institutions providing 'choice' to the consumer.

Local management of schools (LMS) is intended, to have considerable beneficial effects in terms of improving educational standards and providing value for money in terms of the efficient, effective and economic use of resources at the level of the individual institution. It is too early to know whether or not the LMS initiative will achieve the desired results. Some pointers to future developments are to be found in the pilot schemes developed by some LEAs prior to 1988.

An early initiative in local financial management

The Lincolnshire pilot project on delegation which began in 1982 provided valuable experience and some insights into the problems inherent in the implementation of a scheme of delegation. It was clear that the headteachers involved welcomed the greater flexibility to shift resources and make changes. This pilot project developed during a period of financial constraint, however, and some LEA officers feared the consequences of delegation in terms of reducing the influence and the manpower of the LEA. By the time that the county initiated its full LMS scheme in 1987 a number of lessons had been learnt. The whole of the LEA administration, not only the education department, had to be involved in making the necessary changes which would assist schools and colleges with delegated budgets. The arrival of LMS required the establishment of a clear mission statement and set of objectives, changes in the rules (e.g. standing orders and financial regulations), and the constructive involvement of members and officers in all departments. Successful delegation to schools had to be accompanied by a willingness to delegate and a revision of procedures and rules so that they helped rather than hindered the head and governors in the exercise of their duties. The 'climate' was favourable in this LEA with regard to the impending changes because of their willingness to adapt to a new non-monopolistic role. The majority group in the county council, already prepared to move ahead of legislation, had exposed various services to competition, and had begun to develop QTUs (quasi-trading units) that were competing successfully as providers of services. In education they were willing not to oppose applications for grant maintained school status.

The Lincolnshire experience was echoed by the Audit Commission (1988, p. 2):

> These changes will present enormous challenges to all LEAs . . . what is now envisaged is an order of magnitude beyond what has been accomplished hitherto. Moreover the challenges will raise issues for the whole authority, not only the education department. And perhaps most importantly, it will test the management skills of governors and head teachers to the full.

An LEA which is philosophically 'in tune' with the new climate will be prepared to change its role and relationships with schools and to provide support to relatively autonomous schools. An LEA which wishes to preserve its monopoly producer role will find many of the necessary changes unpalatable and may have difficulty in adapting successfully. It is important to look in more detail at certain aspects of the LEA's new role to see the magnitude of the changes required and the difficulties facing an LEA resistant to change.

The impact of LMS on the role of the LEA

Coopers & Lybrand (1988) tried to describe the changes facing LEAs. The LEA would relinquish direct and detailed control and would focus on issues of major importance. In order to make the local management of schools (LMS) work effectively the LEA would need to set a framework within which the schools operate; devise the method by which resources are to be allocated within the framework; determine the total level of resources and support to be made available to schools; monitor schools' performance and provide accountability for the effective use of public funds. The LEA would also have to operate sanctions if necessary. Each of these elements is now examined more closely.

Setting the framework for delegation

As at present the LEA will need to decide on the overall structure of provision such as patterns of school organization and numbers of schools to be maintained. This strategic role is bound to be made more difficult with the emergence of grant maintained schools and city technology colleges and by more open enrolment. The weakening of the LEA planning role may not be cost-effective because the provision of choice may imply an excess of school places and place considerable burdens on LEA budgets.

A second strategic role for the LEA will be the provision of aims and objectives for schools in the context of the National Curriculum. The LEA will be in a position to offer advice on curriculum policies but it will not be possible for it to impose a particular curriculum staffing policy. Such a policy may inform the guidelines for the formula budget but the school will make its own decisions on matters such as the total number of teachers to be employed. All this presents further difficulties for the LEA budget makers. Also, under the terms of the 1988 Act the LEA will not be able to withhold sufficient reserves for schools in difficulty.

The LEA will also have to establish clear guidelines on its expectations in terms of educational outcomes and budget limits. The school and the LEA will require commonly accepted performance indicators providing an objective assessment of educational achievement and value for money. It is essential that there is a clear understanding of what schools are expected to achieve. Whether governors or the local community choose to comply with LEA policies will depend in part on the ability of the LEA to undertake effective consultations with the schools and the communities they serve. Coopers & Lybrand (1988) see the setting of aims and objectives as an interactive process between the schools and the LEA with the schools taking the initial lead. Not all LEAs will be happy to accept a lead from the schools and a reactive rather than proactive role.

Finally the LEA will have to specify the procedures governing the relationship between the LEA and its schools, i.e. definition of powers and responsibilities of heads and governors; accounting arrangements and financial regulations; reporting arrangements and personnel procedures. These detailed guidelines will have to reflect the new relationship between the LEA and the school and many administrators and elected members will have to change their traditional approaches if the new rules are to work constructively.

Devising the method by which resources are to be allocated

The secretary of state's requirements for delegation schemes impinge on the LEA's traditional financial responsibilities. The secretary of state will agree the basis for determining the budget shares of each of the LEA's maintained county and voluntary schools, i.e. its 'formula'. The LEA will be expected to retain the absolute minimum of budgets centrally, moneys saved by a school will accrue to the school and the LEA will not be able to change the level of the delegated budget during the financial year. LEA elected members (councillors) will find it difficult to adapt to this new relationship with schools. They will still be resposible in law for the overall budget but will have to stand back from day-to-day involvement in resource allocation. An area of particular difficulty is presented by the services of the LEA offered to the public through the use of school premises. This is likely to be a contentious issue. Schools will wish to maximize income from school lettings and the LEA may find it increasingly difficult to retain central control in terms of protecting equality of treatment for community education, adult education and the youth service. Those services themselves are likely to move into net budgeting and delegated budgets of their own and may begin to negotiate their own contracts with individual schools.

There is a greater potential threat to the powers of the LEA in the insistence on pupil numbers (weighted) as the main element in the formula. Some see this as a means of introducing a voucher system in order to strengthen the application of market forces and consumer choice and thereby virtually destroying the planning role of the LEA.

Determining the total level of resources and support to be made available to schools

The new relationship with educational establishments will encourage school governors to be proactive in trying to influence the level of resources an LEA puts into education. Governors will be armed with the views of parents through the statutory Annual Meeting with parents (1986 Education Act) and will have detailed data with which to argue the school's case. It may not be too long before governing bodies begin to combine their efforts in order to 'lobby' the LEA. The LEA members may find themselves boxed in by the secretary of state's increased use of Education Support Grants and the LEA Training Grant Scheme to direct priority spending areas, expenditure limits on local authorities set by the Department of the Environment and well-argued and well-orchestrated demands for increased funding coming from governors and parents.

Monitoring educational standards and value for money

Delegation will require an effective means of monitoring compliance with the National Curriculum and educational standards. The LEA will also be the guardian of public funds and their efficient and effective use. The educational and financial aspects of monitoring have been dealt with separately in most LEAs hitherto. Internal Auditors and Education Advisers and Inspectors have acted independently of each other. If delegation is to achieve the desired ends of raising educational standards and applying funds efficiently and effectively to the achievement of educational objectives the LEA has to reshape its monitoring services. It has to 'get its act together' so that educational and financial issues are considered together. This will require a fundamental restructuring of traditional administrative structures.

Applying sanctions

Within statutory limits the LEA will provide the 'rules of the game' for schools with delegated budgets. 'Governing bodies and head teachers will be expected to manage their own schools with due propriety and efficiency. If they do not, they must expect the LEA to act: i.e. to give advice, issue warnings and take direct remedial action as appropriate' (7/88 para. 173). Direct remedial action will include the LEA's ability to charge the delegated school budget with costs arising from a breach of the provisions of a scheme. As a last resort, the sanction of withdrawal of delegation will be available to the LEA where schools are mismanaging their budgets or failing to meet the requirements of the scheme. However, the secretary of state has the last word because there is provision for the governing body to appeal to him where an LEA withdraws delegated powers.

The LEA monitoring of the curriculum also carries sanctions. An LEA can consider withdrawal of delegation where a school fails substantially or persistently to comply with the National Curriculum. The emphasis is on national rather than LEA requirements. Again, the secretary of state has the last word on appeal. His decisions could have budgetary implications outside the control of LEA elected representatives.

The total impact of delegation on the LEA

The emphasis on strategic planning and monitoring could help LEAs to focus on major strategic issues. But the impact of the legislation on parents, governors and heads may bring new pressures which will shape the future role of LEAs. Parents will have clear guidelines and attainment targets for what children should achieve at school. Parent participation on governing bodies and at the Annual Meeting where governors and parents review the school's performance and problems may well result in informed and well-documented demands for more LEA financial support. As the lion's share of the delegated budget is related to pupil numbers this will tempt governors and heads to admit pupils by all possible means, with pressure on the LEA to provide extra buildings.

The provision for opting out of LEA control should encourage LEAs to prepare schemes of delegation that give maximum flexibility to schools. The grant maintained school option also provides parents and governors with a means of putting pressure on an LEA when it is unwilling to provide flexibility or to meet demands for extra resources. The first schools to seek grant maintained school status are doing so because they are threatened with closure or because they have fallen out with the LEA over other matters – e.g. selection procedures. If a substantial number of schools opt out within a local authority area the role of the LEA will be significantly diminished.

A further influence on the role of the LEA arises from the provisions of the Local Government Act 1988. The Act requires LEAs to submit certain defined activities to competitive tendering before they carry out work themselves, either in a functional or agency capacity. The areas defined in the Act are the cleaning of buildings, school catering, grounds maintenance and repair and maintenance of vehicles. Section 2(3) of the Act empowers the

Secretary of State for the Environment to add further activities to the competitive tendering list. The LEAs that have already experimented with competitive tendering find that it creates demands for competitive tendering in new areas of activity. It is certain that schools and colleges with delegated budgets will develop the skills of shopping around for services. If LEAs do not respond effectively to the challenges and opportunities of competitive tendering their direct work with schools will be further diminished. The LEAs will find themselves in competition with other alternative 'producers'. Commercial consultants, higher education institutions and LEAs themselves will be in competition with each other. Already the chief education officer of one London LEA has declared that his college of education is out to secure business wherever it may be found. Educators who begin to run successful trading units for their LEAs may find themselves 'head-hunted' by private firms wishing to expand business among the numerous relatively autonomous LEA schools and colleges, the grant maintained schools and the CTCs. Some schools may be tempted to sell their own services to other schools. Even now it is estimated that there are some 300 to 500 potential providers of in-service training in England and Wales who will be in competition with each other.

Whether or not LEAs welcome their new role it seems almost inevitable that they will be unable to remain as monopoly producers. The impact of financial delegation, the broader legislative changes and the underlying philosophy of consumer choice and the attempt to raise standards through the operation of the market-place will push the LEAs in the direction of their new role as providers, organizers and enablers in the competitive market. LEAs will be arranging contracts for schools, acting as direct contractors, and/or setting standard requirements for others who will produce the services to schools. Schools, further education and higher education sectors will be 'buying' and 'selling' services. Whatever structures are laid down in the Education Reform Act, groups of schools may begin to build up their own 'in-house' arrangements for administrative and educational support services, thus further eroding the services provided directly by the LEA.

In this new context it is possible for LEAs to change their approach and to survive, albeit as agents of central government and providers of services in competition with others. It is difficult to see how LEAs can resist these changes without being declared obstructive and redundant in the new market economy. The financial responsibilities of elected members of LEAs will be increasingly difficult to exercise. It remains to be seen whether or not budding politicians will seek experience at the level of the institution where they can influence spending decisions rather than at LEA level where it may be increasingly difficult to hold the financial ring between the Department of the Environment, a proactive Department of Education and Science, and increasingly independent establishments that, with public backing, insist on having more than their fair share of a finite LEA budget.

The future 'shape' of LEA administration

LEAs are reviewing and revising their administrative structures. The emphasis on strategic planning and the monitoring of educational and financial outputs require considerable changes in staffing requirements. Fewer people will be employed in administration at LEA level. Many clerical and routine administrative jobs will go, as will some personnel posts. There will be a need for more inspector posts and for people able to give advice to institutions on financial, personnel and legal matters. LEAs will use information technology to gain access to information held in schools and colleges. Some LEAs will retain a divisional or area office structure but with a move away from detailed administration and control of schools towards monitoring, support and advice.

The required changes in attitudes and expectations, as well as in administrative procedures cannot come about without investment in training of LEA officers, elected members, heads and governors.

The 'new model LEAs' are likely to develop

- a delegation scheme which gives the fullest possible delegation of the budget to schools and colleges;
- a flexible support service providing advice on legal, financial, personnel and curricular matters. Most or all of these services will be on offer in competition with other providers.
- a flexible workforce of inspectors and administrators, possibly using short-term contracts and secondments.

These changes present a challenge to LEA officers and elected members. There is an opportunity for the traditional separate career pyramids to merge as people pursue promotion in schools, colleges and LEA offices in a more flexible career structure. Elected members will have a more difficult adjustment to make as they find themselves distanced from their former links with schools and colleges. The development of a satisfying and effective strategic role for elected members will be essential if local education authorities are to recruit councillors of sufficient calibre. The achievement of an effective role for councillors may hold the key to the survival of LEAs as an important part of 'a national service locally administered'.

The future role of the LEAs is not theirs to secure in the last analysis. If a substantial number of schools decide to become grant maintained it will be necessary to consider the position of the LEA again. Whatever happens, the schools will need some immediate source of help and advice. If the LEAs are not there to provide it, alternative support systems will have to be created. One option is a national education service which excludes the local authorities from significant involvement.

References

Audit Commission (1988). *Delegation of Management Authority to Schools.* Occasional Paper No. 5, London, HMSO.
Coopers & Lybrand (1988). *Local Management of Schools: a Report to the DES.* London. HMSO.
DES (1988). *Education Reform Act: Local Management of Schools.* Circular 7/88.
Lawlor, S. (1988). *Away with LEAs.* London, Centre for Policy Studies.
McNay, I. and Ozga, J. (1985). Perspectives on policy, in *Policy Making in Education: The Breakdown of Consensus.* Oxford, Pergamon.

17
Local financial management and school effectiveness

Pamela Young

Introduction

This chapter is concerned with financial delegation in the context of school effectiveness, or improvement as it is more commonly known internationally (International School Improvement Project ISIP 1982–1986, reported by van Velzen *et al.* (1985)). There is a brief examination of the government's thoughts about effectiveness and a consideration of the concept popularly called 'effective schools'. What is known about school effectiveness is then reviewed for its contribution to implementing local financial management in schools.

The government's view of effectiveness

The government believes that local financial management (LFM) will improve the quality of learning and teaching in our schools. 'Quality' here means that pupils progress with their reading, mathematics, writing and so on, and do well on associated tests of achievement. There would appear to be less certainty as to whether it applies to other outcomes as well, such as thinking skills, self-esteem, vocational decision making and so on. The government also believes that:

> Effective schemes of local management will enable governing bodies and headteachers to plan their use of resources – including their most valuable resource, their staff – to maximum effect in accordance with their own needs and priorities, and to make schools more responsive to their clients – parents, pupils, the local community and employers.
>
> (Circular 7/88, para. 9)

The basis for belief in effectiveness through financial delegation is largely deduced from theoretical arguments and inferences about responsiveness to client need that originate in decentralized budgeting and management in other sectors of the economy. It may also owe something to the widespread popularity of Peters and Waterman's (1982) book, *In Search of Excellence*, which identified certain characteristics found in successful companies that were capable of reproduction in other settings: keep close to the customer; promulgate clear values and seek active leadership; keep to the centre only that which is necessary; delegate, trust and develop others; maintain a bias for action; stick to what we are best at; experiment selectively and in small steps. As noted later on in this chapter, these characteristics are not dissimilar from those identified by school–effectiveness researchers in the 1970s and confirmed in more recent work. This belief in effectiveness through delegation has not so far been tested, except in a limited way, in any area of social endeavour like education, health, or criminal justice in the UK. Now both education and health are to embark upon a scale of delegation not hitherto experienced. There is, of course, information from a number of LEAs and their schools with pilot or limited cost-centred schemes. These are discussed in chapters 5, 7 and 16 but none of the schools so far have had such an extensive scheme before, for legal reasons as much as anything else.

There are two elements in the government's belief that local financial management will provide effective schools. The first is the principle that those actively engaged in delivering the service to the client are in the best position to decide how resources can be efficiently and effectively utilized. The second relies upon creating a competitive environment for schools. The government contends that self-governing, self-managing budget centres are obliged to respond to the 'market' if they want to survive. It is the 'market' which will be the mechanism for raising standards (effectiveness) and promoting change in the maintained schools. The consumers in the 'market' are parents with school-age children; they have most to gain by efforts to improve the way in which the day-to-day work of schools is carried out.

In suggesting that the school should be the focal point for promoting effectiveness, the government is at one with those who work in the school-effectiveness domain. Both broadly share the ISIP (van Velzen *et al.*, 1985, p. 53) definition of school effectiveness as 'accomplishing the best possible pupil outcomes (defined in both individual and societal terms), with as little wastage of pupil talent as possible and with efficient use of means'. What is missing from the school-effectiveness work so far is a rigorous examination of the effects of varying the quantities of resources between competing objectives. In all fairness to the work there was no opportunity to do this, since most of the work has looked at resources such as salary costs of teaching and non-teaching personnel, day-to-day premises costs, books, equipment and other goods and services as subject to outside control, which limited not only the quantity of individual resources but also the ability of schools to vire between items. What we do have in the school-effectiveness literature, however, are suggestions for structures and strategies that could prove useful.

School effectiveness

The concept popularly labelled 'effective schools' has emerged as a major element of a vision of better schools where all pupils achieve reasonable proficiency in certain basic skills. It has a positive and optimistic outlook about education and its outcomes; in other words, schools matter and are capable of improvement. The word 'improvement' is frequently used instead of effectiveness, notably in North America and more recently in international research. Whichever word is used (and there are some distinctions to be drawn on occasions), both involve notions of achieving 'quality in education' and the 'management of planned change' to achieve quality, effectiveness, or improvement in a process to be worked at continuously and not seen as a single, one-off event. Much of the research, both in the UK and elsewhere, has been prompted by an interest in solving some identified problem like poor learning performance in the classroom, truancy, misbehaviour, or other issues associated with effective learning outcomes. The theoretical approaches adopted in the work have tended to be interdisciplinary; this has resulted in a variety of contributions to our knowledge about school effects and what might be done about them. Although some of the work has been of an interdisciplinary nature, discussions about it as a topic are usually found in the 'school as an organization' paradigm dealt with in Bush (1989), on theories of management in education.

The early studies (mostly American) in the 1960s and 1970s sought out schools that seemed to do better than expected on some schooling criteria. It was noted that such schools tended to have strong and positive leadership; clear goals and a sense of 'mission'; an emphasis on teaching the basic skills; a climate for learning; and a high expectation of achievement on the part of pupils. These findings have much in common with those of Peters and Waterman (1982) cited earlier in this chapter. Later work has confirmed the characteristics and suggested some refinements of some of them, but they are basically the same. What a list of characteristics like this does not tell us is how they might be replicated in other schools. It is not enough to exhort all those concerned to emulate those schools as some commentators have suggested, without making practical suggestions about what might be tried by way of structures and strategies in order to influence the process of school effectiveness; the later work on school effectiveness is much more helpful in this respect (e.g. Rutter *et al.*, 1979; ISIP (van Velzen *et al.*) 1982–6; Mortimore *et al.*, 1988; HMI Scotland 1988; Caldwell and Spinks, 1988). However, before addressing these indicators for school effectiveness, it is as well to consider some of the 'health warnings' for school effectiveness: it can take three to five years before a significant improvement has taken root in an individual school; several changes of differing importance may be going on at the same time; there are phases within the period – initiation, implementation, institutionalization – which cannot be ignored; the people participating in the process need shared beliefs, learning time and a collegial style of decision making; and a system of self-analysis. To ignore any or all of them would seriously impair efforts to achieve an effective school.

Implications for local financial management

There can be no doubt that LMS will give schools both greater scope and greater incentives for developing their own 'school-improvement programmes' than envisaged in the school-effectiveness research to date. There is no need to 'rediscover the wheel' here but to learn from the empirical work so far and to adapt the findings to local circumstances. Many schools will have already discovered for themselves the importance of the 'health warnings' of the ISIP project and will take heed of them when approaching financial delegation.

The following indicators are suggested for consideration in the context of LMS:

1 An analysis of the impact of the surrounding environment on policies directed at influencing school effects.
2 A clear conceptual scheme about what school effects are desired over differing time scales (immediately; in the coming academic year; next year; and subsequent years). This has a great deal to do with a school's management plan with regard to the National Curriculum in the context of the LEA's strategic plan.
3 What supporting structures will be installed is every bit as important: What kinds of committees are to be established? Who will have membership? What will be their powers? What are some of the questions to be addressed? (See Downes, 1988, for headteacher descriptions of such structural matters.)
4 An analysis of the policy, the strategic choices (the costs and benefits that may accrue) to be made, and the operational plan that is to be followed.

1   The environment

Schools, like any other organization, exist in a specific, physical, cultural and social environment to which they must adapt. An understanding of the past conditions of that environment cannot comfortably be ignored (by the government or others) for examining the present and future shape of financial delegation to schools. For example, a number of LEAs have in the past exercised a light-handed, non-directive style towards curriculum planning and delivery but a tight control over financial matters with only limited discretion. The light-handed or 'loose' control is observable in an authority's emphasis upon advice rather than inspection by its advisory team, and a collegial-style relationship between advisers and the teachers in the schools. The Act (DES, 1988, paras 152–5) requires LEAs to have a much stronger role in promoting the National Curriculum and ensuring that the school provides 'quality' education. Thus, monitoring the performance of schools, the giving of advice, and the taking of corrective action if necessary, means much greater prominence be given to inspection than many LEAs and their schools have been accustomed to. Both parties will need to examine the environment in which they work and to consider carefully how it is likely to change, and assess what new structures and strategies are required in order to promote school effectiveness.

2   A conceptual scheme for school effects

Where the LEA in the past has determined the policy goals for its schools, it is no longer able to do so in quite the same way. It has, for example, been able to meet the needs of smaller schools in the light of changing circumstances by movements of funds between schools as necessary without the kind of needs assessment now required by the Education Act 1988. Financial control has passed to the school with the exception of the marginal funding derived from the specific grants and those items which are discretionary, like provision for special needs, on the government's prescription that this does not exceed the 10 per cent maximum – to go down to 7 per cent within three years. This change will require those schools which have tended to be reactive, rather than proactive, in a situation where the goals and the means of achieving those goals have been determined by the LEA, to change radically not only the ways in which they allocate those resources over which they have had discretion but to establish new procedures for dealing with the full range of delegated resources.

Some well-documented LEAs, and others not reported in the media, have taken the opportunities provided by the legislation, Education Act 1944, and the more recent Education Act 1986 (No. 2 section 29), to introduce financial delegation schemes of their own. The number of LEAs has steadily grown since 1986, but others are not disposed to think about delegation even now despite the legislation (Audit Commission, 1988). None of the schemes currently in place in the LEAs, according to the Audit Commission, go far enough to meet the legislation's requirements. Whatever stage an LEA is at, all parties concerned with LFM are faced in the next one or two years with decisions which not only significantly change their duties, but also the environment in which both exist. What, for example, will be the impact of open enrolment on a school where in future each child will have a 'package' of money attached to him or her that goes with them to the school they attend? Large shifts in such 'packages' could have significant implications for medium-term planning of resources to achieve positive school effects.

3   *Supporting structures*

The questions that are set out above cannot be answered here by specific reference to the school-effectiveness literature except to say that there is considerable evidence to suggest keeping aims and goals steadily in mind; and ensuring that they are communicated through structures and strategies of the kind described by the various practitioners contributing to Downes's (1988) book on financial delegation. They suggest collegial decision making to ensure active debate, discussion and action plans that are responsive to clearly identified needs. Schools will certainly require rules and procedures for regulating their own affairs in the form of standing orders and financial regulations supported by a handbook or manual dealing with detailed procedures. Schools cannot be forced to adopt an LEA model – but may be required to adhere to conditions under Section 39(12) of the Education Act 1988 (e.g. conduct of meetings and decision-making procedures for the governing body). Whatever is established, the school-effectiveness findings indicate that they must be responsive to identified needs within a clear conceptual scheme embodied in the school-management plan and known to all concerned. This approach will also ensure that the specific requirement that all schools supply the Chief Education Officer with an itemized budget statement together with an overall month-by-month profile of planned expenditure in advance of the start of the LEA's financial – rather than school academic – year can be matched with actual expenditure as the year progresses to see whether some at least of the short-term desired effects are being resourced according to the school's plan.

4   *Strategic choices*

Some headteachers and their governing bodies view the prospect of financial delegation with relish. The opportunity to determine teacher numbers without, as they see it, the heavy hand of the LEA resting on the financial tiller, and to deploy resources as they think fit, represents a welcome challenge. However, not all headteachers have reacted in the same way. Some see the requirement to manage resources themselves as an onerous task that will get in the way of what they think of as their most important job – that of planning the curriculum and ensuring its delivery. If, however, they see that the achievement of these desired school effects can be more closely monitored by themselves than hitherto, a different climate may be created. The idea of cost-effectiveness, for example, could take on a new meaning. Cost-effectiveness is one of a broad set of cost analysis techniques used as a way of choosing between competing alternatives to produce a stated educational outcome. We tend for the most part to consider only the financial cost of a decision on, say, purchasing additional teaching hours, rather than including a costing of the effects of alternatives. Some school headteachers already practice cost-effectiveness of a kind but do not necessarily give a monetary quantification to the resource. For example, a number of small primary schools might wish to extend their curriculum, but be unable to do so alone because of limited resources. Instead, they form a cluster in order to share teaching and curriculum experiences with a longer-term objective of developing the kind of networks advocated by school-effectiveness researchers for the attainment of identified outcomes. This will be in exchange for known costed teacher time spent in developing the links. Something similar could be done to assist an educational decision to add or subtract from a range of GCSE options. A cost analysis is more likely to yield the types of information that are crucial to such educational judgements than when costs are ignored. At this stage of LMS there are few examples that can be cited of the kind that can be drawn from the school-effectiveness literature. Much more is likely to be forthcoming in the years to come to enable one to say with confidence that a particular support structure or resource usage contributed in an identifiable way to a targeted school effect.

Very little has been said in this chapter about leadership, but it is covered in Riches and Morgan (1989). This and the school-effectiveness material highlight the importance of leadership for positive school effects – visioning, managing the complexity we call a school, designing structures and procedures which promote a collegial culture, are all seen as significant. In the accounts in books like that of Downes (1988) there is ample evidence to support the prominence given to effective leadership. Once LMS is in operation we are likely to see much more evidence not only from the headteacher perspective but from other participants in this new enterprise.

References

Audit Commission (1988). *Delegation of Management Authority to Schools.* Occasional Paper No. 5. London, HMSO.

Beare, H. *et al.* (1989). *Creating an Excellent School.* London, Routledge.

Bush, T. (ed.) (1989). *Management in Education: Theory and Practice.* Milton Keynes, Open University Press.

Caldwell, B. and Spinks, J. (1988). *The Self-Managing School.* London, Falmer Press.

Downes, P. (ed.) (1988). *Local Financial Management of Schools.* Oxford, Basil Blackwell.

Department of Education and Science (1988). *Education Reform Act: Local Management of Schools.* Circular 7/88 DES.

HMI Scotland (1988). *Effective Secondary Schools.* HMSO. Scotland.

Mortimore, P. *et al.* (1988). *School Matters: the Junior Years,* Wells, Somerset, Open Books.

Peters, T. and Waterman, R. (1982). *In Search of Excellence*, New York, Harper & Row.

Riches, C. and Morgan, C. (1989). *Human Resource Development in Education*. Milton Keynes, Open University Press.

Rutter, R. *et al*. (1979). *Fifteen Thousand Hours*. Harvard University Press, Cambridge, Mass.

van Velzen, W. G., Miles, M. B., Ekholm, M., Hameyer, U. and Robin, D. (eds) (1985). *Making School Improvement Work: a Conceptual Guide to Practice*, Leuven/ Amersfoort, ACCO.

Section IV

Performance evaluation

18

Performance evaluation and performance indicators for schools

Geoffrey Hulme

Who needs performance evaluation and for what?

Performance evaluation is assessment of how well an organization or an individual is doing – usually in relation to what they themselves are trying to do – on their own initiative and in response to what others expect of them. Ideally, this is expressed in terms of specific aims and objectives or, where these cannot be precisely defined, in terms of the directions in which the organization or individual is seeking to make progress. Good evaluation improves motivation by giving a sense of achievement over what is being done well, and helping to identify where there is room for improvement and problems to be tackled. It can also help in formulating future objectives and plans to meet them.

The most important evaluation is often self-evaluation, which can be assisted by formal or informal peer review or by management-led appraisal schemes. For a school this means governing bodies, heads and staff periodically evaluating its performance, identifying comparative strengths and weaknesses, and working out how they can build on the one and correct or reduce the other.

Evaluation and monitoring of performance, leading where necessary to corrective action, have long been recognized as essential elements of management control and hence of good management. In recent years there has been increased emphasis on what Peters and Waterman (1982) have called the 'loose–tight approach', in which a minimum of key aspects of performance are tightly controlled and the rest is left to local managers and their staff. Where this approach is adopted, the emphasis of central management is likely to be on assessing overall progress and ensuring that there is local commitment to evaluating and improving performance while leaving the detailed measures to local decision. Peters and Waterman found that 'the excellent companies are measurement happy and performance oriented, the toughness is borne of mutually high expectation and peer review rather than from table-pounding managers and complicated control systems'.

This approach is easier to apply in organizations which have market tests of sales value and profit but the principle of whether local management is subject to market discipline is being increasingly applied and adapted to the public sector. There are signs of this management approach in the DES guidelines on local management in schools, which emphasize the role of performance indicators while leaving choice of indicators to the judgement of schools and LEAs (Circular 7/88).

Evaluation is also an important part of the public accountability which is increasingly required from people who use public money. The future chain of formal accountability will be from teachers to heads to governing bodies and selectively to local education authorities and more selectively to the DES. There will also be increased informal accountability to parents and prospective parents who will have increased power individually to choose schools and collectively to choose systems and management (local-authority or opted-out).

There is potential conflict between the different kinds of evaluation and the information required for these different purposes. For example, people evaluating the work of the school from inside or from outside may assume different objectives and hence use different criteria for evaluating performance, as illustrated in Figure 18.1.

Figure 18.1

A = objectives of political authorities (government and LEA)
B = objectives of school management and staff
C = objectives/criteria against which performance is evaluated

It is the responsibility of political leadership and local management to ensure that there are agreed objectives as a framework for evaluation as in Figure 18.2 which illustrates what is intended under the local management in schools system.

Figure 18.2

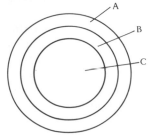

A = total teacher activity including activity left to individual teacher discretion
B = activity to be evaluated against objectives set by local school management (governing bodies, advised by and working through heads); these include
C = objectives of national and LEA policies

If some of the agreed objectives are not mutually consistent, local school management may have to judge the balance to be struck. School and individual self-evaluation require frank discussion of possible weaknesses of a kind that would be damaging if made available as part of the accountability process (e.g. through adverse effects on staff morale and parent and pupil confidence). A point may come when weaknesses are so serious that critical evaluations need to be published as part of proper accountability but in reports on schools, as in company reports, there will be legitimate scope for judicious selection and careful but accurate presentation of the information made publicly available.

Doubts about evaluation

There are a number of reasons for doubts about evaluation. There may be professional defensiveness in response to external criticism. This is common in many professions but is increasingly coming under public challenge from outside and being replaced by more positive attitudes (cf. the growing acceptance in medicine in recent years of medical audit and peer review). There may also be lack of confidence, either fear of being found not to be doing as good a job as one had thought or anxiety that one is not doing a good job and that this will be exposed. Such lack of confidence is likely to be well founded in no more that a minority (probably small minority) of schools and individuals and, where it is justified, there is a strong case for evaluation to assess where improvement can be made. Finally, there is better-founded concern about the technical difficulties and costs of measuring effectiveness and efficiency of activities as complex as education. The available measures are likely to remain imperfect indicators rather than precise guides to performance. Usually they will need to be backed by more subjective judgements and can themselves usefully back and supplement such judgements. Where there are discrepancies they can point to areas where closer examination is needed. Cost needs to be carefully watched in relation to the potential benefits but information technology is increasingly making it possible to manage complex data at acceptable cost.

Benchmarks for evaluation

Operational evaluation requires *benchmarks* against which to compare performance. In tightly managed organizations with established systems, the main benchmark is likely to be that of agreed goals and targets derived from broader aims and objectives. In complex fields such as education it may not always be possible to set precise objectives particularly in the early days of new management systems and the initial benchmark for comparison may be the previous year's performance or the performance of other organizations. One or more years of information on performance may be necessary before realistic objectives and targets can be set.

Framework of analysis

It helps to get to grips with the issues involved in evaluation to see the school or college as forming a *system* of interrelated elements comprising:

- *inputs*, which can be subdivided into *controlled inputs*, i.e. the resources (money, staff, and non-staff cost items) which are (within limits) controlled by education management at different levels (national, local and school), and *non-controlled inputs* basically pupils with different levels of attainment and different family and socio-economic background. These factors are not controlled by education management though it may be possible to influence them (e.g. a school's performance may influence the size and mix of its pupil intake);
- *processes*, educational activities which can be analysed in different ways but include teaching of the curriculum, extra-curricular activities and communication of attitudes and values;
- *outputs*, i.e. results and achievements, which can be subdivided into *intermediate outputs*, e.g. pupils taught English or maths to a given standard, pupils with social skills or physical accomplishments developed at school and *final or near-final outputs or outcomes*, e.g. pupils progressing to higher or further education or to take up employment and applying skills, knowledge, values acquired at school; or, as a final outcome, people developing and taking advantage of life opportunities to an extent that is influenced by their education in school (clearly as one moves along the continuum from intermediate outputs to final or near-final outcomes it becomes more difficult to disentangle the influence of the school from other influences on the individual's life).

Analysis of this kind is called by economists 'production function analysis', but this does not imply that schools have to be equated with factories or supermarkets, nor does it imply simple mechanistic systems. Analysis must and can be adapted to the complexity of the systems and there can in practice be limits to the extent to which quantified analytical techniques can be applied. Numerical measures often need to be combined with softer qualitative judgements. The scope for numerical measurement is limited by what can be made available at acceptable cost and it is often necessary to accept approximate measures (sometimes called proxy measures) which are judged to give a good enough indication of the characteristic at issue.

Design of performance indicators

Because of the difficulties of precise measurement, particularly of service outputs, it is usual to talk of 'performance indicators'. The term 'indicator' was defined by the US State Education Assessment Center as:

a measure that conveys a general impression of the state or nature of the . . . system being examined. While it is not necessarily a precise statement, it gives sufficient indication of a condition . . . of interest to be of use in formulating policy . . . optimally, an indicator combines information on conceptually related variables so that the number of indicators needed to describe the system of concern can be kept reasonably small.

(Blank, 1986, p. 5)

The LMS Initiative (CIPFA, 1988b, pp. 5–7) guide says:

By themselves performance indicators cannot give a full picture of the operation of a school. Rather they give advance warning of areas where management attention may be required; they can also give some indication of how well the school is proceeding towards its objectives.

Management literature suggests a number of desirable objectives to be met in developing performance indicators, including:

(i) relevance to the agreed objectives and management needs of the organization;
(ii) to be as simple and as few as possible consistent with their purpose;
(iii) to be acceptable and credible;
(iv) to be a useful signpost to areas where the questions can and should be asked;
(v) Comparability between organizations similar enough to be able to learn from each other and with national/local standards (which requires indicators to be specific, quantifiable and standardized);
(vi) to be of acceptable cost in relation to the likely benefits (which points to ease of collection and monitoring of the relevant data).

These objectives tend to conflict (for example, concentrating on a few indicators relevant to a school's current management needs, (i) and (ii), may give too partial a picture to be acceptable or credible, (iii), and may fail to identify areas where questions could usefully be asked, (iii) and (iv), and may impede inter-school comparisons, (v). Schools (guided by LEAs and the DES) will need to strike a practical balance between them. A possible approach after a period of local experimentation would be to develop a small set of core indicators which would be standardized nationally for comparison between authorities; there might be a larger set of indicators that are standardized locally and the rest would vary between schools.

Types of indicator

Indicators can be classified by reference to the input–process–output model outlined above, and in particular it is likely to be useful to distinguish between input/process indicators and indicators of output and outcome.

A distinction is often also frequently drawn between quantitative and qualitative indicators, though the distinction is not a hard and fast one. Quantified measures may also give an indication of quality.

In its review of performance indicators in schools (*Performance Indicators in Schools: a Contribution to the Debate*), CIPFA has analysed aspects of the school system which might be the subject of performance indicators under a number of broad management headings (management of staff and the quality of teaching; management of the quality of learning and the curriculum; pastoral management; financial management; liaison with other agencies and the community). This alternative approach involves a good deal of overlap but provides a useful checklist for those not used to thinking in input, process and output terms.

Sources of information

The choice of indicators will depend in part on what information is available or can readily be made available. The main sources are likely to be:

(a) *Routine management information* – new (and usually computerized) information systems will be needed to support local management in schools and will be the main source of information. LEAs will be expected to develop and implement these systems which will be largely common to all schools and will need specialized skills to produce. The schools are expected to take an active role in their design and the management needs of the school should be the primary determinant of the information to be supplied, with LEAs receiving a subset of the schools' needs. The LMS budget manual envisages that information to be provided will include, for example, financial information on budgets and expenditure, operational information (e.g. on staff numbers, class contact hours, pupil numbers analysed by age and curriculum options) and performance information (such as destinations of pupils, results of examinations and assessments made under the National Curriculum).

(b) Reports on internal or external appraisal (e.g. by LEA advisers or HMIs). These will usually provide qualitative information to support quantified indicators but may themselves provide quantified measures, for example, on the extent to which the school processes/activities come up to defined standards.

(c) Surveys of attitudes and opinions of pupils, parents and former pupils may be necessary to supplement (a) and (b), in particular to evaluate aspects of school output not adequately measured by examinations. Many survey instruments are already available and can be adapted to local school needs in collaboration with other schools, LEAs, or institutes of education.

Management and presentation of information

The CIPFA (1988a) paper on performance indicators lists several hundred aspects of a school which could in theory could be the subject of indictors.

Schools have to select those which are most likely to point up opportunities for improvement. It may be useful to group indicators in hierarchies or pyramids with broad first-line indicators at the top and supported by second- and possibly third-line indicators which explain them in greater detail. For example, the input indicator of staff cost per pupil can be subdivided into teaching and non-teaching staff costs, each of which can be subdivided into their components of staff/pupil ratios and cost per member of staff. Staff/pupil ratios can be backed by information on class contact hours, teacher loads, time spent on training and time spent on management, pastoral care, extra-curricular activities and so on. Each indicator can be related to figures for the previous year or for other schools. It will be for local judgement how far to probe down any particular hierarchy after seeing whether the broader indicators suggest that there may be points worth exploring. Computer software can make it easy to scan hierarchies of indicators to pick out those that are worth probing.

Indicators in practice

Schools will want to develop and use the indicators that are most likely to be of practical help in preparing and managing budgets.

Resource use indicators

They will need to take stock of the pattern of spending on teaching and non-teaching staff, on repairs and maintenance, fuel and light and other premises costs, transport, books, equipment and other supplies and services. They should be assisted in this by indicators which show how the cost per pupil compares with that in other schools and enables them to examine in more detail the factors that lie behind a broad comparison.

Output indicators

They will also need to take stock of results, achievements and public reputation which are likely to affect future demand for places. The indicators are bound to include measures of performance in GCSE and National Curriculum tests, probably in terms of proportions of pupils achieving defined results (e.g. five or more passes at grade F or better in GCSE; four or more passes at grade C or better; no graded results). A priority for schools is likely to be to develop supplementary indicators which help to interpret these indicators and put them in context relating them as far as practicable to relative ability of different pupil intakes. As computerization of pupil records develops, it should be possible to classify GCSE and National Curriculum test results by reference to pupils' levels of attainment in earlier years. Pupils might, for example, be grouped in bands of attainment in the test taken at age

11 (and possibly at age 14) and the supplementary indicators would then show the proportions within each of those bands achieving defined results.

Where it is not possible by computer or manually to relate individual pupils' records, more approximate methods will have to be adopted. Pupils' average scores at GCSE could be related to average scores on local or national tests taken at age 11. Schools might be grouped in bands of expectation according to the attainment of pupils at intake age (taking account of proportions with high and low attainment as well as averages) and results at GCSE could be analysed in relation to those bands.

It will also be possible by statistical regression analysis to calculate expected scores, taking account of factors such as scores on tests at entry and social factors (e.g. percentage of pupils from low-income homes as measured by percentage entitled to free meals). Comparison of actual with expected results provides the indicator.

Particularly in schools with relatively small numbers, in which results fluctuate from year to year, it may be desirable to take moving averages of more than one year.

Other indicators

Schools will need to consider what are the most important aspects of their work that are not adequately measured by examination results and where it will be useful to supplement subjective judgements with quantified indicators. The following paragraphs give examples of areas which might be reviewed and the kind of indicators that might be considered.

Social behaviour and discipline

A useful, easily collected, first-line indicator is likely to be that of *average pupil attendance* through the winter and spring terms subdivided by classes.

Other indicators which might be considered include: *proportion of unauthorized absences* (more difficult to collect on a standard basis); *proportion of pupils displaying serious behavioural problems* (derived from pupil profiles on agreed principles and collected for first and one or more later years); *ratio of disciplinary sanctions to numbers of pupils* (unsuitable for use in isolation but may complement other indicators in particular in monitoring trends within a school); *proportion of pupils found guilty of indictable offences* (a controversial indicator which might in schools with high delinquency rates be used to monitor changes over time – it does not imply that schools are accountable for delinquent behaviour of their pupils but a good school in a difficult area may show a positive influence).

Social and cultural activities

Likely to be covered descriptively in school reports. There may be value in quantifying, for example, *pupil participation rates* (i.e. proportion of pupils voluntarily participating in given numbers of activities). Surveys might be used to assess proportions of school-leavers expressing continuing interest in defined activities.

Pupil and parent satisfaction

- Proportion of first-year pupils for whom the school was first choice.
- Proportion of pupils staying on at the school after 16.
- Opinions and attitudes of pupils during first and last years (towards school in general and e.g. curriculum quality of teaching facilities, preparation for work and adult life). (If feasible, surveys of former pupils remaining in the areas might also be undertaken by LEAs on behalf of schools.)
- Opinions and attitudes of samples of parents of a given intake in say first year, a middle year and the final year – towards the school and, for example, curriculum, teaching, disciplines, homework.

Attitudes and values of final-year pupils

Surveys of the attitudes and values which the school may wish to influence, for example, attitudes to work, leisure, healthy life-styles (smoking, drugs, alcohol, fitness), values of honesty, consideration for others, racial tolerance.

Post-16 destination

Proportion of pupils

- continuing with full-time education;
- entering youth training schemes;
- entering full-time employment;
- combining part-time jobs with part-time education;
- remaining unemployed;
- *Employer opinion* – Surveys of opinion of local employers on standards of the school and of the personal and social skills of school leavers whom they employ or interview.

Reports to governing bodies, LEAs, parents

Heads will no doubt consult the governing bodies on the indicators to be reported to them. On current policy reports to LEAs may require subsets of the information prepared for school use.

The annual report of the school is required to contain information about the curriculum and examination results. It is for governors to consider adding other information such as progress of the school towards the objectives set and the measures by which this progress is to be judged and for this purpose they may wish to use one or more of the indicators discussed above.

Conclusion

Presentation of performance information can indeed be seen positively by partners in the education system as a necessary part of public relations. There is likely to be continuing keen competition for resources with other public services and with private consumption. The education service's case for resources is strengthened if it can show that everything possible is being done to make the best use of the resources already provided. The issue for schools and education services is whether they take a defensive line and try to resist the development of indicators or test them out in a positive way and seek to develop them to the advantage of their pupils.

References

Blank, Rolf K. (1986). *Science and Mathematics Indicators: a Conceptual Framework for a State-based Network*, Council of Chief State School Officers, State Education Assessment Center, Washington DC.

CIPFA (1988a). *Performance Indicators in Schools: a Contribution to the Debate*, London, Chartered Institute of Public Finance and Accountancy.

CIPFA The LMS Initiative (1988b). *Local Management in Schools: a Practical Guide.* London, Chartered Institute of Public Finance and Accountancy.

DES (1988). *Education Reform Act: Local Management of Schools.* Circular 7/88.

Peters, T. and Waterman, R. (1982). *In Search of Excellence.* New York, Harper & Row.

19
Using performance indicators: educational considerations

Carol T. Fitz-Gibbon

The need for useful information systems

The major purpose of this chapter is to draw out and explain the *educational* uses of performance indicators: how performance indicators can contribute to improving several aspects of the delivery of education when they are developed with educational considerations to the fore and with due regard to research findings in social science.

The role of performance indicators as a management tool for improvement is distinct from their role vis-à-vis accountability. Educational institutions may be held accountable for the use of the public funds delegated to them under local management of schools (LMS) and part of this accountability may require examination of 'value added' – what has the institution done for the children on whom the money was spent? But if performance indicators were to be produced only as summative gradings of the institution's performance, then a number of unhappy consequences could result.

First, resistance to the system could develop in institutions with poor performance indicators. They might try to fix the performance indicators without actually altering the educational processes which produced them. If the poor performance indicators were combined with no information on how to improve them, then such reactions would be almost inevitable. Cosmetic adjustments to make performance indicators look good would defeat the purpose of the monitoring system and result in time wasted in battles about appearances. It would certainly be vigorously argued that the information cost more than it was worth.

It cannot be expected that the numerical indicators which constitute performance indicators will be universally welcomed. Old conflicts between qualitative and quantitative approaches to social science will surface with comments like 'Not everything that goes on in schools can be measured on a scale'. Whilst not everything can be measured, this does not mean that nothing can be measured. How measurements can be made which are fair and useful is, then, the topic of this chapter.

We will start with a brief case study from which we will then extract some general principles for the characteristics of acceptable, fair and beneficial performance indicators in education.

A case study: the COMBSE A-level project

The project called Confidential, Measurement-Based Self-Evaluation (COMBSE) started in 1983 with twelve comprehensive schools representing a wide range of social backgrounds. Performance indicators were developed for two of the most heavily subscribed A-levels: English and Mathematics.

Confidentiality was maintained by giving each school a code-name chosen by the school (e.g. COLDITZ, SHUT, ETON) and known only to themselves and the researcher. This confidentiality was probably important in the production of reports and in the schools' decisions to allow the reports to be put into circulation via the School of Education's library at the University of Newcastle.

The term 'performance indicator' was not in widespread use in 1983 and the question which had to be asked was: 'In order to investigate the effectiveness of A-level provision in a school, what "variables" need to be measured?' To-day the question would be posed in terms of 'performance indicators' rather than 'variables' but the term 'variables' is mentioned to draw attention to the fact that what today may be called 'monitoring' is only different in its ongoing, cyclical and collaborative aspects from what was and is *research*. In particular that line of investigation called 'school-effectiveness' research was very close to providing the information needed for the design of information systems (Gray *et al.*, 1983; Reynolds, 1985; Willms and Cuttance, 1985; Fitz-Gibbon, 1985; Willms, 1987).

What indicators would be fair and beneficial in monitoring A-levels? A logical place to start is to consider goals. What are we striving to provide to A-level candidates? Good examination results? Broadening and educational extramural experiences? A congenial environment at school or college? Since all these were considered legitimate aims for sixth-form provision, we tried to collect performance indicators for each of these aspects. Examination results were collected to see if they were good considering the particular student and what should be expected of that student. We asked about participation in extramural activities so that institutions could see how their students' experiences compared with those in other institutions. And we asked students questions to elicit their attitudes to the institution and their attitudes to the subjects they had been studying. These, then, might be seen as major *output* indicators:

- examination results,
- participation in extramural activities,
- attitudes to school,
- attitudes to subjects studied.

At the time, one indicator in widespread use was the percentage pass rate for examinations. There are many inadequacies in this indicator, its only virtue being, perhaps, that it is simple. But such a virtue is not sufficient. Indicators should also be fair and beneficial. In Figure 19.2 the inadequacies of the percentage pass rate as a performance indicator are summarized.

Having selected some *outputs* which were considered important, the next task in developing a useful set of performance indicators was to collect information on those *inputs* which might be related to the outputs. For example, if we were going to look at examination results as indicators of school effectiveness, we could not fairly compare the results from, say, a group of pupils most of whom had As at O-level with those from a group of pupils most of whom had Cs at O-level. To make fair comparisons you must

Figure 19.1   Example of a less-than-desirable performance indicator

The percentage pass rate is not a fair or beneficial PI for several reasons:

- no account is taken of the kinds of pupils entered. A 70 per cent pass rate might be a greater achievement than a 90 per cent pass rate if a group of not very able students took the examination in the former class. This lack of adjustment for intake is the most serious problem and applies to any raw set of examination results, such as numbers of passes at various levels.
- barely passing is counted in the same way as getting a high grade, with the result that no extra credit is given for higher levels of achievement. The focus is purely on the pass/fail dichotomy. Since we know that the level of a pass is important to employers and selectors for higher education the reliance on a simple dichotomy is unjustifiable.
- the percentage pass rate may push institutions to allow only potentially successful candidates to attempt examinations.
- the percentage pass rate if calculated for an institution ignores the curriculum balance. Not all A-levels are equally difficult. There is evidence to suggest that a D in A-level Mathematics is about as academically difficult to get as a B in A-level English. An institution attracting many candidates into Mathematics might thus be at a disadvantage when percentage pass rates are examined.
- an inevitable question is 'percentage of what?' Vagueness on this allows the indicator to be strategically manipulated. Are adults counted? What of those who take the examination through some other institution? Are re-sits included?

If an indicator like percentage pass rate is used institutions may be tempted to be guided in their advice to students by considerations relating to the PI rather than relating to the students' long-term prospects, educational needs and interests.

either compare like with like or make some adjustments to take differences into account, or, preferably, take both precautions. How inputs can be taken into account for examination results is the topic of Figure 19.2.

In summary, output indicators were assessed because they represented goals of the institution and inputs were assessed to make comparisons of outputs fair and to give a better indicator of 'value added' by the schools.

In order to take account of differences in intakes, that is, to 'control for' differences in intakes, we needed to find characteristics of the students which were correlated with their A-level grades. The best correlate was the average grade a pupil obtained at O-level, hereafter called the *O-level grade point average*. Since the O-level grade point average was a measure of prior achievement, when it was taken into account we were looking at a measure of 'value added': the increase in a pupil's qualifications. However, there were some problems associated with relying on this measure of intake alone.

Probably the most important problem was that O-levels were set to change (to GCSE) so that we would not have comparable data across the years if we relied only on O-level grades as predictors. To obtain comparable

Figure 19.2   Example of a fairer and more beneficial performance indicator

---

How is a fairer PI for A-level examination results to be calculated? If we knew what grade to expect for a student, then when the A-level grades became available, we could see whether or not the student had lived up to expectations. If many students in one school achieved better than was expected of them, we might consider that to be a positive PI for the school. Even though all students got Es this could be a very good result if one would have expected them all to fail.

How can we know what to expect of a student? Obviously we cannot know accurately for one student but if we consider, say, a few hundred students, we can make some predictions based on the general pattern. To invent a simple example, suppose over several hundred students we found that the pattern relating GCSE grade to A-level grade was this: at A-level a student tends to get one grade lower than at GCSE. We would then have a 'prediction equation':

$$A\text{-level-grade} = GCSE\text{-grade}\quad minus\quad one$$

or

$$A = G - 1$$

The outcome (A-level grade, A) is predicted from the input (GCSE grade, G). The relationship between GCSE grades and A-level grades is not quite so simple but it *can* be represented by an equation like the one above.

Example: in 1988 the best predictor of A-level was the students O-level grade point average (GPA). These O-levels were scores as A = 7, B = 6 etc. The

A-levels were scored A = 5, B = 4 as in the 'UCCA' scale (University Central Council on Admissions). On the basis of 1988 data, the equation which best predicted A-level Mathematics grade from the average O-level grade obtained by the pupil was:

$$A \text{ grade} = 1.85(\text{O-level GPA}) - 8.71$$

Thus for pupils who had an average of B at O-level the expected grade at A-level was 1.85 times 6 minus 8.71 which works out at 2.39, representing an average of a D or slightly better.

For English, the regression equation was:

$$A \text{ grade} = 1.50(\text{O-level GPA}) - 5.77$$

What grade would therefore have been predicted for A-level English for students with a B (6.0) for an average O-level grade? (Answer at the end of the figure.)

The essence of the idea is that if we know something about a candidate, such as his or her O-level grade, and if we know how O-level grades in general, in all the participating schools and colleges, related to A-level grades, then we have the basis for predicting the A-level grade each candidate might have been expected to get. If the candidate got a grade higher than the one predicted then that is a positive point for the school. If the candidate got lower than predicted, that is a negative point. *The difference between the actual grade a student gets and the grade predicted for the student is called a residual.* Positive residuals indicate better-than-predicted performance. Negative residuals represent worse-than-predicted performance. By averaging the residuals for a school we can see if, on average, a school's results are better or worse than would have been predicted on the basis of the prior achievement of its candidates.

Of course, a particular candidate's over- or under-achievement may be nothing to do with the school but if a pattern builds up of, say, most candidates doing better than expected then it would look like a positive indication. It is certainly a fairer indication than percentage of passes: it uses all the information (not just a pass/fail dichotomy) and enables outcomes to be compared *having taken account of* O-levels. Statistically this process is referred to as 'controlling for' O-levels. In the COMBSE project, the residuals were averaged for each department in each school, thus providing fair performance indicators for the department.

We have used the example of GCSE grades for simplicity, but of course other characteristics of the students could be 'controlled for': home background, ability, prior achievement on all O-level and CSEs rather than on just the subject matching the A-level subject, and so on.

Indeed, several predictors can be 'controlled for' (taken into account) at once. The procedures for doing this are known in statistics as multiple regression analysis.

(Answer to the regression equation question: Students with O-level grade point averages of B = 6.0 would be expected to get 3.23 in A-level in English, on average, i.e. grades averaging to a little better than C.)

data we turned to testing ability. Three different ability tests, each designed for high-ability students such as A-level candidates, were tried: the AH6 from the NFER, Raven's Advanced Progressive Matrices and the International Test of Developed Abilities (ITDA). The last proved to be the most effective predictor.

Another factor which might be thought to influence A-level achievement was home background. We tried out various measures of this based on father's and mother's occupation and educational levels but on the whole no measure of home background was strongly correlated with achievement at A-level. Although the correlation between measures of home background ('socio-economic status', for example) and achievement may be stronger in earlier phases of education, even there such measures are unlikely to be as strongly related to achievement as are measures of prior achievement or ability. The latter measures are therefore the ones which it is most important to take account of as 'inputs'.

Process variables were also assessed in order to see whether they related to outputs. For example, we considered whether or not some styles of teaching were associated with better outcomes and also looked at amounts of homework reported and allocated instructional time. This we view as just a beginning. Seeking adequate measures of process variables, of what schools do, is the most difficult part of the information system but it is the part which might be of most help in the long run. To locate effective process variables (which may be different in each subject area and different with different kinds of students) will require long-term and close collaboration between those who collect and analyse the information and those who use it.

How was all this data actually collected? By personnel from the university going directly into schools and colleges, giving the ability test under standardized conditions and administering a questionnaire immediately afterwards. One visit to each school or college was generally sufficient. We asked for the students taking A-levels in the coming summer to be brought together under 'examination conditions' for 1.5 hours. These conditions were requested partly because of the need to administer the ability test but also because it was better that the questionnaires were answered without discussion among students so that the answers were their own opinions, independent of others. That no school dropped out of the system may well be a reflection of the fact that at least we made few demands on school personnel.

Over the years since 1983, more schools and colleges have joined the project voluntarily and in 1988 a sudden expansion took place as it spread to five LEAs and included nearly 50 schools or colleges. It was also extended to monitor eleven subjects rather than just English and Mathematics.

When LEAs started to support the project financially, the confidentiality aspect changed: some LEA personnel wanted to see the data and know which code-names represented which institutions. (To signal this change the project was renamed in 1988, becoming ALIS: the A-Level Information System.)

Using performance indicators in management

Each year reports were produced which summarized the data on inputs, processes and outputs. The summaries were provided for each *department*. By perusing these reports heads of departments could locate institutions similar to their own (from the tables of inputs), and then compare their performance on the outcomes (examinations, participation rates and attitudes) with those of the similar institutions.

The tables of greatest interest were probably the tables of residuals for the examination results. For each student a predicted grade had been computed based on information about the student and on the pattern of results in the entire sample. When this predicted grade was compared with the grade the student obtained, it could be seen whether the student had done better or worse than expected. If the student had done better than expected then this yielded a positive residual. A negative residual represented doing worse than expected and a residual of zero represented a performance in line with expectations. By summing up and averaging the residuals in each department it could be seen whether the students in the department tended to have done better or worse than expected. In other words, the 'residuals' (explained in Figure 19.2) provided fair performance indicators for examination grades and they were aggregated at the level of the *department*, not summed for the whole school. Here it should be noted that a department would get good performance indicators if it had obtained results in line with students' abilities (or better). Since each student counted equally, the implication for schools was in line with desirable professional practice: to care equally for each student. To get good residuals bright students must get good grades and less bright students must get grades appropriate to their ability. Using residuals as performance indicators, rather than using percentage pass rates, meant there was no temptation to implement exclusive entry policies just to boost the indicator. Entry policies would not affect the indicator and could therefore be based on educational considerations rather than being made with a view to the subsequent statistics.

Were the performance indicators in the COMBSE project educationally useful? Because of the 'self-evaluation' nature of the project and because at the time of writing there has been little systematic research on this question, it is difficult to provide an adequate answer. Perhaps some schools or colleges stayed in the project because they found the data useful in ways which have not come to our attention. However, from the uses we have heard of, examples can be given.

1 Some schools frequently look unsuccessful when compared with other schools simply because the other schools have a more privileged intake and consequently get a 'better' set of raw examination results. Parents may then ask questions, wondering if the school is responsible for the poor results. One of the schools in the sample was in this kind of situation. It was one of the few schools offering Further Mathematics and it sent students to

Oxbridge colleges, despite being located in a far from privileged part of town. An interesting observation about this same school was that although it was attracting many more students into mathematics than normal (about four or five times as many as took English, whereas nationally this ratio is about 1.4) and getting very good results considering its intake, it was not recognized locally as particularly good. Lecturers visiting it in connection with teacher training actually gave the mathematics department a 'below average' rating in an off-the-cuff set of ratings collected to look at the reputation of schools and among a dozen teachers, eight could give it no rating at all. The four who could give a rating gave two above-average and two below-average ratings. Gray and Hannon (1986) drew attention to the inability of HMI to notice when a school with a 'poor' intake did well. The existence of fair performance indicators allows such events to be observed and this school in particular found the COMBSE reports useful in its relations with parents and governors and in reassuring and encouraging its own staff.

2 A second example can be given from quite a different kind of school. This school could be described as having been coasting along happily with a privileged intake and many high examination scores. Concern developed when a selection of students' responses to an open-ended question were included verbatim in the annual report. Comments like 'We're just like fifth formers only without the uniform', 'They don't treat us like adults', 'Staff are sarcastic', were worrying, especially when the proportion staying into the sixth was found to be declining. A staff meeting was called to discuss the findings. Following a request for more information from the data base, *all* students' comments were reported back to the school (suitably edited for anonymity) and the tenor was certainly not uniformly negative – which reassured staff somewhat. Nevertheless the performance indicator on the attitude scale was placing the school each year consistently among the two or three schools with the least positive attitudes among its sixth-formers. Plans were made to improve the sixth form with a view to increasing the satisfaction of students.

Now perhaps it doesn't take a data base to tell you if the atmosphere is good in a sixth form, but the data base did add to the evidence and did convince some who thought there was no problem that there might be a problem. Furthermore, the data could be related to ability groups and rule out the idea that it was only low-achieving students who were dissatisfied: dissatisfaction was across-the-board. However, the interpretations made must be cautious. It could be that the kind of students typical of this school, the sons and daughters of professionals, tend to be more critical in the sixth form than the students from more working-class backgrounds. This negative correlation between attitude and parental occupational status did hold in the COMBSE data base accumulated over five years, and this possible relationship is being further investigated as more data becomes available.

3 Another use made of the COMBSE data was to investigate differences in difficulty between A-level subjects. An investigation of the difference in difficulty level of Mathematics and English suggested that a D in Mathematics was indicative of the same level of academic ability as a B in English (Fitz–Gibbon, 1988).

Limitations

Although some instances of use of the data have been provided, the information was less useful to schools than it might have been and the reasons for this need to be considered.

First, the project provided a set of performance indicators, a data base, but did not provide a person to ensure the data were understood or used. One meeting a year was not enough for this purpose, especially when there were no other pressures towards paying attention to indicators.

Another possible hindrance was the nature of the reports: they were heavy and indigestible. There was a good deal of information and much of it appeared complicated at first sight. The mathematics department heads might have taken the report home for light reading but the English department heads, quite understandably, may have largely ignored it. The single best-recalled part of the reports appeared to be the verbatim comments from students.

It might be thought that the tables should be simplified and verbatim comments should be reported back more often, but there are a number of aspects to be considered before such a recommendation could be accepted. Leaving the tables in a somewhat complex form discouraged trivial and precipitous interpretations by uninformed persons. The information system was for the colleges, schools and LEA; it was for a professional rather than a lay audience. Better to concentrate on training managers to cope with the tables than to oversimplify. Furthermore, there would have been costs involved. The tables used were taken directly from the computer output, which ensured there were no transcription errors and was quick, even though some tidying was needed to make them more elegant and intelligible. To re-work the tables further would have increased the costs of the production of the reports.

The costs argument applies acutely to the question of feeding back the verbatim reports. Before they can be fed back they have to be carefully read to remove remarks which betray the institution's or the student's identity. They also have to be typed, which is costly; and they take up many pages, which increases reprographics charges. Nevertheless, such is the interest in these comments that at least a one-in-five sample of the comments should be reported back to institutions. If resources were less limited, formal coding procedures could be used on the entire set of comments. The problem is entirely one of cost.

To evaluate school performance, the indicators must have two important features: they must be *comparative* and at an *appropriate level of aggregation*.

Much of the usefulness of the data derives from its *comparative* nature. Take, for example, just the responses to the invitation to agree or disagree with the statement 'I would recommend to others that they take their A-levels here'. What percentage agreeing with the statement would be acceptable? Thus even simple figures need to be considered in three ways: (1) Is the figure satisfactory taken at face value? (e.g. is 70 per cent positive response acceptable?) (2) How does the figure compare with that from other schools like ours? (3) Does the figure need to be adjusted for intake differences? The last two questions can only be answered with a comparative data base across institutions.

The *level of aggregation* must be appropriate. Much of the discussion of performance indicators has been couched in terms of 'good schools' and 'poor schools', but is it not the case that the same school may be good or poor in different ways? Take examination effectiveness, for example. Good and poor departments exist in the same institution. Adding up the residuals given to each department, in order to obtain a school average, would simply obscure the information about the more and less effective departments and give no indication of which departments the school might most appropriately seek to improve. Much more research is needed before we know if there is a 'school effect' which influences work in every department, and meanwhile it would seem wise to aggregate only at the level of the department, not up to the school level.

Discussion: lessons from the case study

Case studies are illustrative; they do not establish proof that the lessons drawn from the individual case will generalize. Nevertheless, it is useful to try to see some general patterns in a case study which might apply to other situations. In the following pages we will look at characteristics which, partly on the basis of the experience gained with the A-level Information System, seem to be important. These desirable characteristics will be discussed under headings which reflect the steps you might use in developing an information system (see Figure 19.3).

Approach

If LEAs are to make a success of the monitoring role which the Coopers & Lybrand report and the DES circular 7/88 suggested, then their approach to the institutions they will monitor needs to be carefully considered. The view put forward here is that the approach needs to be very much in the spirit of *collaboration* with schools and colleges: collaboration in information seeking and interpretation, with the overall goal of improving the delivery of

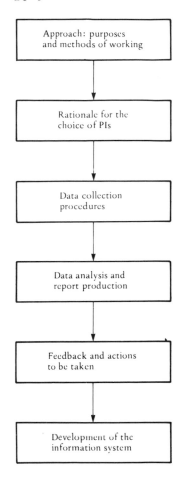

Figure 19.3 Steps in developing an information system

education. This kind of approach is strategically advisable for reasons argued at the beginning of this chapter but it is also, quite arguably, the only intellectually defensible approach. Not a great deal is known about the effects which schools have on pupils, about how much effect schools can have on attitudes, achievement, 'demeanour', delinquency rates and so on. In the absence of a strongly established research base, the monitoring must be investigative, not conclusive. Schools cannot be held responsible for outcomes over which they have little control: no accountability without causality! But little is known about which outcomes can be directly affected by schools, and even less is known about what changes to make in order to improve the outcomes. In the face of this situation no strong-arm judgemental system is defensible.

Rationale

Not every number which spews from a computer or a budget is worthy of the term 'performance indicator'. A performance indicator should have some observable and arguable, if not proven and evident, relationship to performance. Performance indicators are taps into a model of how the system is working. Thus, in the COMBSE project, outcomes were selected which were consistent with widely accepted goals. Then input indicators were located which needed to be taken into consideration because they had a bearing on the output indicators. Process indicators were selected to try to find actions which the schools took which might relate to *how* the schools' goals were attained. The need for there to be comparative data which has been derived from pupil-level data suitably aggregated was stressed above and the criterion added here is that the indicators should be chosen because they are elements in an explanatory model of the system being monitored.

Data collection

The data collection method should be designed to produce credible and defensible data of research quality while making few demands on staff and students. In the COMBSE study, data were collected specifically for the information system, by persons independent of the school. This represented a cost but seemed worthwhile in terms of credibility, convenience and efficiency.

If schools were asked to administer their own questionnaires about students' levels of satisfaction would the data be seen as credible? Would the students believe an offer of anonymity if their own teachers were collecting in the questionnaires? It might be argued that the questionnaires could be completed anonymously but that would mean that the questionnaire data could not be linked with examination data. One could not, for example, investigate whether positive attitudes were expressed by a range of students or only by students who were doing well academically.

Another problem which could arise in the questionnaire administration is the building up of a group ethos by comments spoken aloud when the questions were being answered. There might be some mileage in having students discuss the attitudes in groups but a few vocal students can sway the opinion of the group quite considerably. It seems safer to aim to get each pupil's individually considered response, at least in the first instance.

Then again, the atmosphere set by the way the task is presented and explained to students could influence their responses on the questionnaire. In the COMBSE project the explanations were put on a tape and this was played to each group. Thus all participants heard the same explanation in the same tone of voice.

It is not only attitude measurement which needs careful attention to the conditions of administration. The tape we used also timed the test. It takes schools no time at all to realize that they can improve their residuals based on controlling for ability by obtaining low scores on the ability test, making it appear they are working with less able pupils than is in fact the case. Simply shortening the administration time could provide a boost to such residuals.

Data analysis

The first step in data analysis is to ensure that the data are accurately entered into the computer and are being read accurately, so-called 'data cleaning'.

As a furhter check on the accuracy of the data it is important to build in some checks which can be made by schools and colleges. In COMBSE the raw unadjusted mean A-level score was reported. If our figure was different from the institution's figure the problem could be investigated and was usually due to absence at the time of the administration of the test and questionnaire. One point on which there is certainly consensus is that the basic achievement and attitude data should be collected and analysed *pupil by pupil*. School-level aggregates can be seriously misleading as well as un-informative about the details (Aitkin and Longford, 1986; Woodhouse and Goldstein, 1988).

Feedback and actions consequent upon it

Feedback is an important concept both inside and outside social science (as in the entire science of cybernetics). There is some evidence that feedback in and of itself is motivating, without the need for contingencies dependent upon the level of performance.

Quality circles, a concept familiar in management, would seem to be the way to ensure that indicators are examined and, where appropriate, actions are taken. A quality circle might be established within each school with a brief to: evaluate a department's performance taking into account the PIs on outcomes which are valued; consider what actions are needed in view of the evaluation; if improvement is sought, to consider the process variables which have been found to correlate positively with residuals and ask if any of these might be adopted or, if already used, exploited further; to consider explanations for the PIs and where appropriate suggest how information in the data base might be used to check the hypothesized explanation. Initially, someone may need to work with school personnel to develop these activities.

There were two pieces of information on the COMBSE questionnaire which could be directly related to the costs of providing an A-level course: the minutes per week of instruction and the class size. Comparative data on these variables can help managers to see if their courses are very much more costly or very much cheaper than courses provided elsewhere. They will also want to know if the residuals relate to minutes per week or to class size. Adding this kind of information to good educational judgement might assist managers in reducing costs without damage and/or in putting money where it is needed to improve results.

Development

It has been argued that a data base needs a human interface; it needs to be part of an information system. People are needed who sit down and talk through the data with management teams at each school, who explore possible explanations with the management teams, who listen to ideas from management teams for other data which should be collected to explore other facets of the education system being monitored, facets which might explain the indicators.

The lack of a management system to facilitate the flow of information into the data base (e.g. revisions of the questionnaire) and the flow of information from the data base to schools in a way which made it useful, was a serious deficiency in the COMBSE project and highlights an important point: management information systems require more than performance indicators and information. They require people to make them operate effectively. The most likely people, it seems, are LEA advisers whose new roles include being inspectors as well as advisers.

Research

A monitoring system produces huge amounts of very valuable data. It would be sheer profligacy not to ensure that the data base is mined for valuable information. In addition to the examples which have already been given (the difficulty level of examinations in different subjects, the difficulties of the same subjects with different examination boards, the extent to which schools can actually influence PIs, no accountability without causality, . . .) there are many other questions. There are many opinions about formal, didactic, experiential, pupil-centred approaches but few empirical studies. And what of the effectiveness of schemes like supported self-study or other ventures into distance learning? Are some textbooks ideal for some syllabuses? Or for some pupils? What is the effect of students' having jobs outside school? There are many questions which participants may think of each year. Someone should attempt to answer them in collaboration with the institutions.

Who will do this research? During the heady days of development of the information system you can probably find university or polytechnic researchers only too keen to participate in research and development. Eventually perhaps every LEA will have a thriving R&D unit. Indeed, after the LEA has distributed the money according to the formula, then goal setting, monitoring, evaluating, and research and development may be *the* role which is left. It is a very important and beneficial role if undertaken in a spirit of collaborative research.

References

Aitkin, M. and Longford, N. (1986). 'Statistical modelling issues in school effectiveness studies', *Journal of the Royal Statistical Society. Series A*, 149(1), 1–43.

Coopers & Lybrand (1988). *Local Management of Schools*. London, HMSO.

Fitz-Gibbon, C. T. (1985). 'A-level results in comprehensive schools: the Combse project, year 1', *Oxford Review of Education*, 11(1), 43–58.

Fitz-Gibbon, C. T. (1988). 'Recalculating the standard', *The Times Educational Supplement*, 26-8-88, p. 15.

Gray, J. and Hannon, V. (1986). 'HMI interpretation of schools' examination results', *Journal of Educational Policy*, 1(1), 23–33.

Gray, J., McPherson, A. F. and Raffe, D. (1983). *Reconstructions of Secondary Education Theory, Myth and Practice since the War*. London, Routledge & Kegan Paul.

Reynolds, D. (ed.) (1985). *Studying School Effectiveness*, London and Philadelphia, The Falmer Press.

Willms, J. D. (1987). 'Differences between Scottish educational authorities in their examinations attainment', *Oxford Review of Education*, 13(2), 211–32.

Willms, J. D. and Cuttance, P. (1985). 'School effects in Scottish secondary schools', *British Journal of Sociology of Education*, 6(3).

Woodhouse, G. and Goldstein, H. (1988). 'Educational performance indicators and LEA league tables', *Oxford Review of Education*, 14(3).

20

The dominion of economic accountability

Ernest R. House

[. . .] The dominant theme today is economic efficiency and its purpose is control – control over the behavior of pupils, control over the behavior of the staff, control over schooling.

At the risk of oversimplification let me outline this mode of account-ability, which I call economic accountability. It is an economist's view of the world. Basically it presumes that the purpose of education is to supply manpower to other institutions of the society, particularly the economic ones. The skills needed to run the social machinery can be formulated in specific terms, so educational goals are mandated by technological demands. The goals being specific and set, the job of educators is to maximize these goals (usually forms of student achievement), with the greatest efficiency possible. Ultimately then the goals of education become economic and the attendant accountability system is economic. [. . .]

Now there are serious problems in applying economic analysis to education in a pluralist society. Where objectives or outcomes are not known, economic theory offers no way of determining them. And where there are competing viewpoints of what education should be doing, the maximizing solution does not even apply. In a pluralist society such as ours, there are irreconcilable differences as to what the outputs of education should be. At best one can compile a great list of possible outputs and try to relate inputs to them, thus establishing a collage. But this solution does not have much practical appeal to administrators who want to make decisions. [. . .]

The alternative is to reconcile these differences into a few set goals – which is what I believe the demands for economic accountability are attempt-ing to do. [. . .] In this scheme students are shaped to prespecified ends, educators are efficient at producing those ends, and education is more closely wired to the economic institutions of the society. The whole social system is more efficient, but the cost is terribly high: it is our cultural pluralism and our humanity. For this mode of accountability simply reduces to this: the individual is accountable to the institutions, but the institutions are not accountable to the individual. [. . .]

The same principle of economic efficiency shapes both the accountability system and the nature of education. Managerial education dominates when the schools are assessed by the usefulness of their 'product' to the dominant institutions of the society. In our society this means that the schools are held accountable for effectively and efficiently meeting the demands for educated manpower. To the extent that the economic institutions maintain their voracious appetite for technical skills and to the extent that school credentials become the primary means of placing people in the structure, managerial education will predominate.

Contrast this with humanistic education in which schools are assessed in terms of what they do for people – independent of their contribution to other institutions. The humanistic credo, often expressed as the impossible goal of 'developing each individual to his fullest', is the official ideology of most educators. It seeks, not to shape the individual to a predetermined end, to some criterion of external utility, but to cultivate independence and individualism. [. . .] The production-line model calls for elaborate prespecification and quality control. Emphasis is placed on that which is replicable, easily quantifiable, readily discernible, and unambiguous. Education becomes engineering and, finally, industrial production. Evaluation becomes greatly simplified: one need only compare the prespecification to the final product.

PPBS – an accountant's dream

Thus we get simple business management tools applied to education – as in the PPB system California is implementing. The system promises no less than the

> information necessary (1) for planning educational programs that will meet the needs of the community; and (2) for choosing among the alternative ways in which a school district can allocate resources to achieve its goals and objectives.
>
> (California State Department of Education, 1969)

According to the state's lucid and well-written manual here's how the system works:

The school arrives at a set of *goals*, which are the cornerstone of the system. From the goals is derived a set of objectives, which must be measurable. Based on these objectives the *program* is developed, which is a group of activities to accomplish the objectives including attendant resources and schedules. This completes the program development. Then the *program description package* is drawn up, which includes the course content, objectives, and method of evaluation. Then the *program structure* is set up which is a hierarchical arrangement of programs. [. . .]

Finally the *program code* is built, which means each program is assigned a number, the *program budget* is completed, and the *multiyear financial plan*, a five-year cost projection, is constructed. All is neatly rational and internally consistent – if you believe in an abstract 'economic man'. Actually any relation between the PPB *system* and reality will be purely coincidental.

Figure 20.1   PPBS element form

Goal Statement

To provide all students the opportunity to develop skills in typing, shorthand, bookkeeping, and office machine operation.

DEVELOPED BY _____

Objective Statement and Evaluative Criteria

Ninety per cent of graduating Business Curriculum students shall meet the following standards:

Typing – 70 words per minute as measured by the IBM Test with 90 per cent accuracy

Shorthand – 100 words per minute as measured by the Gregg test.

Bookkeeping – Demonstrate understanding of journals, income statements, and balance sheets as determined by decision tests.

Office Machine Operation – Mean score equal to national average on NCR test.

DEVELOPED BY _____

Program Description Summary

This program is designed to allow students to develop skills in the areas of typing, shorthand, bookkeeping, and office machine operation sufficient to gain employment using these skills. This program will include practice with typical problems and situations found in actual employment situations. Contacts will be maintained with the local business community to aid students in obtaining employment.

DEVELOPED BY _____

PROGRAM TITLE _____

PROGRAM ID. NO. _____   PROGRAM NO. _____

SUPPORTED PROGRAMS _____   PROGRAM LEVEL _____

SUPPORTING PROGRAMS _____

The problem of defining goals in a pluralist society has already been noted. The PPBS manual spends no time explaining how to arrive at goals, and with good reason. Defining goals is a political, not an economic, process. Empirical studies of business organizations have shown that their goals are changing, multiple, inconsistent – and the organizations survive quite nicely. [. . .]

Assuming that the goal problem is overcome, one must then develop a set of objectives that are measurable – the old behavioral objectives problem. [. . .] The program description package is prepared after the program has been 'developed'. A sample is illustrated in Figure 20.1. [. . .] Something as complex as a classroom cannot be reduced to a ledger sheet. I submit that, with this form completed, you would know almost nothing worthwhile about any program. Here is also implicit the interesting idea that 'program development' is completed when these activities are specified. This is not how good programs develop. Our own data indicate that program development is a complicated process that occurs when an 'advocate', perhaps a parent or teacher, becomes interested in developing a program for children. This advocate organizes a group of people, secures resources, and proceeds to build a program. The development of the program is never complete.

[. . .]

Finally these artifacts are coded and related to the budget – which I suspect was the purpose all along. The code numbers can then be manipulated as if they meant something – which they clearly do not. The manual is peppered with statements such as 'Assessment of results is essential' and other exhortations to evaluate these programs, do cost–benefit analyses, and so on. But actual procedures for doing so are glossed over at great speed. Well they might be, for there is absolutely no legitimate way now in existence to collect the measures and make the comparisons the system demands.

The end result is what I always find in dealing with systems analysis – a lot of hazy generalizations that seem reasonable on the surface but are actually impossible to implement. All the objections to this system that I have raised are based on either empirical evidence or experience. But one thing I have found with the systems people is that they are never disturbed by data. They simply say 'You aren't doing it right', which means that people are not behaving in accordance with the rationalist–economic model that underlies the system. If they did behave properly the model would work – a brilliant piece of circular logic. [. . .]

My prognosis is something like this. My worst fears are that the system will actually succeed in doing what I see as its real design. In that case, we will have a high level of managerial education. The repression and dullness of the classroom will increase and we will have succeeded in crucifying our children on the cross of economic efficiency. My most hopeful prediction is that people will realize the restrictiveness of this sytem and subvert it into an information system that attends to the needs of the children instead of simply shaping them to the needs of the institutions.

But I do not think that either of these projections is likely in the near future. I think the schools will stay pretty much as they are now. Schoolmen will get by just as they got through chemistry lab. – by filling out forms the way they are expected to regardless of what is happening in reality. [. . .] The end result will be a slightly less efficient system that looks more efficient. But even that is certainly preferable to the first choice I outlined [. . .]

I wish I had a well-worked out alternative to economic accountability that would solve all our problems. I do not. But let me suggest a different mode of accountability in which institutions are accountable to persons rather than persons accountable to the institution. Such an accountability scheme would provide feedback on the clients' well-being instead of just how well they are 'shaping up'. Teachers might be responsible to students and administrators to teachers. The information system for this accountability would revolve around the question 'Is this information going to help the institution adjust to characteristics of the student or will it result in shaping the student to the demands of the institution?' [. . .]

Reference

California State Department of Education (1969). *Conceptual Design for a Planning, Programming, Budgeting System for California School Districts*, Sacramento, California State Department of Education.

Author index

Subject index

R